W9-CJS-925

DISCARDED

Solving the
Productivity
Paradox

Solving the Productivity Paradox

TQM for Computer Professionals

Jessica Keyes

McGraw-Hill, Inc.

New York   San Francisco   Washington, D.C.   Auckland   Bogotá
Caracas   Lisbon   London   Madrid   Mexico City   Milan
Montreal   New Delhi   San Juan   Singapore
Sydney   Tokyo   Toronto

Library of Congress Cataloging-in-Publication Data

650
.028
K 44

Keyes, Jessica (date)
    Solving the productivity paradox : TQM for computer professionals
/ Jessica Keyes.
        p.   cm.
    Includes index.
    ISBN 0-07-034476-0
    1. Information technology.   2. Total quality management.
I. Title.
T58.5.K48   1994
650'.0285'42—dc20   94-30141
                                                                CIP

1 2 3 4 5 6 7 8 9 0   DOC/DOC   9 0 9 8 7 6 5 4

ISBN 0-07-034476-0

*The sponsoring editor for this book was Ronald D. Powers, the editing
supervisor was Caroline Levine, and the production supervisor was
Pamela A. Pelton. This book was set in Palatino by McGraw-Hill's
Professional Book Group composition unit.*

Printed and bound by R. R. Donnelley & Sons Company.

Contents

Part 1.   The Productivity Problem

A look at some of the subtle, insidious problems plaguing the information technology (IT) industry. Is IT alone responsible for flat productivity gains despite massive investments by management? Or did IT have a little help from its friends? Sure to dismay you, but not to surprise you.

Part 2.   Sampler Solutions to Productivity Problems

All problems suggest a solution. The ones in this book are no different. Whereas Part 1 presented some seemingly uncorrectable problems, Part 2 provides some ideas on how to counter the effects of the resulting productivity losses by instituting programs sure to enhance not only productivity but quality as well.

Foreword

I've been mulling over the subject of the productivity paradox for some 10 years or so—way before there was even a name for it. I discovered that there was a lot more to productivity than meets the proverbial eye. What this book is about is how information technology (IT) itself contributes to the productivity paradox. Yes, there's stuff in here about lack of training and poor management; but there are some discussions in this book that are bound to surprise you. These are about the hidden causes of the productivity paradox. And that's what makes this book so unusual. For what I discuss between its covers is a real departure from anything you've ever seen in print.

I say things right out loud that you've been whispering about for years. Things like how the computer press is swayed by advertising dollars, perhaps giving us too rosy a view of certain technologies or vendors; and how the trend in hiring managers with more pomp than circumstance gives rise to more than just inefficiency. And although we laugh heartily when we hear the joke about the consultant asking for our watch before giving us the time, there's more behind this joke than just a few chuckles. I'm going to air our dirty laundry. Secrets that this industry thinks about, whispers about but, ultimately, does little about.

The goal of this book is nothing short of laying bare our foibles so that we can correct them. Toward that end, I present a collection of insight, ideas, opinions, methodologies, and procedures, collected from some of the industry's leading experts, that are sure to spur you to action. For after all, if you identify the sickness you're motivated to find the cure.

Ultimately, many of you may disagree with what's in this book. But I'll bet that many more of you will agree with my assessment of the situation. And gleefully. It's my bet that those who grumble will be those that I verbally assault squarely between the eyes. The consultants who steal your watch. The journalists who "just don't get it" and as a result weave errors into their writing. The people who will complain loudest about this book have the most to lose. But their loss is your gain.

This book wouldn't have been possible without the help and encouragement of many people. First of all, I'd like to thank my husband, Robert, without whose unwavering support it would never have been finished. I'd also like to thank my parents, who were always on the lookout for yet another tidbit about the subject.

But I'd also like to thank the many experts who gave willingly of their time and expertise. People like Hamilton Technologies' Margaret Hamilton—a true pioneer in the field. These are the real heroes. I know they, as I, hope this book will become the wings that finally make the productivity paradox fly away.

Jessica Keyes

Preface

It comes creeping in the middle of the night. That nagging feeling that there's something wrong. That the systems you are building just don't hit a home run. That instead of making it easier for your end user to do his or her job, they are making it more complicated. Or that the solution you've chosen isn't as efficient as you thought it might be.

Choices. So many choices. It's much different now than it was 20 years ago—or even 5 years ago. How can you be certain you're making the right decisions? What if you're the one who's responsible for a part of the "productivity paradox."

Yes, you!

The productivity paradox is a puzzle in which, with all the hardware and all the software and all the money you've poured into IT, you can't quite make your organization more productive. And like Humpty Dumpty, all the king's horses and all the king's men can't put productivity back together again.

This book is about that puzzle—from an IT perspective. We're going to take a long, hard look at our profession. And we may not like what we see.

To help you see the light, I've divided *Solving the Productivity Paradox* into two parts. In Part 1, as promised, I air some pretty dirty laundry. Based on my over 18 years of experience plus extensive conversations with your peers, I've culled what I consider to be some of the most insidious problems facing our industry today. Of course, you might not agree with my assessment. In fact you may well have uncovered some other fatal flaw. So I encourage you, welcome you, to call me, fax me, email me. I want you to barrage me with your ideas on the subject. But first in Chapter 1 we're going to find out if there is a productivity paradox at all. Even if it's not a paradox, it's certainly a problem that as we'll see in Chapter 2 can lead to a distinct competitive disadvantage.

And what we're going to discover is that some of the reasons for the productivity problem come out of left field—from places you wouldn't expect, like building the wrong systems, which we discuss in Chapter 3. Or from mismanaging people or being mismanaged, a problem we discuss in Chapter 6.

The two chapters that will simultaneously surprise and disturb you are Chapter 4, where we discuss how journalists may just be responsible for leading us astray, and Chapter 5, where I offer stern advice against hiring the consultants that I've named the "bottom feeders."

And you might be surprised by Chapter 7 where I question whether client/server is a productivity buster. But don't worry, I do more than question; I also offer some very specific advice on client/server.

Where Part 1 offered some insights into what might be causing IT not to reach its fullest potential, Part 2 offers some tangible advice on how to re-engineer your organization to achieve the biggest productivity and quality payback. Now there are many books on *quality*, more on *productivity*, and even more on TQM (my own book, *The Software Engineering Productivity Handbook*, fits into all three categories); therefore it would be impossible for me to offer a total treatise on the subject. Instead, I'll do what I do best; I'll abstract and excerpt. In other words, I'll do the footwork for you.

From all those papers, books, and articles I've selected what I consider to be the surest shots. As a "hands-on" technologist what I offer you in Part 2 is advice that you *can* follow. Not some "pie in the sky" abstract and usually entirely unworkable notion on how to improve productivity. Not some esoteric advice from a consultant who has never been awakened at 3 a.m. when a system crashes. Not some hackneyed advice from a freelance writer who has misinterpreted the "experts" she was assigned to interview. What I offer you is solid, usable, and workable—like what to do about legacy code.

If legacy systems are one of your problems, then you might find Chapter 8 just what the doctor ordered. Now how many of you use a methodology? My research indicates that usage hovers somewhere around a pitiful 10 to 15 percent. Does this surprise you? What may surprise you even more is that developing a system without a concrete methodology is akin to driving thousands of miles to a place you've never been—without a road map. Within this context, I offer up Chapters 9 and 10, which will guide you through the painful process of understanding the concept of methodology. Chapter 10 will also introduce you to what I consider to be the most radical advance in the field of IT—the *development-before-the-fact* methodology. In my opinion, this particular methodology is a sure shot on the road to productivity and quality.

And there's plenty of that in this book—guidelines to achieving productivity and quality, I mean. Chapters 13 and 14 offer you some specific procedures to get you there. And the chapter on partnering, 12, and the one on smart systems, Chapter 11, give you some concrete examples of systems to aspire to.

Handling legacy systems, partnering to achieve economies of scale, building "smart systems," methodology, and a grass roots look at some procedures and policies to put you on the fast track to quality and productivity—this, in essence, is what Part 2 offers you. So read on and read well. Maybe you can put Humpty Dumpty back together again after all!

Jessica Keyes

Solving the
Productivity
Paradox

The Productivity Problem

Yes, deadlines are rough. And they keep changing. As do the requirements. But is this alone responsible for the much ballyhooed lack of technological productivity we are experiencing?

There has been much press lately about this issue. The chapters to come explore it in great detail, so the issue won't be delved into here. I would like you to mull this over, though. Given the enormous amounts of money and resources that have been thrown into the proverbial technology soup, what did we really end up with? Do we build better systems? Do we build systems that users want? And can use? Do these systems speed up the works? In the end, do these systems make the organization that has invested in them more competitive?

Certainly, many systems do. But many more don't. The question is: Why do we have so many failures? Read on. The chapters in Part 1 are full of many of the reasons—subtle, and not so subtle, I and many others think we're not as productive as we could be. But before we draw that conclusion, let's discuss the very idea of the "productivity paradox." Let's find out if it's for real.

The Productivity Paradox

Over the last couple of years a debate has been raging, albeit ever so quietly. You can hear folks discuss it over lunch. In their fuzzy-walled cubicles. In oak-paneled boardrooms. And most certainly around the watercooler in the pressrooms of nearly every computer- and business-oriented magazine and newspaper in the country. The question? Given the untold billions that this country has invested in computer technology over the last decade, have we really become any more productive?

The answer is about as nebulous as the question itself. It is entirely possible to find contingents of academicians and economists who will point to trunkfuls of colorful charts showing statistics that prove technology's beneficence. On the other hand, an equal number of academicians and economists have an equal number of colorful charts showing an equal number of statistics proving that computer technology is not the panacea it's reputed to be.

Ultimately, the question "Is there a productivity paradox?" is wrongly put. Technology is neither a boon nor a boondoggle. Yet it can be both, depending on who is using it. For the question of whether technology is productivity—enhancing or productivity-reducing is entirely dependent upon the organization and individuals using it.

The question is intriguing, however. It indicates a nagging doubt on the part of many that computers really solve the problems that spawned their creation.

The Productivity Paradox—A Definition

The premise behind the productivity paradox is rather simple. Businesses that expected a big productivity payoff from investing in technology are, in many cases, still waiting to collect. According to research by Paul Attewell, former professor at the State University of New York at Stonybrook, there is an absence or paucity of productivity payoffs from *information technology* (IT), despite massive investment in IT over the last 25 years.

In 1988 alone, U.S. companies invested some $51 billion in hardware, $20 billion in purchased software, and over $44 billion in computer services—a figure representing 25 percent of corporate capital stock. This huge commitment was made at the expense of other kinds of investments while the United States placed its bet that IT investment would raise economic productivity.

During the 1980s U.S. businesses invested an awe-inspiring $1 trillion in information technology with little payback (see Figure 1.1). Economists invented the term *productivity paradox* as a way of explaining the anomaly of massive investments in technology which unexplainedly resulted in flat profits and stagnant productivity gains.

The most troubling piece of the puzzle is that the service sector, which alone accounted for $800 billion in IT investments, experienced the most sluggish growth of all.

The big debate

Since the recession bottomed out in 1991, some have argued for the debunking of the productivity paradox. *Business Week* for one has engendered yet a new catchphrase—the *productivity payoff.*[1] The gist of the *Business Week* premise is that a coupling of technology and sweeping changes in management and organizational structure (i.e., re-engineering) has paved the way for the productivity payoff.

The statistics to support this view are compelling. In the years since the end of the recession, productivity (measured in output per

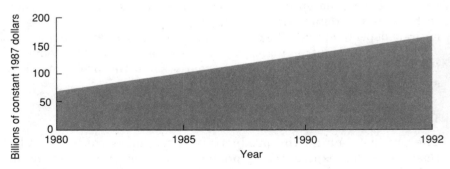

Figure 1.1 The investment in information technology. (*Source: Morgan Stanley & Company.*)

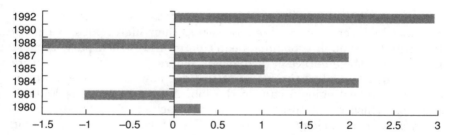

Figure 1.2 Productivity gains. (*Source: U.S. Commerce Department.*)

hour) has increased at an average annual rate of 2.3 percent. In 1992 alone, that rate jumped to a long-awaited 3 percent (see Figure 1.2).

Even more encouraging is the fact that corporate profits are up. Although some economists, including the Federal Reserve's Alan Greenspan, believe that this profit surge can be attributed to higher productivity, not every economist is convinced that we are on the road to a productivity explosion.

Both sides of the debate provide studies to back up their position. On the productivity explosion side, Erik Brynjolfsson and Lorin Hitt of the Massachusetts Institute of Technology's Sloan School of Management report that the return on investment in information technology averaged 54 percent for manufacturing and 68 percent for all businesses surveyed. In spite of these encouraging statistics, naysayers are pointing to stagnating wages, an unemployment rate persistently hovering at 7 percent, and lagging job growth (see Figure 1.3).

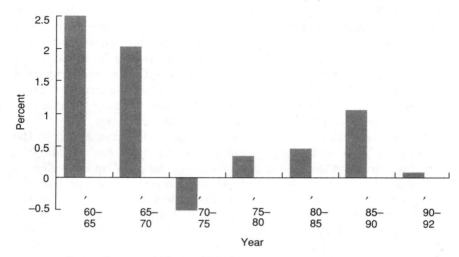

Figure 1.3 Stagnating wages. (*Source: U.S. Commerce Department.*)

One reason for the lag in employment statistics is the unprecedented rate at which corporations are downsizing their hierarchies. A part of this trend, although economists can't determine which part, is most likely due to the embrace of technology. Where dozens of workers were once needed to control the information flow, now one solitary worker, armed with technology, can do the job. A case in point is Federal Express, which rose to prominence on the back of its automated package-tracking technology, Cosmos. And Wal-Mart, the superstore king, uses technology to keep its stores stocked and its prices low.

But there are always two sides to a story. Sometimes technology only adds more confusion to an already confused situation. Look at General Electric. After aggressively spending a big part of its profits on technology in the 1980s, the megaconglomerate has begun reassessing its position—to the point of taking automation out of the factories altogether. The reason? GE believes that in many cases technology impedes productivity.

Ultimately, this just might be a case of whose statistics are more correct. IT defenders insist that macroeconomic data produced by the U.S. Departments of Commerce and Labor isn't reliable and doesn't accurately reflect the benefits being derived from information technology. For example, a shift to a service economy would be reflected as a decrease in labor-factor productivity. Additionally, the greater complexity of service-sector work calls for an increased level of output to do the job. But macroeconomic statistics simply do not capture these vagaries; therefore, it is impossible to measure productivity increases or decreases as a result of technology.

Perhaps the great leveler is a view proposed by Raymond Panko, head of the Department of Decision Sciences at the College of Business Administration, University of Hawaii. During 20 years of researching the measurement of computers and productivity, Dr. Panko has drawn the conclusion that investments in IT aren't as massive as everyone assumes. Compared with the economy as a whole, they're actually quite small—only about 1 percent of gross domestic product (GDP). This figure is far too small to serve as a true test of whether or not IT investments affect the economy.

The person with the most insight into this problem just may be the economist who coined the term *productivity paradox*. Morgan Stanley's Stephen Roach has been studying the problem for well over a decade. Roach's position is that we've had a very serious problem for the past 15 years, not because of any inherent deficiencies in the machines or in the software, but because of managerial ineptitude in applying technology to productive endeavors. In other words, we're not adequately using technology to cope with the great deluge of information we must confront each and every day.

Buried in Information

Pick up a copy of *The New York Times*. There is more information contained between the front and back pages than we can possibly digest. Add to this the other 99 papers we'll read this year. Or the 3000 notices or forms we'll read or complete, or the 2463 hours of television we'll watch, or the 730 hours of radio we'll listen to. There are 11,520 newspapers, 11,556 periodicals, and 500 million radios in the United States. Some 40,000 new book titles are published every year (300,000 worldwide), and more than 60 billion pieces of junk mail litter our mailboxes. It all adds up to something called the *information explosion.*

According to Linda Costigan Lederman, who in 1986 wrote a treatise entitled *Communication in the Workplace,*[2] these figures don't even take into account the number of hours spent exchanging information in conversations.

Experts predict that the amount of information that we are expected to absorb will double every 4 to 5 years. Even now, more new information has been generated for mass distribution in the last three decades than in the previous 5000 years.

Perhaps it's more than an information explosion; perhaps it's more like a glut. And with this glut comes the breakdown of our ability to process or even retrieve the information we so labor to possess. Akio Morita, chairman of the Sony Corporation, believes that our capacity to retrieve this information is declining. In fact, he believes that out of all we absorb, we can retrieve from our memories only a paltry 5 percent.

Alvin Toffler,[3] in his much-acclaimed 1970 book, *Future Shock,* paints an even bleaker picture. He writes of an actual breakdown of human performance under these extraordinary information loads and demonstrates its relationship to psychopathology.

Increasingly, we are doing work in our heads rather than at our desks in an effort to cope with this massive information overdose. Further, the information we must assimilate has become more and more abstract as technological innovators find new and clever ways to present it.

This increasingly large information flow is forcing us to adapt to mastering it and making judgments about it in shorter and shorter periods of time. The burgeoning quantity of information can be likened to an algae-infested pond that no longer has enough oxygen to support its fish. We may actually be pushing the physical limits of our ability to process information. When that begins to happen, great amounts of information will be passing by, which we cannot evaluate.

Born of this glut is a new phrase that all agree has distinct meaning in our lives. *Information anxiety,* a nice turn of phrase coined by

Richard Saul Wurman in his 1989 book of the same title,[4] is that chasm between what we think we should understand and what we really need to understand. As those papers and magazines and books pile up at bedside, and countless computer-generated reports stack up on desktop, we grow increasingly uneasy at our ability to keep up the pace. Information anxiety, according to Wurman, is the black hole between data and knowledge. It happens when information doesn't tell us what we need to know.

And perhaps there is no denser black hole than in the realm of information technology.

Quill pens and visors

The more avant-garde among us have been toying with the strategic use of technology to turn the tide of information glut. But, for the most part, we're still using the same old methodologies that we've been using since the computer took over the basements of our office buildings. According to Wurman, these old formulas and systems for data processing are impotent against the complexity of information we must assimilate today.

The New York Stock Exchange automates a system that displays a profile of the organizations that it regulates. This profile pours so much information on-line that it tops out at over 91 display screens. Rumor is that no one has ever seen the ninety-first screen.

The Securities and Exchange Commission must process thousands of free-form financial filings on a daily basis, far exceeding the capacity of the human reviewers.

Entering insurance underwriting data into the computer is so difficult that it takes one midwestern company 6 months to train each new employee.

The process of credit authorization depends on dozens of variables and is fraught with human error. Factors that need to be considered include payment history, seasonal variation, and even pattern of spending. Complexity grows exponentially as the number of cardholders rises and with it the request for more authorizations in a shorter span of time.

"The common denominator today is that the insurance agent is totally befuddled," says William LeStrange, president of one of the largest of the independent insurance agencies. "The agent is no longer able to answer the questions that were simple to respond to only 5 years ago." LeStrange's complaint can be traced to the power of the computer, which spawned countless new policies. The problem with the insurance industry is that companies can't get the information fast enough, can't process it quickly enough, and can't get it back in a format they can deal with.

Technical

Tactical

Strategic

Figure 1.4   Relative quantity of information needed, by decision type.

So the problem is not getting the information. The problem is that once you get it into the computer, you have a heck of a hard time getting it out. We have just begun to realize that by changing how this information is evaluated or aggregated, we can alter the dimensionality or structural content of the information to provide a different input to a different level of decision making.

There are three types of decision makers, as shown in Figure 1.4. At the bottom of the corporate hierarchy are the paper pushers. These are the people who *do* need to see all the data. They are the check processors, complaint takers, order takers, and customer service staffers. These *technical* users need to input and review a wealth of data. Given the nature of this task, they usually work in a rote fashion without resort to complex decision making. At the other end of the spectrum are the organization's senior managers, who use information gathered at the lower rungs for *strategic* purposes. A whole range of vendor-sold executive information systems (EIS) are now in vogue. They sport flashy colors, touch screens, and sparse information displays. Data displayed here would mostly likely be sales projections, profitability numbers, and key competitive stats. In the middle of the spectrum are the *tactical* users. In organizational terms, these are the individuals right on the firing line who need the most careful balance of data. They are the staffers who suffer most from information anxiety.

Companies have always collected data and stored it in diverse and hidden corporate databases. Automobile manufacturers keep massive amounts of data on file concerning their supplies and dealerships. For a long time no one saw any strategic value to this mass of detail. Then one year Chrysler fell into the black pit of insolvency. Lee Iacocca, boss of the ailing car maker, tweaked this very set of databases to save Chrysler from a fate far worse than rust. By moving to a different level of information analysis, Iacocca was able to convince members of Congress to support the loans that infused life into the veins of his company.

Whereas Chrysler is a company that learned to deal creatively with its glut of information, the nuclear facility at Three Mile Island is a case study at the opposite end of the spectrum.

Before Three Mile Island became synonymous with nuclear disaster over 15 years ago, information technology—as in so many organizations—was a necessary evil. As a result, information flow was haphazard at best. On March 28, 1979, when the plant's core overheated because of a stuck valve, the control room operators were suddenly deluged with information on a sequence of events. Each event resulted in a screaming alarm. Unable to absorb this growing mountain of data effectively or efficiently, the operators just succumbed. The result was that Three Mile Island was shut down for over 6 years. The facility didn't come back on-line until it could assure the public and the Nuclear Regulatory Commission that its reactor was safe. Part of the guarantee was that better information would be provided to the control room operators.

Today's Technology Is Not Working

In spite of Roach's protestations that inadequate hardware and software are not the cause of the productivity paradox, I believe that they are exactly the cause of the problem. Unfortunately, up until now corporate IT departments have applied the "pitch, hit, and run" theory to most systems development. Little, if any, consideration has been given to the diverse levels of decision making. Many kluges spew out unneeded and irrelevant data to users. These besieged users then unceremoniously toss the results onto the very crowded scrap heap. The result: the productivity paradox that this chapter is about.

Broken systems, broken dreams

Things have changed little in 25 years, despite the advent of faster processors, more powerful software, and more programmers. Systems are still delivered late, with more than their share of attendant bugs, and they rarely deliver what they promise to the ultimate end user. The result is the scrap heap referred to above.

The Association for Computing Machinery (ACM) publishes one of the few worthy magazines in the industry, though it is a bit high-tech for most people's tastes. Probably the best part of *Communications of the ACM* is a column written by Peter Neumann. Actually it's less a column and more a tale of woes. Neumann painstakingly collects system horror stories either told directly to him or written up in the various business and industry press. What follows is a sampling of his collection. ("War stories" with footnotes were severe enough to warrant press consideration. The other war stories were culled from Internet messages by those involved in the untidy situations.)

The state of Virginia acquired a new system for distributing child-support checks, but experienced massive delays, confusion, lost checks, delayed payments and improper seizure of tax refunds. Operations costs were expected to be triple the original estimates.[5]

The Bank of America spent $23 million on an initial 5-year development of MasterNet, a new computerized trust accounting and reporting system. After abandoning the old system, the bank spent $60 million more trying to make the new system work and finally gave up. Departed customer accounts may have exceeded billions of dollars.[6]

In 1982 Allstate Insurance began to build an $8 million computer to automate its business, with Electronic Data Systems providing software. The supposedly 5-year effort continued until at least 1993, with a cost approaching $100 million.

In 1984 Richmond, Virginia, hired Arthur Young to develop a $1.2 million billing and information system for its water and gas utilities. After spending almost $1 million, Richmond canceled the contract for nondelivery. Arthur Young retaliated with a $2 million breach-of-contract suit.

Business Men's Assurance began a 1-year project in 1985 to build a $500,000 system to help minimize the risk of buying insurance policies held by major insurers. After the company spent $2 million, the completion date was slipped to 1990.

Oklahoma hired a major accounting firm in 1983 to design a $500,000 system to handle its workers' compensation claims. Two years and more than $2 million later, the system still didn't work. It was finally finished in 1987 for nearly $4 million.

In late 1983 Blue Cross and Blue Shield United of Wisconsin hired Electronic Data Systems to build a $200 million computer system. It was delivered on time in 18 months, but didn't work, issuing $60 million in overpayments and duplicate checks. By the time the system was completed in 1987, Blue Cross had lost 35,000 policyholders.

The U.S. Office of Surface Mining spent $15 million on a computer system intended to prevent violators of strip-mine laws from getting new permits. The system could not keep identities straight, and the Government Accounting Office called it a failure.[7]

Thousands of Los Angeles County homeowners were billed retroactively for up to $15,000 in additional property taxes—an oversight which had resulted from a 1988 glitch in an $18 million computer system that was subsequently rewritten from scratch. The county was unable to collect $10 million in taxes.[8]

The B-1 bomber required an additional $1 billion to improve its ineffective air-defense software, but software problems prevented it from achieving its goals.

The software for the modernization of the Satellite Tracking Control Facility was about 7 years behind schedule, came in about $300 million over budget, and provided less capability than required.

The Airborne Self-Protection Jammer, an electronic air-defense system installed in over 2000 Navy fighters and attack planes, was $1 billion over budget, 4 years behind schedule, and only marginally operationally effective and marginally operationally suitable.

General Bernard Randolph, head of the Air Force Systems Command, commented: "We have a perfect record on software schedules—we have never made one yet and we are always making excuses."

The C-17 cargo plane being built by Douglas Aircraft had a $500 million overrun because of problems in its avionics software. A GAO report noted that there were 19 on-board computers, 80 microprocessors, and 6 different programming languages. It stated: "The C-17 is a good example of how not to approach software development when procuring a major weapons system."

Note that the majority of these failures were government. This is not to imply that the government is inept (although other factors may well hint at such a conclusion) or that the commercial sector is happily developing systems and meeting target deadlines. It's just that commercial failures rarely come to light—corporate public relations is just too good at covering up. The government, on the other hand, is required to issue very public reports detailing its successes as well as its failures. Therefore, a careful reading of government literature provides some excellent insight into why technology often goes wrong.

Case Study: Poor Management Results in Unmet Needs and Wasted Millions

The National Institutes of Health (NIH) is one of the biggest computer users in the country. With all that horsepower, NIH's IT organization must be streamlined and efficient. As we shall see, in spite of its best efforts, NIH was anything but. What went wrong?

In September 1988, NIH awarded IBM a total system contract that encompassed all aspects of a major computer system, including hardware, software, and related services. The contract, with a term of 1 year and nine 1-year options, was a jackpot for the lucky vendor—almost $806 million.

First, a little techno-history on the project. NIH uses the IBM system to process administrative data; some of its scientists also use the system to support research. Additionally, the system is operated as a federal data-processing center that provides computer-processing time to other components of the Department of Health and Human Services and about 30 other federal agencies. Portions of the system are operated on a fee-for-service basis whereby users are charged fees in order to fund the system's operations.

Federal policies and regulations require agencies to conduct specific activities to help ensure that their computer resources are effectively and economically managed. For example, agencies must prepare a strategic plan and determine system requirements to help ensure that systems will meet user needs.

But like the rest of us, NIH is anything but perfect. Again, because it is a government agency, public records document NIH's shortcomings. These records reveal that NIH did not effectively manage four key aspects of the IBM total system contract, resulting in unnecessary costs and a system which did not meet scientists' computing needs. Sound familiar?

First, NIH's information resources management organization did not assert leadership or exercise its authority over the acquisition. Second, the acquisition was not addressed in strategic-planning efforts. Third, computer center personnel did not collect or analyze data to identify the needs of scientific users. Fourth, as a result of ineffective capacity management, NIH not only acquired excess computer capacity but spent over $16 million on unnecessary computers after the contract was initiated in October 1988.

But they tried hard

NIH probably has more computer power than the average Fortune 100 company. The Division of Computer Research and Technology, which has operational responsibility for NIH's main computer center, operates a system of five IBM mainframe computers—available for scientific and administrative processing. This is the cornerstone of NIH's computer system. The computer center also has a Convex mini-supercomputer dedicated to processing scientific data. Other NIH computers that are outside the computer center include a Cray supercomputer facility, about 40 minicomputers that are used primarily for scientific work, and over 6500 personal computers.

The computer center's IBM system has about 19,000 individual users. About 51 percent of total users are NIH personnel who perform biomedical research or administrative processing. The remaining 49 percent are users in non-NIH organizations, including components of the Department of Health and Human Services and about 30 other federal agencies.

The computer center's current mainframe system has evolved through a series of contracts since the 1960s, when NIH converted its Honeywell-based system to IBM. NIH's 1981 contract with IBM is its first agreement based on a total system concept. That is, a single contractor is responsible for system operation and is required to supply specified levels of computing resources—hardware, software, communications, personnel, maintenance, and related services.

Interestingly, despite its bad ratings, NIH has endeavored to organize itself for maximum efficiency. NIH's information resources management (IRM) organization consists primarily of the IRM council, headed by NIH's senior IRM official, with supporting committees staffed by NIH personnel on a part-time basis. Although the council's responsibilities are broad-based, they include some specific activities such as strategic planning. In general, the council is responsible for (1) overseeing and coordinating NIH-wide IRM functions and (2) providing leadership to the NIH staff and offices (such as the computer center) that have functional responsibility for IRM. The IRM organization's deputy director is the council's chairperson. Council membership includes high-level NIH officials as both permanent and rotating members.

In spite of all this involvement, NIH was still deficient.

So what went wrong?

First bad move.   The IRM organization was simply not involved in the acquisition. NIH established a council, headed by its senior IRM official, to oversee and coordinate IRM functions. However, this council did not provide leadership or oversight for the acquisition. Further, committees that were supposed to support the IRM council were not involved. For example, the computing resources group was established to review acquisition proposals and provide advice and assistance to the council on acquisition requirements. Despite its potentially major role in NIH's acquisition, this group was never asked to provide advice or assistance. Lacking leadership and oversight, NIH's computer center mismanaged the acquisition.

Second bad move.   NIH's strategic planning was deficient. The IRM council did not address this major computer contract in its strategic plans. The 1986 and 1988 plans it prepared did not even discuss the acquisition. Further, a strategic planning effort undertaken by the Division of Computer Research and Technology identified a trend away from mainframe computing toward greater use of personal computers, but did not discuss the implications of this trend for the total system acquisition, which was in progress. In the absence of a strategic plan that included the total system contract, the computer center adopted an acquisition approach that did not consider whether the contract would meet scientists' changing needs.

Strike three?   Requirements were inaccurate. NIH officials stated that the IBM system was being acquired for use by biomedical research scientists. However, they did not obtain detailed input from the scientific community to identify needs. As a result, the scientists' need for the UNIX operating system was not identified and was not met by the initial system under the contract. Also, the computer center did not collect and analyze data to justify its requirements for the latest technology and a full-sized dedicated backup computer. After the contract was awarded, two NIH committees independently determined that the contract did not effectively meet the needs of NIH's scientific community.

Strike four? Oh, oh. It was found that inadequate capacity management resulted in unneeded computers. NIH overestimated the capacity requirements for its IBM contract. Consequently, NIH acquired more computer capacity than it needed and subsequently upgraded its already underutilized computers. This situation occurred in part because the computer center limited its capacity management primarily to monitoring system responsiveness. Further, NIH did not take steps to identify excess capacity and opportunities for efficient operation. A secondary study showed that two of NIH's six computers were unnecessary. Over $16 million in equipment leasing costs were wasted on these two computers and additional millions could be saved by eliminating them.

And finally, efforts to obtain competition were unsuccessful. NIH took several steps to promote competition, including soliciting industry comments on its draft request for proposals, offering up to $1 million to competitors that successfully completed a required benchmark, and extending its proposal deadline at the specific request of a potential competitor. However, only IBM bid on the system. A major acquisition feature that limited competition was NIH's insistence on the total system approach. NIH officials believed this approach was necessary to facilitate management of the computer center. However, they did not collect data or perform any analysis to justify their position. Although NIH officials believed they struck an appropriate balance between features that inhibited and enhanced competition, they were ultimately unsuccessful in attracting more than one vendor.

Sound familiar? These problems are all too typical in any organization—profit, nonprofit, or government. But at least NIH can account for what made the project go astray. Many organizations are not so lucky. There are other, less obvious, reasons that IT creates its own productivity paradox.

The Hidden Part of the Productivity Paradox

There is no doubt that computers have made many organizations far more productive. But there is also no doubt, at least in my mind, that the road to productivity through technology is littered with land mines any of which can explode with potentially disastrous results.

Although Lotus 1-2-3, WordPerfect, and their kin have proved a productivity boon, for the most part, to knowledgeable workers the disasters described earlier in this chapter should have a sobering effect.

How could NIH have gone down such a path? What led Electronic Data Systems to bungle the Allstate project? How could the Bank of America spend over $80 million on its MasterNet project and still wind up with a nonworking system?

The common denominator in all these cases is not that the technology was inefficiently applied but that the technology was inefficiently developed. Whenever the technology paradox arises in discussions, we hear little about the foibles of the system development process itself. Aside from the most obvious of system development woes such as nonuse of methodologies and improper application of tools, there is a whole category of "hidden" reasons that system developers come up with much less than perfect systems. And essentially, that's what the rest of Part 1 is really about.

References

1. *Business Week,* June 14, 1993.
2. Linda Costigan Lederman, *Communication in the Workplace,* Oxford University Press, New York, 1986.
3. Alvin Toffler, *Future Shock,* Random House, New York, 1970.
4. Richard Saul Wurman, *Information Anxiety,* Doubleday, 1989.
5. *Richmond Times-Dispatch,* June 8, 1987, p. B1.
6. *Business Week,* November 7, 1988.
7. *The Washington Times,* February 15, 1989.
8. *The Los Angeles Daily News,* February 25, 1991.

2

Competitive Advantage and the Computer

How prepared are the workers of the future? Reports over the past few years on adult and student performance in math, geography, and other areas present a less than reassuring picture:

- 75 percent of American adults can't point to the Persian Gulf on a map
- 61 percent can't find Massachusetts
- 60 percent of American 13-year-olds can't solve two-step math problems

Each year the United States graduates over 700,000 students who can't read at a fourth-grade level. It's no wonder that the nation repeatedly finishes dead last in comparative studies of math and science skills of 13-year-olds across five countries.

"We are as bad off as it seems," says Albert Shanker, president of the American Federation of Teachers. "The evidence is very clear and it's incontrovertible."

Welcome to the workplace of tomorrow.

This book is certainly not a sociological treatise on what's wrong with American education. These sad statistics are mentioned only because a corporation's foundation rests on the skills of its workers. If that foundation is weak, the corporation will falter. And in spite of American industry's investment, to the tune of about $25 billion a year, in teaching employees the basic skills that should have been learned in school, the outlook is still bleak.

An antidote to this corporate woe just may be technology. Savvy organizations have long realized that technology could be used, not only to *replace* assembly-line clerical workers in doing repetitive and mechanical tasks, but also to *assist* white-collar workers in performing their functions more productively. And more accurately.

Nowhere is this pattern more evident than in the initial productivity boon that followed the introduction of the personal computer. From the simplest task of writing a word-processing document and then spell-checking it to produce clean copy to the more complex task of building a series of interlocking spreadsheets, for the first time the worker had a sort of built-in personal assistant. This automated assistant could relentlessly correct, recalculate, and tutor the worker so that documents could be delivered to clients, superiors, or subordinates in spotless form. In fact, in the office of the 1990s it's getting more and more difficult to discern where the knowledge of the worker ends and the sheer horsepower of the word processor—or spreadsheet or desktop publishing system—begins.

We need not dwell on the knowledge amplification abilities of computers to see that technology has become more than a nicety in American corporations. It has become a necessity. But the coming dearth of talented and able workers will make it even more necessary to automate functions that are now deemed marginally automatable. These are the functions marked by reasoning and logic. As John Diebold, one of technology's spokespeople, puts it: "You got a lot of people showing very elegant sets of figures all worked out in great plans, but with the same sorts of lack of judgment you would have had without the computer."[1] Here are the workers who need to be automated if American corporations are to stay their current competitive course.

But is it *enough* to stay the current course? With global competition intensifying and closing in rapidly, will we wind up, as *USA Today* once so succinctly put it, as "an easy target in the slow lane"?

This particular phrase came from a description of a report produced by 16 Massachusetts Institute of Technology (MIT) faculty members in 1989. The 344-page, $1.3 million study concluded that the nation is slipping—and that industry, not government, is primarily responsible. Although the report, *Made in America,* targeted many culprits, perhaps the most interesting was a target labeled "outdated corporate strategies." One of these outdated strategies might well be the omission of technology from the corporate weave.

A company's technology strategy is often subordinate to its business strategy. Typically a management committee, or some other planning body, meticulously develops the company's long-range plan. The technology chiefs are called from their basement perches only to plan for one or another automated system as it meets a comparatively short-term goal from one or more of the business units. But in some companies, the process of planning is more akin to weaving.

In manufacturing fine cotton, for example, thread after thread is woven so tightly that, when complete, the cloth's individual threads are nearly impossible to distinguish from one another. The strength and resiliency of the completed cloth is the result of this careful weaving.

A company is also made up of many threads. Each has its own strategy. It's only when all these unmatched threads, or strategies, are woven together that a successful general competitive business strategy can be formulated. If the technology thread is not as tightly woven as the others, the final strategy will be like a cloth that is missing threads—full of holes and weak.

The Technological Advantage

A McKinsey & Company report, published in late 1990, gives an opinion of the strategic use of information technology that parallels what is presented in this book. According to the McKinsey study, there are three "information technology levers" that can be used to raise a company's performance.

At the lowest rung is the *information content lever*. The objectives of this approach are to approve only those IT investments that directly support business strategy. A number of initiatives can accomplish this end. One is to translate the corporate business vision into guidelines that will be followed by the IT unit in development and implementation of strategic systems. Another methodology is to use information value analysis methodologies to ensure that IT expenditures produce net economic benefits.

The middle lever is referred to by McKinsey & Company as the *technology lever*. Here the objective is to reduce the distance between the information generators and the users. Again McKinsey provides some suggestions for initiatives that can accomplish this goal. One is to decentralize IT capabilities to support front-line decision makers. A second is to ensure that application development involves interaction with users—an obvious suggestion, but one often overlooked.

The final lever is referred to as *delivery capabilities*. Here the goal is to develop internal and external capabilities allowing IT to support business strategy.

According to the report's authors, McKinsey & Company director Tom Tinsley and principal Andrew C. Power, this approach is designed to "guarantee superior delivery of information by developing and rewarding internal and external technology staffers who not only support the company's business strategy but help change it in ways that realize much more of the potential of information technology than is currently being tapped." Accomplishing this goal requires focusing resources on pivotal IT jobs and linking IT support to business change.

While McKinsey talks about levers, I prefer the concept of levels. And while McKinsey describes three levels, I think there are two more. On the very lowest level are those companies that have not as yet understood the value of the use of information technology as a partner to business strategy. These firms, according to Fred Smith of Federal Express, will most certainly be "combatively annihilated." Such firms, unfortunately, are not small in number.

On the very highest level—beyond delivery capabilities—are those *techno-businesses* whose very existence relies on the wholesale use of technology. These five levels, then, form a technology continuum. I firmly believe that the more complex, competitive, and unstable the marketplace becomes, the more we need to stay on a high technological level to keep even.

The Power of Tomorrow's Machines

Over the last 10 years the growth of technological advances has proceeded geometrically. It's a well-known fact that if the automobile industry had proceeded at the same rapid clip as the computer industry, we'd all be driving sports cars that cost $100 and get 100 miles to the gallon. It is reasonable to expect that this trend will continue. Computers will keep getting smarter and smarter. The more innovative among us will use these advances to make their competitive move and forever retain a leadership position in the marketplace. Look to Federal Express as an example. When Fedex "invented" its hand-held supertracker, there was no similar technology in the industry. As a result of this and other innovations, Fedex has managed to garner a lead that will force others to play catch-up for years. And all during those years Fedex will be developing a satisfied customer base that will be loathe to switch to the competitors once Fedex's innovations are matched.

In 1989, *The Wall Street Journal* interviewed several computer industry notables to get their perspective on what to expect from "tomorrow's hot machines."[2] Their insight and vision will be useful to business managers who are searching for that particular piece of technology that can set their company apart.

William Gates is chairman and chief executive officer of Microsoft in Redmond, Washington. Today the software produced by Microsoft is running on nearly every IBM-compatible personal computer that has been purchased since the early 1980s. Gates envisions PCs as being a staff member's window on the world. When you walk into work on any given day the computer, which already has been advised of your preferences, will display anything and everything relevant to your interests.

Computers will be about 20 times faster than they are today. Displays will be very large—two pages will fit onto every screen. People will walk around with handwriting machines that they can use to scribble information.

Gordon Bell, vice president of research and development at Ardent Computer in Sunnyvale, California, is one of the foremost computer designers in the world. He expands on Gates's vision by forecasting that by the year 2000 there will be a tremendous turmoil in the computer industry as the price of hardware "goes south." He envisions being able to walk around with a $10 card computer in his pocket. This card computer will be totally voice-operated.

Alan Kay agrees wholeheartedly with Bell but goes one step further. Kay, an Apple Computer fellow, has been on the front lines of personal computing since its beginnings in the early 1970s. He forecasts being able to put your grocery list on a new tiny personal computer and carrying it out of the store with two bags of groceries. He also forecasts head-mounted displays which look like eyeglasses. This concept, called *virtual reality,* is getting "red hot" at the moment. For now, it is limited to design, gaming, and some analytics, but in the future it is hoped that an analyst will be able to use it readily to get "inside of information" to better understand the relationships involved and therefore make better decisions.

In essence, these forward-looking thinkers envision a day when hardware and software will combine to form *information utilities,* making it easier and cheaper to more accurately size up data and make good decisions. If these devices are on their way, the question then becomes more pointed: Is corporate America ready for them?

Strategic Applications for the 1990s

Of course, this is all so much future thinking. We are, after all, only in the middle 1990s. But even in the 1990s there is much in the way of technology that a company can take in hand and use as a competitive weapon.

Most companies spotlighted by the press are fairly large and well-known. It is important to note, however, that small- to mid-size companies, have not been left out of this discussion. In fact, these companies, whose founders are closer to the technology grapevine, are most aggressively pursuing this path. Some even suggest that these very companies have the best shot at creating strategic systems. Why?

One reason has already been mentioned. The flattened hierarchy in smaller companies shortens the distance between a typical CEO and his or her technology unit. This closer relationship, once forged, provides mighty pluses. Fred Smith's Fedex started in this way, and continues on this path until this day. But there are others.

When you think of the fast-food industry you probably envision waiting in line at McDonald's for a hamburger, some fries, and a soft drink. What you probably don't think of is the state-of-the-art computer systems that get all that food delivered correctly and on time.

Grand Rapids, Michigan, is home to Sunneveldt, probably the most high-tech wholesale food distributor in the country. But exactly where do computers fit into the hamburger and french fry picture that we're so used to? "Where don't computers fit in?" counters Gene Goulooze, vice chairman and CEO. "We couldn't operate without computer systems."

Goulooze ticks off the two main reasons that state-of-the-art computers are so important to Sunneveldt: These computers require relatively few people to operate, and their reliability, dependability, and uptime have been very good. Such attributes take on a major significance in any attempt to do what Sunneveldt has done so successfully—that is, to create a far-flung, distributed network which links a company to its hundreds of customers and suppliers.

Sunneveldt's customers use their own personal computers to access the mainframe in Grand Rapids. Through this automated link, Sunneveldt customers can perform a plethora of activities, including automated order entry, store-level statement printing, and electronic mail. This E-mail feature permits customers not only to send messages and get responses from Sunneveldt but also to send messages to any other customer or store on the network. For customers with multiple stores, E-mail has provided a great way to communicate daily information without the expense, and ritual, of the daily telephone call.

Sunneveldt's mainframe acts as a hub for all these activities and more. Through EDI, the company is hooked up, mainframe to mainframe, with its hypermarket supplier, achieving efficiencies unheard of in the paperbound world. Sunneveldt's tentacles also reach out to Fort Worth, Texas, where a sister company utilizes the mainframe, as well as to Dayton, Ohio, which houses a second facility.

Even down at the warehouse level, computerization is the norm. The Sunneveldt system keeps track of every one of the hundreds of items stored in the warehouse. The system even knows where the oldest products are located. Replenishers—those folks who load orders into "palettes"—use hand-held units to indicate what they're "picking." Once an order is complete, data can be uploaded back into the system, completing the cycle of automation. The cycle begins at the customer site with remote order entry, goes out to the supplier through EDI if necessary, passes down to the warehouse for actual order fulfillment, and finally ends up back with the customer for inquiry, statements, and E-mail.

Smith and Goulooze seem to be representative of those CEOs who have an intimate awareness of what technology can do for an organization. Therefore, they "push" their companies to find the most innovative solutions to their business problems, with extremely profitable results.

F. Warren McFarlan, the Ross Graham Walker professor of business administration at Harvard University, would agree that Fedex and Sunneveldt demonstrate the vast improvements in performance that companies can achieve through imaginative use of information technology.

In the University of Western Ontario School of Business Administration's summer 1990 *Business Quarterly,* McFarlan expounds on how innovative companies are likely to use information technology as this decade progresses. He suggests that "information-enabled time compression" as a competitive weapon will be perhaps the most important IT application area. Reducing production-run times is equally applicable to all industries. For the automakers, information technology can pare days from the production of a new car. For the financial services industry, even the shaving of a second can make a trader more competitive than his or her neighbor.

Second on McFarlan's list is cost displacement and asset utilization, which will occur over extremely long periods of time. One example of this strategic application is in the drug wholesale industry, in which distribution cost as a percentage of sales has dropped precipitously from 16 to 2.5 percent over the last 19 years. The drop is due largely to the increasing use of information technology.

Guidelines for Using Information Technology Strategically

If this chapter relays any one principle, it is that senior executives must take an active interest in the merger between technology and business in their organizations. If successful firms have one common denominator, it is the availability of a senior executive who understands and appreciates the value of technology coupled with a strong advocate, who understands business, in the technology department. This dynamic duo possesses the understanding, and ultimately the know-how, for using information technology strategically.

Unfortunately, few firms have achieved this ideal. Ronald B. Wilkes, an assistant professor of management information systems at Memphis State University, has done extensive research in this area and has uncovered some interesting factors which might account for the failure.[3]

Although systems have often been described as strategic—more specifically, as "competitive weapons"—it appears, according to Wilkes, that the *same* systems are being described "ad nauseam." The small number stems from a lack of "strategic information systems vision." According to Wilkes's study, technology managers and executive-level managers view strategic use of the IT resource very differently. Although strategic issues are important to both levels of management, it has been found that technology managers are much more complete and accurate in identifying potential strategic technology strengths and weaknesses than are executives.

The root of the problem is this difference in perspective about the strategic use of information technology. It is worthwhile, then, to examine the components of strategy and how they relate to information technology.

Components of strategy

According to Wilkes, three factors define strategy and strategic processes: the scope of strategic decision making, the domains (factors or forces) to be considered in formulating a strategy, and the approach to strategic planning.

The scope of a decision defines its impact on the organization. For a decision to be strategic, it must deal with the organization's relationship with the external environment and must have some impact on the success of the organization as a whole.

Wilkes's study uncovers seven key domains which typically comprise strategic decision making:

Basic mission

Customer mix

Product mix

Service area

Goals and objectives

Competitive advantage

Outside relationship

Another perspective on the same issue comes from Michael Porter,[4] who has identified several competing forces which need to be considered in strategy formulation. These are bargaining power of customers, bargaining power of suppliers, current competitors, threat of new entrants into the market, and threat of substitute products or services. These forces are affected by barriers to entering or exiting markets. Porter advises that a company should flexibly employ its assets to ease its entry, mobility, and exit in a market area. Alternatively, the company can attempt to put up barriers to other companies' entering the marketplace. One advantage of this strategy is "cornering the market," but it may be more than offset by the expense involved in doing so.

The process of strategy formulation consists of many activities, according to other business theorists.[5] In the best-case scenario:

- A strategic profile is developed that encompasses how the company defines itself as well as the steps it has taken to be competitive.

- A strategic forecast of the environment is created. The forecast encompasses political, economic, market, product, competitive, and technological issues.

- An audit is performed to assess the strengths and weaknesses of the organization.

- The audit results are compared with the environmental scan. From this comparison, a set of strategic alternatives is developed.

- The consistency of the alternatives is tested to make sure that they fit the capabilities of the organization as well as the external opportunities defined by the organization. These alternatives must also be consistent with the profile that the organization has created for itself. This step permits the company to align what is possible in a particular environment with what the company has the capability to do.

- The alternatives are reviewed and a choice is made.

Wilkes has identified many differences in how the IT resource is used strategically. He has devised a series of questions that attempt to uncover the meaning of the strategic use of this resource:

1. Does strategic use of the IT resource refer to support for the strategic decision-making process or to information technology as an organizational resource?

2. Is the focus on classifying existing systems or on identifying potential systems which will have the greatest impact on the success of the organization?

3. At what level of planning is the IT resource considered? In other words, are systems developed to confront operational problems of efficiency and reduction of errors, or are systems developed to implement known organizational strategies?

4. Is the IT resource considered in the formulation of corporate strategy?

There is an important distinction between using information technology to support the strategic-planning process and considering it to be one factor in the strategic-planning process. It has been found that when technology managers say that their department is being used strategically what they really mean is that reports generated by their department are used in strategic planning.

Strategic levels

It is important to be able to determine the strategic level of an existing, or potential, system. One methodology is the framework developed by Harvard professor F. Warren McFarlan.[6] McFarlan's framework assesses the strategic significance of a system to an organization. As shown in Figure 2.1, the McFarlan grid is two-dimensional, showing four different types of management environments.

In *strategic firms,* the relationship with technology is very tight. These firms have, according to McFarlan, an "excruciating" dependence on technology. Systems developed by strategic companies are critical to competitive success. *Turnaround firms,* while considering technology to be very important, don't quite have the dependence on technology that strategic firms do. These firms are making the transi-

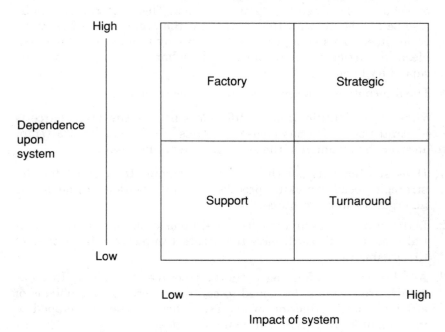

Figure 2.1 Framework for assessment of strategic importance of an IT system. (*Source: F. Warren McFarlan and James Cash.*)

tion to the strategic level. Their current systems are not considered strategic, but the development of new ones is and such development is crucial to the competitiveness of the organization.

In *factory-type firms,* although technology is heavily depended upon for the smooth running of operations, it is not seen as a major differentiator. In *support-type firms,* technology is considered important and useful, but it is not on the short list of things that the company needs to do.

McFarlan's grid is designed to assist a company in determining its classification and the appropriate way to manage the IT resource, depending on whether that resource serves a support or strategic role in the organization.

The dual nature of technology in relation to business strategy calls for the utilization of different sets of techniques.[7] When the IT resource supports the mission and strategy of the organization, a well-known technique that is often applied is *strategy set transformation:*

- Identify the "strategy set" of the organization. This consists of the firm's mission statement, its organizational objectives, the organizational strategy, and strategic organizational attributes.

- Identify stakeholder groups within the organization.

- Identify the operating objectives of the stakeholder groups and the constraints related to the development of systems.

- Develop information strategies on the basis of these results.

When information technology is considered a strategy in itself, it is useful to envision a three-level impact on business: industry, firm, and strategy.[8]

- Technology can change the products and services offered. An example is the publishing industry, which is now offering electronic versions of publications.

- Technology can change the markets served by the industry. For example, the proliferation of automated teller machines (ATMs) has expanded the banking marketplace by broadening geographic range and customer base as well as by lowering costs.

- Technology can change production costs.

McFarlan sums up nicely by posing several questions to help determine if an opportunity exists for an organization to use technology strategically:

1. Can technology be used to build barriers to entry?

2. Can technology change the basis of competition?

3. Can technology be used to generate new products?

4. Can technology be used to build in switching costs?

5. Can technology change the balance of power in supplier relations?

Finally, a technique commonly known as the *customer's resource life-cycle model* can assist in uncovering new strategic opportunities for the successful application of technology. The technique is based on the stages of a resource's life cycle. Each stage must be reviewed independently to search for a way to utilize technology to provide a competitive edge. Here are some examples:

Specify	Many products today are sent out to distributors with attached computer cards. When a card is returned to the manufacturer, the information is entered into a system which can assist in determining when something needs to be restocked.
Order	CompuServe and other national on-line networks provide an electronic shopping mall. Consumers can shop at any number of stores directly through their personal computers.
Authorize	Automated teller machines provide immediate authorization.
Acquire	CompuServe and many other networks provide news directly on-line.
Test and accept	Computerized pharmacies have the capability of making sure that patients are receiving the proper medications.
Integrate into Inventory	Airline systems used automated reservations systems to balance their flight loads.
Monitor	Inventory systems monitor usage and indicate when it is time to reorder.
Upgrade	Supermarkets use sophisticated systems to keep track of sales.
Maintain	Most appliance companies keep track of sales to notify customers of renewal of service contracts.

Information technology may either assist in the strategy-building process or serve as a component of it. All the research indicates that the componetization of technology into strategy services an organization best.

Doing Systems Right

Perhaps part of the problem is that American corporations have chosen the wrong systems to automate. We not only will have to build systems right, but will also have to build the right systems.

To ensure technological productivity, technologists must go beyond the traditional approaches of system development to be able to make a correct match between technology and process, between problem and solution.

One way this can be done is by evaluating each critical success factor (CSF) of a business or business line. Managers are intimately aware of their missions and goals. But they don't necessarily consciously define the processes required to achieve these goals. In other words, how does the company get there? In these instances, technologists must depart from their traditional venue of top-down methodologies and employ a bottom-up approach. They must work with the business unit to discover the goal and work their way up through the policies, procedures, and technologies that will be necessary to arrive at that particular goal.

Suppose that the goal of a business line is to be able to cut down the production and distribution cycle by a factor of 10 and provide a customized product at no more cost than what has been true for a generic product in the past. To achieve this goal, the technology group needs to get the business managers to walk through the critical processes that need to be invented or changed. It is only at this point that any technology solutions are introduced.

An IBM approach to determining CSFs

Maurice Hardaker and Bryan K. Ward encapsulate rather neatly IBM's approach to helping a team develop a specific plan of action for a particular approach. The technique, called *process quality management* (PQM), makes use of the concept of critical success factors.[9]

IBM originally developed PQM to solve a persistent problem that plagues most companies: How do you get a group to agree on goals and ultimately deliver a complex project efficiently and productively? PQM is really a combination of methodologies that many companies use independently. IBM synergistically culled these diverse techniques with the effect of creating a method that is used today by a broad array of companies, including Time Warner.

PQM is initiated by gathering, preferably off-site, a team of up to 12 people who can be considered essential to the project. *Essential* is the operative word here. The team members should represent all facets of the project. Obviously, all teams have leaders and PQM teams are no different. In teams set up at the request of the technology department, the desire to appoint the head of technology as team leader will be strong. However, this choice should not be seen as mandatory and, in fact, may not be in the best interests of the project.

The team leader chosen must have a skill mix closely attuned to the projected outcome of the project. For example, in a PQM team whose assigned goal is to improve plant productivity, the best team leader just might be an expert in process control, even though the eventual solution might be in the form of enhanced automation.

Along with the team leader, a discussion leader is selected. Care should be taken to ensure that the discussion leader has no vested interests in the outcome of the group's work. Often, outside consulting firms are brought in to fulfill just this role.

Assembled at an off-site location, the team first seeks to develop, in written form, a specific statement of its mission. With an open-ended goal such as "Determine the best method of employing technology for competitive advantage," the determination of the actual mission statement becomes an arduous task. The best approach is to segment this rather vague goal into more concrete and specific goals, such as:

Goal 1   Determine how other companies use technology competitively

Goal 2   Assess the company's technological strengths and weaknesses

Goal 3   Assess the company's product line strengths and weaknesses

Goal 4   Research new technological advances

Goal 5   Tie together

When the mission statement has been written down and agreed upon by all team members, it is time for a quick, open-ended brainstorming session in which the team lists all the factors that might inhibit the mission from being accomplished. The session should take no more than 10 minutes, and the results should be a series of one-word descriptions. For example, in goal 4 above, mission inhibitors could be cost, time, and integration. Given the 10-minute time frame, the objective is to identify as many of these inhibitors as possible without discussion and without criticism.

At this point the team turns to identifying the critical success factors—the specific tasks that it must perform to accomplish its mission. Each CSF must adhere to the following four requirements:

1. All team members must agree on the inclusion of any item.

2. Each item must be absolutely necessary for the successful completion of the mission.

3. Each item must stand alone. That is, no conjunctions of the form *and* and *or* are to be allowed.

4. Taken as a unit, the CSFs must be sufficient to accomplish the stated mission.

It is vitally important that the entire team reach a consensus on the CSFs. Hardaker and Ward describe a study which asked the top 10 managers in 125 European companies to individually identify their companies' most critical objectives. The rules for this exercise were to produce a minimum of 5 objectives, with a maximum of 50. It seems that the managers of the 40 most profitable companies agreed on 6 to 12 objectives. For the 40 least profitable companies, the range was from 26 to 43. Apparently, the top executives of the poor performers had no shared vision of what they were trying to do.

The next step in the IBM PQM process is to make a list of all the tasks that are necessary to accomplish the CSFs. The description of each of these tasks, called *business processes,* should be declarative. Each should begin with an action verb such as *study, measure, reduce, negotiate,* or *eliminate.*

Figures 2.2 and 2.3 show the *project chart* and *priority chart,* respectively, used to diagram the Hardaker and Ward PQM technique. PQM requires that the team fill out these charts as well. The team's mission, in the example presented, is to introduce *just in time* (JIT) inventory control, a manufacturing technique that fosters greater efficiencies by stocking inventory only to the level of need. In this case, the team identified 6 CSFs and 11 business processes labeled P1 through P11.

The project chart is filled out by first ranking the business processes according to their importance to the project's success. Each busi-

Business process		Critical success factors						Count	Quality
		1	2	3	4	5	6		
P1	Measure delivery performance by suppliers	x	x					2	B
P2	Recognize/reward workers					x	x	2	D
P3	Negotiate with suppliers	x	x	x				3	B
P4	Reduce number of parts	x	x	x	x			4	D
P5	Train supervisors					x	x	2	C
P6	Redesign production line	x		x	x			3	A
P7	Move parts inventory	x							E
P8	Eliminate excessive inventory buildups	x	x					2	C
P9	Select suppliers	x	x					2	B
P10	Measure				x	x	x	3	E
P11	Eliminate defective parts	x	x	x				3	D

CSF 1 = Rapid access to parts
CSF 2 = Supplier cooperation
CSF 3 = Products engineered for JIT assembly
CSF 4 = Supportive work force
CSF 5 = Worker knowledge of JIT procedures
CSF 6 = Supervisor knowledge of JIT procedures

Source: Maurice Hardaker and Bryan K. Ward.)

Figure 2.2 Project chart.

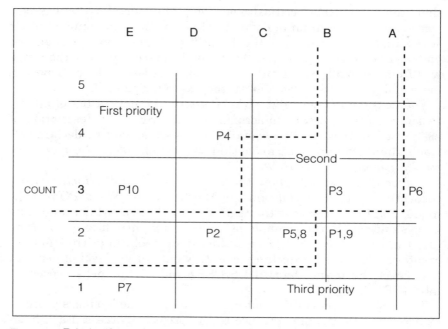

Figure 2.3 Priority chart. (*Source: Maurice Hardaker and Bryan K. Ward.*)

ness process is evaluated against the set of CSFs. A checkmark or "x" is placed under each CSF that relates significantly to the process. In our example, business process P1 is to measure the delivery performance by suppliers. Two marks are assigned to this process (note the Count column). Process P1 is quite important to rapid access to the parts CSF as well as to the supplier cooperation CSF.

This procedure is followed until each of the business processes has been analyzed. The Hardaker and Ward technique recommends assigning one to four business processes to specific members of the team. In practice, however, ranking the importance of business processes is more effective when done by the team as a whole.

The final column of the project chart permits the team to rank each business process relative to current performance, using the following scale:

A = process performed in an excellent manner
B = good
C = fair
D = bad
E = not applicable or not currently performed

The project chart can be thought of as a preliminary to the priority chart. But it is the priority chart, when completed, that will steer the mission to a successful, and prioritized, conclusion. The two axes to this graph are Quality, using the A through E grading scale above, and Priority, represented by the number of checkmarks that each business process received. These can be lifted easily from the Quality and Count columns, respectively, of the project chart.

The team's final task is to decide how to divide the priority chart into different zones representing first priority, second priority, and so on. In our example, the team has chosen as a first priority all business processes that range from a quality of "fair" to a quality of "not currently performed" and that have a rank of 3 or greater. Most groups employing this technique will assign priorities in a similar manner.

Determining the right project to pursue is one factor in the push for competitive technology. It is equally important to be able to "do the project right." That is, it is paramount that the company run a productive and quality-oriented software factory.

The Quality Issue

The quality issue is necessarily inseparable from the productivity issue if a company is going to "do systems right." Quality in the short term translates to productivity in the long term.

Quality is frequently overlooked in the race to implement on or before deadline. However, no matter what the time pressure, certain measures—undertaken seriously—can enhance the quality of output of any software investment. What follows is a look at some interesting techniques that organizations are using to promote quality. Before you read on, remember one thing. Library shelves are filled with books on the subject of quality techniques. What these companies discovered, however, was that some techniques are more practical for "real" situations (as opposed to textbook, theoretical cases) than other techniques. Although each company must tailor a quality program to its individual needs, the best research the company can undertake is to find out what its peers are doing. It is in this vein that I offer up solutions that I consider to be among the best of the lot.

Microsoft's search for quality

Few firms understand the value of quality better than the giant in Redmond. With so many software products, and so many customers, Microsoft regards quality as an important issue. James Tierney is the testing manager in the multimedia products group. He is responsible for making sure that the quality of each Microsoft multimedia offering is high enough to warrant shipping the product. Despite the growing trend toward viewing after-the-fact bug detectors as quality assurance tools, Tierney insists on being able to *predict* problems before the fact. He wanted some software to track "trends in how the software was doing." He wanted to be able to track bug trends and bug density so that he could more accurately determine the final release date and thus allocate resources better.

Tierney found his solution in a company called Software Quality Tools Corporation (SQTC). Microsoft is not the only client that this Westborough, Massachusetts company supports. Its customer roster also includes such heavy-hitters as Apple Computer and Cray Research Inc. With Microsoft, Cray, and Apple heavily investing in "defect removal" strategies, corporate IT managers are beginning to sit up and look more closely at the quality factor.

The software quality management system (SQMS) implements software reliability models by measuring the reliability of a product in development. SQMS is based on a theoretical technology that goes back to 1972. Of the software reliability models that were then being popularized, the most prominent were the two developed at AT&T by John Musa: the *basic execution time model* and the *logarithmic poisson model.* These two models are used to predict mean time to fault detection and the number of faults remaining in the code. A good read on software reliability can be found in John Musa's book on the subject.[10]

In SQMS, data is collected either through access to automated problem logs or through analysis of the volatility of the code—that is, determination of how much the code changes on a day-to-day basis. Data culled from the problem reports is used to compute mean time to fault repair, while the volatility data is used to calculate the *software volatility index.* Ultimately, a *software quality index* can be calculated giving the ratio of known and corrected faults to the predicted total number of faults.

These measures are produced through the *testing module,* which is only one of five that underlie SQMS. Other, related modules are the *complexity module,* which evaluates software design and predicts testability and maintenance problems; the *integration module,* which recommends the optimum testing path for subprogram integration and measures the resulting reliability of the integrated system; the *costing module,* which uses several industry standards, such as the constructive cost model (COCOMO), to calculate the total cost of developing the software, including maintenance; and the *tracking module,* which provides management reports, including the option to identify critical paths. Like factory scheduling, tools such as SQMS help managers allocate resources better.

The Hewlett-Packard way

Perhaps one of the best examples of a company tracking the quality and productivity of its software from an engineering perspective comes from Hewlett-Packard (HP), based in Cupertino, California. Quality and productivity have been part of HP's corporate objectives for years. But only within the last few years has this concept filtered into the world of software development. To help develop and utilize metrics companywide, HP created a software metrics council. Today, 80 productivity and quality managers within HP perform a variety of functions, from training and communicating the best software-engineering practices to establishing productivity and quality metrics.

HP has adopted a methodology called *total quality control* (TQC). A fundamental principle of TQC is that all company activities can be scrutinized in terms of the processes involved; metrics can be assigned to each process to evaluate effectiveness. HP has developed numerous measurements for TQC (see Chapter 14).

The TQC approach places quality and assessment high on the list of software development tasks. When projects are first defined, along with understanding and evaluating the process to be automated, the team defines the metrics that are to be used to measure the process.

When HP decided to revolve the future of the company around a new type of computer architecture, software reliability was deemed critical. Creation of the system software for this enterprise was the largest development effort in HP's history, and the first that required multiple divisions to produce a software system.

Charles A. Krueger of the University of Wisconsin in Madison points out the productivity paradox of budget versus getting to market: Is it more important to stay within the targeted confines of money allocated or to get the product out on time? Krueger quotes a McKinsey & Company study which indicates that going over budget by 50 percent and getting a product out on time reduces profits by only 4 percent. But staying on budget and getting to market 5 months late reduces profits by two-thirds. Obviously, productivity is really a measure of how successful you are in achieving your results.

Hewlett-Packard came to the same conclusion as Krueger, and the company insisted on reliable software and delivery on time. HP established a system software certification program to ensure measurable, consistent, high-quality software through defining metrics, setting goals, collecting and analyzing data, and certifying products for release. This program developed four metrics for its new architecture:

- *Breadth.* Measures the testing coverage of user-accessible and internal functionality of the project

- *Depth.*   Measures the proportion of instructions or blocks of instructions executed during testing.

- *Reliability.*   Measures the stability and robustness of a product and its ability to recover gracefully from error conditions.

- *Defect density.*   Measures the quantity and severity of reported defects and a product's readiness.

HP's results were impressive. Defects were caught and corrected early, at a time when costs to find and fix were lower. Less time was spent in the costly system test and integration phases, and on maintenance. The results were lower overall support costs and higher productivity—along with increased quality for HP's customers. HP's success demonstrates what a corporatewide commitment to productivity and quality measures can achieve.

References

1. Peter Coy, "1980s PC Awaits a Transformation," *The Boston Globe,* December 12, 1989.
2. "Computer Gurus Cast Their Eyes Toward Tomorrow's Hot Machines," *The Wall Street Journal,* June 23, 1989, p. 15.
3. Ronald B. Wilkes, white paper, Memphis State University, 1991.
4. Michael Porter, *Competitive Strategy,* Macmillan, New York, 1980.
5. H. Uyterhoeven, R. Ackerman, and J. Rosenblum, *Strategy and Organization.* Richard D. Irwin, Homewood, Illinois, 1977.
6. James I. Cash and F. Warren McFarlan, *Competing Through Information Technology,* Harvard Business School Video Series, 1989.
7. G. Parsons, "Information Technology: A New Competitive Weapon," *Sloan Management Review,* vol. 25, no. 1, Fall 1983, pp. 3–14.
8. B. Ives and G. P. Learmonth, "The Information System as a Competitive Weapon," *Communications of the ACM,* vol. 27, no. 12, December 1984, pp. 1193–1201.
9. Maurice Hardaker and Bryan K. Ward, "How to Make a Team Work," *Harvard Business Review,* November-December 1987, pp. 112–120.
10. John Musa, *Software Reliability,* McGraw-Hill, New York, 1990.

3

Building Systems Wrong, Building the Wrong Systems

From the popular press one would get the impression that the advent of the computer is akin to the second coming. Not quite. But computers do give organizations and individuals the ability to do things that they could never do before and to speed up the things that they could do before.

Still, the computer is a machine. And like any machine, it has appropriate and inappropriate uses. Let me try to explain. A fork is an implement (a sort of machine). You use it to scoop and pick up. While a fork works fine on one or two leaves of lettuce, you wouldn't use it to pick up a head of lettuce.

So too with computers. Just because they're here and available doesn't mean that they offer an appropriate solution to every business problem.

Now this may seem obvious, but it isn't. Not from some of the stories you'll read about in this chapter. When I got my M.B.A., the teaching methodology employed was to present case histories to make a point. Well, the case histories presented below make this point all too clearly. Not all computerized solutions work. If we're going to pursue the elusive goal of enhanced productivity, then not only do we have to "do systems right," we have to "do the right systems."

Boilerplate Lawyering Irks Judge

From *New York Newsday*[1] comes this war story:

> In an A&P supermarket in New York's Greenwich Village, Thomas Rich got into an altercation with a clerk about food stamps. When the clerk

grabbed a 5-pound sack of potatoes and flung it against his back, Rich went out and got a lawyer.

The defense lawyer retained by A&P filed highly specific motions to the court. But the district attorney responded with a one-size-fits-all "boilerplate" reply spewed out of a computer. Unfortunately, the reply referred to demands for hearings that A&P's defense attorney never made. It also ignored issues raised by A&P.

A&P's defense attorney, Neil Checkman, had this to say about computer boilerplates: "Lazy. Sloppy. And I see this often. Doesn't anyone bother to think anymore?"

Criminal Court Judge Arlene Goldberg feels the same way. "The indiscriminate use of the word processor has resulted in the mass production of boilerplate responses which often bear little relevance to the motions they are ostensibly designed to answer."

The result of this practice is that some lawyers fill in the blanks on all-inclusive, formulaic motions. Thus autopsy photos might be demanded in a drug bust. Or a gun in Medicaid fraud. And some boilerplate motions by one side respond to boilerplate motions by the other. As Judge Goldberg puts it: "It's become the War of the Machines." Caught in all this computer crossfire are overworked judges who have to read the whole dense mess.

In some states, the debate about boilerplating has gone all the way up to the supreme court. A decision by Justice Patricia A. Williams seeks to end this: "Judges should not be asked to wade through a paper swamp and identify those few items that stand on solid, relevant ground. It appears to be assumed that this is quality legal representation. This court, for one, says it is not. The practice will not long go unsanctioned."

Is PC Software Really Up to It?

On some major roadways, PC stores are about as ubiquitous as gas stations. Go inside any of them and you'll see sleek displays of even sleeker-looking boxed PC software. And all these boxes are saying, "Buy me."

A *Computer Market Letter* survey finds that, on average, there are four software packages installed on an end user's PC.[2] The breakdown is usually a word processor, a spreadsheet, a database package, and some presentation software. From the start, the user knows he or she is in trouble when the installation program just doesn't work.

I had this problem recently when I installed a copy of Adobe's Photoshop. The installation program asked for my serial number, which I dutifully entered. Unfortunately, it wouldn't accept what I entered the way that I entered it. It turns out that Adobe had used a not-so-great printer to print serial numbers, so what looked to me like PVV was actually PW. Chalk one up to lousy printers.

Perhaps my best war story involves the installation and running of the optical character recognition (OCR) software that came with my Microtek scanner. For me, OCR is a wonderful boon to productivity. Unless, of course, I encounter persistent and sometimes unexplained problems with my hardware or scanner.

I installed OmniPage Direct by Caere, using what is referred to as the Twain driver. It installed and worked like a charm for 2 weeks. Then, all of a sudden, OmniPage wouldn't "recognize" the typed page. The scanner was working. I knew this because I could scan pictures into my image-editing software. I presumed OmniPage just got cranky.

I called Caere. Its service technicians weren't interested in discussing what I considered to be an "unsolved mystery." They merely told me to download (at my own expense) an alternative driver and use the new one instead. I did. It works. But to this day I'm waiting for it to become temperamental and call it quits.

Then, of course, there's the now-famous bug in Microsoft's DOS 6. Some people found out the hard way that compression software is tricky business. Of course, Microsoft isn't the only culprit here. I had much the same problem with Stacker.

I had used Stacker on my NEC computer. When I bought an ALR (Advanced Logic Research) PC and began to run out of space, I decided that Stacker was just the thing to solve my problem. Unfortunately, I didn't read the `readme.txt` file. I should have. It would have told me that, for some reason, ALR and Stacker are mutually exclusive. I found that out the hard way when I wound up with an unusable 120-million-byte file. But at least I got more disk space.

I don't think there is a user out there without one or more war stories like these. The bone I'd like to pick with software vendors is that there should be nary a complaint. In spite of vendors' protestations to the contrary, PC-based software is neither carefully tested nor quality-assured—at least, not in the same sense that mainframe software is. Again, *Computer Market Letter* found that users perceive the error rate to be 75 percent higher in PC-based software than in mainframe-based software.

There may be many reasons for this high error rate. Certainly, the quality of the programmer is one. And the sheer number of software products that need to interact on a little PC is another. The immaturity of the field and of user-expectations is yet a third. Accept less than quality and you get less than quality. The worst offender, however, is the constant drive to "get it to market"—a dictum that pushes products out the door before they're ready. In other words, a mainframe beta test is a PC product.

Some years ago, a wine producer ran a series of TV commercials claiming that it would "sell no wine before its time." Since we apparently can't rely on all computer industry vendors to be so honorable, I recommend that you not buy versions of software that offer radically altered functionality (unless, of course, you really have to have it). Wait until the vendor shakes the bugs out. This is exactly what happened in the Microsoft DOS 6 case. After a few hundred organizations fumed that they had essentially killed their hard disks and lost hundreds of productive hours, Microsoft fixed the bugs. Those of us patient enough to wait got the new functionality without the trauma.

Even the press gets the blues

Everyone in the PC field is created equally. The staff at InfoWorld recently reported on a brush with PC bugamania.

Apparently Apple Computer sent a Macintosh Workgroup Server 95 to InfoWorld's Nicholas Petreley, Nancy Durlester, and Laura Wonnacott. The first bad omen was that the floppy disk drive didn't line up exactly with the slot where the floppy is inserted. The second omen was that Apple neglected to send along the color monitor.

Then the InfoWorld folks opened the box that presumably held the keyboard. Wrong. No keyboard either. But the box did contain a few manuals, a CD-ROM, a cord, and a mouse. After stealing a keyboard and a monitor, the intrepid team put it all together and turned on the machine. A few screen flickers and then—nothing.

Finding what they thought to be the answer to the problem, the InfoWorlders reseated the SCSI card, only to encounter trouble getting a good fit. Once that was accomplished, they attempted to test out the misaligned floppy—again to great unsuccess, since the floppy got stuck and not even a paper clip would get it out.

The team persevered, and ultimately a screwdriver did the trick. But an hour after it booted, the beautiful color screen developed a wee bit of an alignment problem.

Finally, the team gave up, took the bait, and asked Apple for a new server. That delivered, the team tried again, getting past the hardware intricacies only to be foiled by the software installation. Although the instruction manual assured the team that it would be able to run PING, a TCP/IP connection test facility, no PING was anywhere to be found. So back to Apple tech support.

The first question raised by tech support was whether or not the team was following the manual. The answer was a resounding yes. Tech support replied: "Well, there's your problem. The manual is wrong."

So, what's the answer to this dilemma? Apparently, PC software vendors, or at least the majority of them, are too busy getting the goods out to market to concentrate on quality. And their lack of quality is making you less productive than you think. The solution, it seems to me, is to get the vendors on the quality bandwagon.

ISO 9000 is a standardization process that is rapidly gaining acceptance worldwide. The reasons include internal quality improvement, market positioning, and customer or regulatory requirements, particularly those connected with the European Community. Firms seeking ISO 9000 registration must go through a grueling process of analyzing their quality shortfalls. And then they must develop and implement steps that lead to a better-quality product.

If software firms would embrace a standards ideal, many of the problems discussed in this chapter would simply disappear. The problem is that not enough firms are making a commitment to ISO 9000. Perhaps if we all clamor loud enough, this will indeed come to pass.

Nightmare on Wall Street

Financial institutions use hard data. As millions of securities are sold to millions of customers daily, the business of doing business becomes extremely paper-intensive. And the business of reporting on this highly regulated industry constitutes a veritable paper chase—from financial statements, loan agreements, and complaints to stock information and customer statements.

But to the hapless souls who need this mountain of reporting data, the deluge is never-ending and usually keypunched with less than complete accuracy, forcing the back office to verify, verify, and verify again until the data is 100 percent clean and accurate.

It is at this point that complex, multi-million-dollar information systems take over to analyze data, looking for potential financial or operational problems, monitoring trends that could lead to problems, or even forecasting future problems. So on the one end you have these expensive, souped-up systems being choked at the other end by endless streams of paper and a burdensome keypunch operation.

Enter the microcomputer. Brilliance strikes an organization only a very few times, and in the case of deciding to use the microcomputer to transmit required data, it is still unclear whether this choice is brilliance or sheer luck. Whatever it is, microcomputer reporting is a lot harder than it looks.

The firms on Wall Street are as different from one another as they are similar. From the large, technically sophisticated firms to the small mom-and-pop companies with no computers, a microcomputer-reporting requirement compounds the problem in proportion to the number of firms transmitting information.

Unfortunately, transmission of data to regulators and other destinations is generally delegated to the lowest rung on the employee hierarchy ladder—in other words, to whoever is available. To make matters worse, many of these transmissions are made monthly or quarterly rather than daily. Infrequent transmissions mean a continuous stream of users on the lowest end of the learning curve. And dealing with the bottom of the learning curve means increasing levels of support, costing cold, hard dollars.

At one firm, a clerk named Peggy called the help desk at her data's destination to complain that the data was not transmitting. She had entered it all successfully, and it had passed all the edit checks, she said. She ran the transmission program, which she had run a hundred times before, but got no message from the host indicating that the send was successful. Pat, a member of the help desk staff, asked Peggy if her modem was working properly. "What modem?" Peggy asked.

"You know, that little box sitting right next to your PC," Pat answered.

"Oh, yeah. It's not there."

A simple problem—a missing modem—but time is still spent in trying to resolve the difficulty.

Then there is the story of the no-name computer. When a new application is targeted for PC transmission, some firms send out a questionnaire to be completed by a technical staffer at the transmitting firm. A typical questionnaire asks for such mundane information as brand of PC, model number, modem type. These questions are asked so that the data-entry and transmission diskettes can be properly configured.

Getting accurate answers to these questions can be surprisingly difficult. It often turns out that the PC described in the questionnaire bears no resemblance to the machine actually used for transmission. To be on the safe side, each of the firms is called personally to confirm the information on the questionnaire. At one transmitting firm, the person on the other end of the phone vehemently insisted that its computer was not an IBM, not a Leading Edge, not a Compaq, but a Computerland.

Help desks breathe numerous sighs of relief when a user firm has finally achieved that pinnacle of success, the high end of the learning curve. But too often despair soon follows when the expert quits. This happened to one firm when it moved across the Hudson River from New York City to New Jersey. At 4 p.m. on the day before a transmission, the regulator got a call from the new hire, who requested that someone sail across the Hudson to train him in the intricacies of automated regulatory reporting. All in a day's work.

Ask Not Thy Supervisor

Sometimes computer systems make wonderful excuses for somewhat lazy staffers. Consider this short take. A British insurance giant installed a computer system to speed the processing of claims. Unfortunately, the system came to a near halt, deluged by a flood of claims. It seems that the clerks had quickly discovered that the insurance system had rules built into it to weed out dubious claims. They also discovered that asking the computer to decide on a dubious claim was much easier than asking a supervisor or fumbling through obscure rule books. This extra volume quite literally flooded the system.

More Is Most Definitely More

One food company used to generate monthly reports of product sales and shipments for the purpose of making marketing and promotion decisions.[3] A few years ago, technology made it possible to turn the reports out weekly. Now they arrive daily.

The actual amount of information has not increased. The food company is still getting the same information, only faster. The problem in this case is not the technology, but rather the belief, shared by many organizations in the technology age, that more is necessarily better.

In the case of the food company, nothing more has been accomplished by crunching numbers daily than used to be achieved when the statistics arrived monthly. The numbers are simply not time-sensitive enough to create a competitive advantage for the company by being generated daily. Further, the company does not have the employee resources to study the data each day.

Yet, in a classic "climb the mountain because it's there" approach, the data is produced daily simply because it can be. This creates the illusion that it needs to be dealt with daily. Unable to accomplish this feat, employees are forced to choose between becoming hopelessly mired in reports or giving the data only superficial attention. The technology defeats its purpose. Instead of making work faster, less tedious, and easier, it wastes valuable time without creating significant productivity or quality gains.

The Institute for the Future, a California think tank, predicts that by 1995 some 90 percent of American white-collar workers will have their own PC. Given everything a computer can do today, and everything it is projected to do tomorrow, we need to ponder the role that computers should really play in business.

The hardest problem posed by computers is that they are so flexible. They can do all sorts of things. So, increasingly, the right question to ask is not "What can the machines do?" but "What do we want them to do?"

References

1. Mary Voboril, "Boilerplate Lawyering Draws Ire," *New York Newsday,* October 31, 1993.
2. "The PC Myth," *Computer Market Letter,* May 1993.
3. Randall Johnson, "Technology Use Must Match, Not Exceed, Human Needs," *Total Quality Newsletter,* November 1992, pp. 1–2.

4

How Journalism Is Doing IT Wrong

I run great risk in writing this chapter. The risk that this book will never be reviewed. Or that it will be reviewed in less than a polite fashion. The reason I make such a pronouncement is that the chapter deals with what I consider to be the undue influence of computer trade publications on the IT profession.

But it's more than just undue influence. It's misinformation as well. What this chapter will uncover is that a large number of the most popular computer publications are written by folks who simply do not have an adequate grasp of information technology. And ignorance usually begets misinformation. In other words, take what they say at your own risk.

When I was a junior programmer some 18 years ago, the IT field (at least the commercial part of it) was still in its infancy. There was most definitely an aura of professionality about the field. It was well reflected in the publications we read and the trade shows we attended.

Back then there were trade shows like the National Computer Convention (NCC)—a serious mix of academia and commercialism. Today's trade shows seem to be full of pomp but very little circumstance. There's lots of glitz—from a cappella singers to famous boxers—but very little substance. Where the NCC had speeches and seminars hosted by heavyweights, today's trade shows seem dominated by the perennial magazine editor as keynote speaker. True, some editors and writers do have technical backgrounds, but for the most part today's editors and writers are journalists. And journalists are having a bit of a credibility problem today in all sectors.

On the Objectivity of the Press

Not too long ago, the TV news program *Dateline NBC* came under fierce attack for jury rigging a car explosion. The motives were innocent enough—to expose a safety hazard. The methodology was anything but. As a result, the *Dateline* disaster has become synonymous with what's wrong with journalism today.

Howard Rosenberg of *The Los Angeles Times* called the fiasco an "electronic Titanic—an unprecedented disaster in the annals of network news and perhaps the biggest TV scam since the Quiz Scandals." What *Dateline* had the audacity to do was to stage a crash test that was rigged for a particular outcome. They purposely concealed from the public's view the hidden rockets and the overfilled and loose gas tank that precipitated the crash. And if many thought the *Dateline* scandal was a freak or bizarre departure from accepted network standards, they were wrong. Both CBS and ABC had previously run the same sorts of grossly misleading crash videos and simulations, while also withholding material facts about the tests.[1]

Perhaps the most serious of misjudgments on NBC's part was in trusting "experts" who were deeply involved in litigating against the target of the exposé.

The June 1993 issue of *National Review* focuses on one salient topic: "The Decline of American Journalism."[2] Although the publication has a bias admittedly right of center, the 40-odd pages devoted to this topic are rare in their self-exposure. The basic message of this series of articles is that journalists themselves are biased, and that they write through the haze of their bias. In other words, since most journalists are quite liberal in their political stance, liberal causes are written about supportively while conservative topics are written about less enthusiastically—if at all. Those astute readers who have noticed the seeming embrace of the "politically correct" movement by the press will understand immediately what I'm referring to. How else can we explain the dozens of magazine lead stories and TV specials on AIDS? Granted it's a most dreadful scourge, but if the truth be known, many more cases of breast cancer are diagnosed each month than are cases of AIDS. How else can we explain the press's seeming fascination with people like Donald Trump and John F. Kennedy, Jr.? Most of us have little interest in these people. Much less frequently, it seems, does the press write stories that reflect our true interests and needs.

Criticism of the press is not limited to right-of-center publications. A literature search in the public library on the subject turns up these gems:

> Junk stories are slowly eroding the public's faith in the media. The press is being used as dupes for lawyers and other charlatans who want to

implicate public figures. Seeking to satisfy what they perceive to be the tastes of the American public, the press is printing first and asking questions later.[3]

The centrist bias of the U.S. media. Neither left nor right, but biased just the same.[4]

It seems that the love affair with the media is just about over, although not everyone appears to have gotten the message. Press people have as many foibles as the rest of us. They make errors. They take shortcuts.

Unfortunately, somewhere around third grade or so, it was hammered into us that the printed word was gospel; "If it's in writing, it must be so." This is a habit that's hard to break. But break it we must if we are to make informed decisions.

The English Major and the Expert

When I first started my business, I decided that I had a lot to say and that the best place to say it was in the computer trades. After all, I was an experienced systems developer with a flair for words. What more could the computer press ask for? I figured they would welcome me with open arms. Actually some did—publications that were edited by experts and written primarily by experts. But the most well-known of the trades were, and still are, dominated by "professional journalists" who write sleek, packaged articles instead of engaging experts whose writing may need some tidying up.

I have no grudge against journalists in general. At least I didn't until I started writing for some of the more major publications and saw the "art of journalism" from the inside out. The sad fact is that the majority of the trades we read prefer to have "professional journalists" write the articles rather than spend the time in editing any article that would be handed in by an expert. This is no mere opinion on my part, this was actually told to me by an editor for a major trade that you probably have on your desk right now.

Although journalism thrives in the political, economic, and social arenas, it somehow deteriorates when applied to the professions. Twenty-odd years ago, when all there was to write about were some IBM 360 computers and batch systems, journalists served the important function of "reporting" on trade news. Reporting is still an important function today. However, the computer press seems to have branched out and is now offering opinions, commentary, and advice. I have no argument with such commentary, as long as it's pertinent and accurate. The problem is, it often isn't.

I wrote the "Marketplace" column for one of the most senior of trade newspapers for a little under a year. During that time I had two editors, neither of whom was particularly knowledgeable about high technology. Yet these same editors would appear in the newspaper regularly, offering advice about some esoteric computer topic or another. Two English majors, who didn't quite understand the difference between a client and a server, giving "expert" advice on such technical topics as downsizing and managing projects!

Apparently, this is prevalent. Pick up your favorite trade publication and flip through the pages. How many bylines indicate expert status? The vast majority of articles and columns are written by in-house editors, in-house columnists, and a sprinkling of freelance writers. What all these folks have in common is a very limited grasp of the very high-tech world of information technology. And they have absolutely no experience in developing any of it.

At the end of my tenure with the computer newspaper in question, I decided to prove to the editor-in-chief my contention that a publication with a majority of "English majors" as opposed to expert writers actually did a disservice to its readers. In the prior week's paper, there was a rather large, in-depth article about expert systems—an area that I have considerable experience in. In other words, I was an expert.

With yellow marker in hand, I carefully read through the article, searching for inconsistencies and inaccuracies. I didn't have to wait long. By the time I had finished the article, virtually every other sentence was underlined. If these errors had been obvious, readers would have known that what they were reading was full of holes. The problem was that the errors were subtly wrong. What this meant was that, unless readers of the article were themselves experts in artificial intelligence, they would never know that what they were reading was fatally flawed.

A similar incident in the now defunct Ziff publication *Corporate Computing* backs me up on this point. I submitted a "Technology Outlook" column on computer-assisted software engineering (CASE) to the editor (nontechnical, of course), who immediately decided he didn't like my opening. He didn't merely change the semantics; he rewrote the entire opening. He added some gobbledygook about how "when Von Neumann invented the computer, little did he think that one day computers would program themselves." Now I was in a quandary. I didn't want to offend the editor (yes, they're easy to offend) but my angst about including such an obviously wrong statement under my byline got the best of me. So I told him that not only is Von Neumann not the inventor of the computer, but CASE does not mean that the computer is programming itself. A few months later Ziff scrapped the magazine. I wonder if fatal flaws such as the one I caught had anything to do with it?

Think of the ramifications. A company decides that it would like to explore the potential of expert systems. In collecting information about the subject, the project manager comes across the article in question. It is entirely possible that the manager will decide to go in a particular direction as a result of the flawed article. It is also entirely possible that the technology will be applied wrongly as a result of the article's advice.

A Headline with Substance

One day stroll over to your public library and take a good look at the trade publications in other fields. For the most part, the trades that cover the professional industries (law, medicine, and so on) are written and edited by the profession itself. The IT field does have a counterpart in a handful of computer journals. Although often neglected by information technologists, these journals are the real voice of the profession. The articles may be written with less than a journalistic flair, but their content is meaty, topical, and extremely valuable.

Then come the computer trade publications. And with their proliferation comes heavy competition—that is, competition for advertisers. Since the majority of trades are free, advertising makes up 100 percent of the revenue stream. Trade editors are hard at work making their particular publication as palatable as possible to potential advertisers. But doesn't this draw the focus of the magazine away from the reader? If there are literally hundreds of vendors making client/server products, isn't it to the benefit of the publication to tout the demise of the mainframe and the rise of the client/server kingdom?

Whether the magazines they write for are advertiser-biased or not, journalists tend to paint a very rosy picture of the world that technologists live in. To hear them tell it, every IT shop from the Atlantic to the Pacific practices "headline technology." UNIX. Client/server. CASE. These are some of the hot-ticket technologies that are making headlines in the publications most of us read.

Although most IT shops have embraced these new technologies, it is questionable whether many have actually used them productively. In other words, it's substance over form.

Howard Rubin of Hunter College in New York City, an expert on productivity and CASE, quotes an alarming statistic: Even though perhaps 50 to 60 percent of IT shops have ventured forth into CASE, only about 10 percent have used it effectively.

MIT's Chris Kemerer has long been searching for an IT shop that has used the same CASE tool more than once—with the same programming team. What's wrong? Why do we hear so many stories of these newer technologies ending up as so much shelfware?

Part of the reason is that when the press touts a technology as the latest trend, organizations get caught up in a "keeping up with the Joneses" mentality. This means that whether or not they're prepared, they'll invest sometimes huge sums in the latest gizmo—often with disastrous results.

I recently interviewed a large number of people for an article which attempted to answer the question "Is there a role for the mainframe in CASE?" I surveyed an equal number of product vendors and system developers. Now, mind you, the backdrop for all this is the resounding cry by most of the trades that the mainframe is long dead. The results of my interview showed a wide divergence of opinion between the vendors and the developers. The vendors almost uniformly dismissed the mainframe as a dinosaur. Most developers, however, while admitting to a downsizing trend in their organizations, indicated that the mainframe would remain in their computer rooms at least until the turn of the century. Long live the mainframe! Note that, again, the advertisers and vendors were on a similar wavelength, with the actual users of the products being somewhere out in the VHF band.

The latest example of buzzword madness is the *information highway*. Somehow this term has become the nom-de-charge for all things that deal with—now let me get this list straight—the Internet, cable, telephone, multimedia, videoconferencing, and on and on.

Now here's a term that's essentially meaningless. What is an information highway? Presumably, it refers to some sort of network in which information (images, voice, data, video) can travel in two directions. Well, I thought that we had something akin to this. And I thought it had been around for quite a while. If services like Internet and the increasingly popular CompuServe aren't bidirectional highways, what are?

The information highway got its big boost with the proposed, but ultimately unsuccessful, merger between Bell Atlantic and TCI. With the Clinton White House backing the idea, if not necessarily the monopolistic merger, the information highway (or at least the term) took over in the popular press and unfortunately the trades, as the catchphrase of the moment. Headlines such as *Computerworld*'s "Bell Atlantic/TCI Deal Could Pave Way to 'Information Highway'" really do the industry no service.

I can see it now. Corporate CEOs all over the country clamoring to climb on board the information highway shuttle. Never mind that what Bell Atlantic/TCI has to offer will be years in the making. Never mind that it will be a hard sell to the consumers who will ultimately provide the funding when they see their already high cable bill pushed to stratospheric new heights. (I now pay $46.10 a month in New York City for basic cable and one premium channel—all of it quite boring, so I'm loath to spend another cent on it.) And will these consumers shell out the big clams to pay for the new high-definition television (HDTV) sets that I presume they'll need to be able to "read" all this information? (Did you ever try to read text when using your TV as a monitor?)

Of course, consumers are really only a means to an end. They will be the ones to shoulder the cost of rewiring the nation for the broadband wire or fiber needed to carry all this stuff. What the IT field wants out of this is the transport itself.

But if all that IT managers want is the capacity to move data (i.e., voice, text, images, and video) quickly over the network, then maybe they should look no further than companies like Hayes. Amid all the brouhaha about the information highway, Hayes quietly announced a new, extremely high-speed modem that will enable connection to a remote computer at the speed of a local connection. If advances like these are forthcoming, aren't we already going top speed on the info highway?

The Computer Journalist as Rock Star

I don't know when it happened, but somewhere along the line journalists achieved "star" status. Perhaps it started with Barbara Walters and her celebrity interviews or possibly with the million-dollar-plus talk show hosts. However it happened, journalists became celebrities in their own right. In general, this has amazed me. After all, reporters just "tell" the news, they don't "make" the news. I for one am far more interested in the interviewee than the interviewer. This journalist-as-expert mentality reaches its zenith in *The McLaughlin Group,* aired on NBC in New York City. Each Sunday John McLaughlin invites three or four journalists to comment on the topics of the week. While they offer interesting points of view, they are simply not experts. NBC would do better to invite three or four politicians to comment on the topics of the week.

Lately the computer trades have begun to market their editors and columnists in much the same manner. The next time you get a flyer for yet another trade show, check out exactly who is making the keynote speech. More often than not, it is one editor or another, one publisher or another.

There has also been a rise in journalism as gossip. The following profile, taken directly from a recent issue of *InfoWorld,* demonstrates the seeming lack of technical background and the less than professional bent of a new breed of computer journalist:

In Focus: Robert X. Cringely, columnist

Profile: Former war correspondent, Stanford University professor, hack writer. Sex symbol. Fired by several pioneering PC companies. Author of *Accidental Empires: How the Boys of Silicon Valley Make Their Millions, Battle Foreign Competition,* and *Still Can't Get a Date.* Speaks widely and semicoherently on the state of the PC industry. Writes *InfoWorld*'s "Notes from the Field," a column of industry secrets and philosophy.

This profile of Cringely (presumably a pseudonym) epitomizes exactly what I'm rallying against. A less-than-tech-expert journalist who flippantly writes about topics that are of crucial importance to IT managers. Of course, Cringely may well be an expert. His Stanford professorship may well be in the computer sciences. But if this is so, why isn't *InfoWorld* touting his credentials?

InfoWorld, which by the way does have some very fine, expert columnists, has lately begun to publish quite a few of these three-quarter-page profiles of its stars. From what I have seen, not a one sports any crucial technical credentials, though many have years and years of reporting or editorial experience.

Most disturbing of all is that *InfoWorld* doesn't seem to think that anything is missing from its editorial mix. This is true for most of the other computer trades as well. Business, it seems, is business. And entrepreneurs will be entrepreneurs, nonexperts with a flair for spotting golden opportunities.

All the News That's Fit to Print

Information technologists would do well to understand that the computer trades are not always the gospel truth. The tack I take in reading the trades is as follows: I read all the news, look at all the ads, and then read only the columns or articles written by people with a byline that indicates a technical background. I also assiduously avoid articles written by "free-lance writers."

Although free-lance writers have a definite way with words, they are usually even less well versed in a given technical field than are a publication's in-house staff. Most free-lancers are generalists, although several do specialize in the high-tech arena. How can you expect a writer who writes about the environment one week to write lucidly about the IT field the next week?

Interestingly, the IT field has become somewhat of a cash cow for the dozens of free-lance writers who work with the two score or so computer publications. *Writer's Digest* is the trade magazine of choice for most writers. I recently came across a compilation of its best articles, entitled "The Basics of Earning Big Bucks in Business Writing,"[5] which explored ways to make "good money" writing for a living. Prominent among these articles was one describing how to break into the "high-paying high-tech market." The author, Ronald Benrey, is the veteran of more than 1000 articles on "difficult subjects" (his quotes) and 6 books about computers and electronics. The problem is he is admittedly a low-tech person. Let me quote you a bit of his advice:

> I earn a big chunk of my free-lancing income writing interesting words about, well—let's be brutally honest—dull subjects....Writing about tech-

nology is one of the steadiest, most dependable, least crowded, most lucrative free-lance specialties you can choose....I don't appreciate every scientific nuance. And yes, my knowledge is shallow. But I do have enough understanding about the subject matter with a confidence that convinces my readers they're in good hands....If you're merely "underinformed" about advanced technology, jump right in.

Unfortunately, in the field of information technology, Benrey is not an exception but the rule. Why take advice from an admitted nonspecialist who spent a mere 2 or 3 days boning up on a topic that could have productivity and economic consequences for your company?

Somehow when it comes to matters pertaining to business, we are all too willing to take the advice of whoever happens to be writing in this week's publication. We rarely check the credentials of the author. Would we do the same in matters pertaining to our personal lives? Don't we check the credentials of the person who comes to wallpaper our walls? Or the doctor who's going to remove our appendix?

Advertising Dollars Speak Louder Than Editorials

At the tail end of 1992, my company did a survey to determine whether system folks were cognizant of any correlation between the amount of dollars vendors spent in advertising in a publication and the amount of favorable editorial treatment vendors received from that publication. Although editors will roundly denounce this allegation, the simple truth is that it does happen. Maybe not in all the publications all the time, but at least in some of the publications some of the time.

In skimming through thousands of trade magazines and newspapers over many years, I discovered that the vast majority of articles, news tidbits, and even user-profiles concerned products from advertised companies. Seeking to determine whether others noticed this aberration, my company decided to devote an entire issue of the *Computer Market Letter* to the subject.[6] The results were intriguing, as shown in Figures 4.1 to 4.5.

The base for our survey was 223 technical managers. Out of several dozen magazines, we chose the following six market leaders:

Corporate	*Corporate Computing* (now defunct)
Software	*Software Magazine*
CW	*Computerworld*
InfoWeek	*Information Week*
InfoWorld	*InfoWorld*
OpenSys	*Open Systems Today*

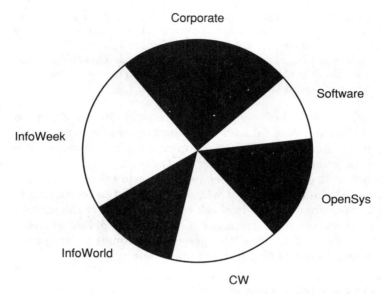

Figure 4.1   Trade publications of preference. (*Source:* Computer Market Letter.)

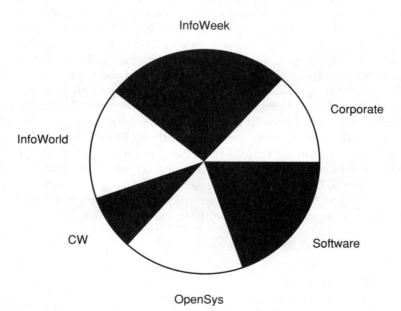

Figure 4.2   Quality of writers. (*Source:* Computer Market Letter.)

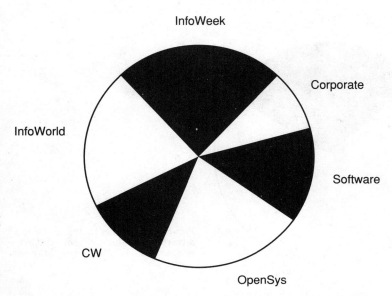

Figure 4.3 Quality of editorial content. (*Source:* Computer Market Letter.)

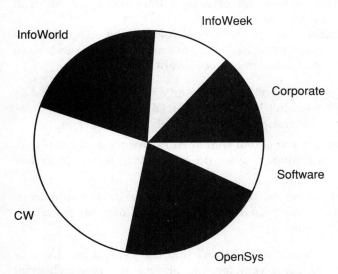

Figure 4.4 Quality of coverage. (*Source:* Computer Market Letter.)

No

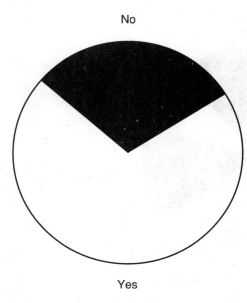

Yes

Figure 4.5   Correlation between advertising dollars and editorial coverage. (*Source:* Computer Market Letter.)

Evidently, the majority of respondents felt the same way. They too saw a positive correlation between advertising dollars spent and editorial coverage received (see Figure 4.5).

Even more disturbing is the occasional coercing by some publications to get advertisers into the fold. Several of my contacts have reported this subtle and sometimes not-so-subtle tactic:

- A research firm "implied" to a company whose product it was reviewing that it wouldn't hurt the product's review for the company to take out a subscription for the research firm's services.

- A technology company was told that shrink-wrapping an advertisement into a certain magazine would generate a favorable article about the company.

- A well-known publication indicated that its writers would work with the company to provide a glowing profile if only an advertisement were forthcoming.

Idealists among us would like to think that if we spend hundreds or even thousands of dollars a year for the services of a research firm, what we get from that firm will be unbiased and accurate. If the picture my contacts paint is accurate, then even "professional" reports are suspect. Of course, these experiences may just be aberrations. One way to tell is to ask to review what you're subscribing to. Then ask for a list of other clients of the research firm. If the research firm's high-tech clients are all graced with glowing reviews, think hard about the credibility of whom you're doing business with.

Ultimately, a publication's editorial must stay apart from its advertising. But it seems that the two are coming closer and closer together.

The Press Release That Got Away

To a one, technology vendors lament the way their companies are treated by the computer press. A key area of discontent relates to the new products (or product watch) section of magazines and newspapers. All publications have some sort of section that keeps track of the latest happenings in industry. Vendors, when they have something new to report on, dutifully send out press releases to several hundred editors and writers in the computer press. The question the vendors voice is this: Just how does one press release get picked over another to get reported on?

Computer publications receive literally hundreds of press releases a day. Obviously, not all of them can make it into print. So writers and editors must be performing some sort of journalistic triage—picking what they deem to be the most worthy. But just what constitutes worthy?

One public relations executive for a large computer manufacturer laments the fact that the press releases on his company's line of mainframes no longer make it into print. Given that (as we've already seen) the computer press thinks the mainframe is long dead, a lack of mainframe coverage is quite understandable. But what service do the trades perform—especially for the large number of installations that are still running part or all of their systems on "big iron"?

Just what is lost as a result of inadequate or incomplete new product coverage? I know of several small companies with astonishingly innovative products, but tiny advertising budgets, that never get press coverage at all. If they're not advertising heavily and the press doesn't cover them, how will we be able to benefit from their innovations? Perhaps the easiest solution to this dilemma is to pay serious attention to the types of publications that we read.

General publications such as *Computerworld, Software Magazine,* and *Datamation* are literally besieged by press releases, product announcements, and other sundry notices from eager product vendors. These publications literally cannot cover the entire techno-front. Therefore, the chances are that news about your particular field of interest will be sparse or sporadic.

Your best bet is to subscribe to one of the segment-specific publications. There are many to choose from. For example, in the field of artificial intelligence (AI), you can read *PC AI* or *AI Expert.* Since both publications concentrate on a limited subfield within information technology, you can bet (or hope) that their coverage will be complete. Also, since these magazines tend to rely on experts, you can be sure that their articles will be accurate as well.

The Symposium Connection

Lately, many publications have taken on a new role—that of seminar promoters. Add to this mix the ever-burgeoning number of trade conferences and you definitely have seminar overload. More and more of these conferences are a triumph of form over substance.

As noted earlier in the chapter, some of the more popular conferences have deteriorated in a sea of a cappella singers and boxing champs. And, according to the *Computer Market Letter* survey described above, many IT managers agree. Figure 4.6 shows how these managers evaluated information vs. glitz in the following trade events:

UnixExpo
PCExpo
CASEw   Case World
NetW   NetWorld
Mac   MacWorld
Win   Windows & OS/2

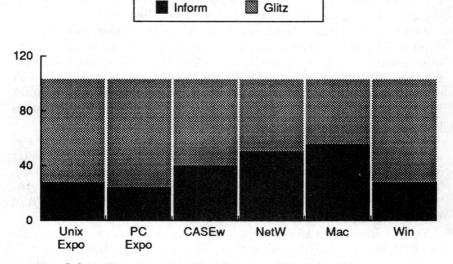

Figure 4.6 Information versus glitz. (*Source*: Computer Market Letter.)

Complaints over the lack of substantial "learning" at these conferences notwithstanding, I think that attending them is beneficial in that you can see a wide array of technological advances all in one room. And the nice thing is that the conference promoters usually provide their exhibitors with unlimited guest passes, which means that you have a very good chance of getting in for free—to the exhibits only, of course. From my perspective, that's good enough. Spending hundreds of dollars on seminars only to hear the vice president of marketing of a hardware firm, or an editor of a trade publication, is just not worth the money in my book.

There also seems to be a rather obvious correlation between speakers and exhibitors. Take a look at the next trade show brochure you receive. See for yourself whether or not the majority of speakers have also rented exhibit booths on the show floor.

You'll also note that some trade shows invite the same speakers back (presumably for the same seminar) year after year. DCI (Digital Consulting, Inc.), which seems to have become a leader on the show circuit, follows this pattern. Every year I see the same names over and over again: Ed Yourdon, Howard Rubin, and so on. Now I like Ed and Howard, and they both have much expertise to share—but please, not every year!

Perhaps the most informative of all trade shows are those offered by the various nonprofit associations and trade groups. Show organizers, usually experts themselves, take care in putting together a show that is low on glitz and high on content.

The American Association of Artificial Intelligence (AAAI) puts on a yearly show that I find to be mind-boggling in scope. A happy mix of academia and commercialism provides a real learning experience—which is, after all, what we really should go to trade shows for. There's no lack of exhibitors either.

The periodic "Technology Day" trade shows sponsored by the Data Administration Management Association (DAMA) really hone in on what is of interest to the association's members. As I write this chapter, I just received an invitation to a DAMA tech day on the subject of client/server systems.

Et Tu, Brutus?

This chapter was written to provide an awareness of the dangers of relying on trade publications and for-profit seminars to bring you up to speed in your particular area of expertise. Trade publications serve an extremely valuable purpose if they are used in conjunction with other sources of education. But always be cognizant of the credentials of the writer or speaker.

If you don't already belong, I urge you to join an association in your field of interest. At a minimum, joining (Association of Computing Machinery) ACM and IEEE will broaden your outlook and extend your professionality immensely. Their conferences and publications may be less slick than the for-profit ones, but I guarantee that you'll benefit far more from them. One final hint: The publications with the best information are those that are geared to the vendors themselves. Peruse *Computer Reseller News* and you'll see what I mean.

References

1. Walter Olson, "It Didn't Start with *Dateline NBC*," *National Review*, June 21, 1993.
2. *National Review*, June 21, 1993.
3. Mark DiIonno, *The Sporting News*, April 20, 1992.
4. Jeff Cohen, *Utne Reader*, September–October 1990.
5. Ronald Benrey in "The Basics of Earning Big Bucks in Business Writing," *Writer's Digest Guide*, vol. 14.
6. *Computer Market Letter*, vol. 2, no. 2, January 12, 1993.

5

The Bottom Feeders

When the field of information technology was a closed shop—that is before the advent of the PC—it was rather easy to keep tabs on just how professional your staff was and just how professional your consultants were. But when the PC knocked on the door, the software that entered with it put the art of computer consulting on a newer, more complex level.

IT managers used to be senior in more ways than just their paychecks. Today it is entirely conceivable that IT managers are less than comfortable with the vagaries of all the new technologies. Object orientation. Client/server. Local area networks (LANs).

But when the door opened, more than just the PC and its software entered. A whole new breed of consultant came in as well. A breed of consultant that gives new meaning to the term *caveat emptor*.

In this chapter we'll take a look at the field of players who go by the name of consultants. You pay them big bucks. But what are you really getting? In other words, do "consultants" add or detract from the bottom line?

Smaller Computers, Smaller Skills

There's a joke about consultants. It goes something like this: "A client walked up to a consultant and asked him for the time. The consultant grabbed the client's watch and proceeded to give the correct time to the client." This very silly little story sums up the general belief that consultants get paid for sucking in everything a client tells them, reorganizing it, and then spitting it back out at the client in the form of an expensive report.

There are good consultants and there are bad consultants. There are good consulting experiences. And then there are bad consulting experiences. I had one encounter with a very well known Big Six consulting firm that was anything less than positive. I was working at the New York Stock Exchange at the time. We were in the midst of developing a system that had congressional oversight.

We really had no need for consulting help but brought the firm in anyway because of the panache of its name. It just added credibility to have our project associated with the Big Six. If only celebrity meant quality. I'm sure that each of you can recount a similar experience.

To be fair, the Big Six does have some of the most experienced IT people in the league. And consultants, in general, are really worth the money you spend on them if you take care to check their credentials very carefully and then monitor their work very closely. (Of course, I'm naturally biased, since I'm a consultant myself.)

Credential checking entails much more than taking a gander at résumés. It means probing consultants on the extent of their experience. How many Sybase installations have they done? In what kind of environment? What types of problems did they run into?

When PCs came onto the scene, a lot of nontechnical people were taken with the ease of using them. Because some of the software, such as spreadsheets and databases, provided a macrolike form of programming language, naive users began to think of themselves as professional programmers. After all, they reasoned, they could program. They knew how to connect a PC to a LAN as well as set up a computer. Why not go into business?

Around the same time, a series of articles and books appeared on the subject of how to turn your computer into a gold mine. And what a gold mine it was, as literally thousands of newcomers hung out their shingles as computer consultants.

Don't you see the problem here? If your goal is to merely connect a PC or two, then by all means go out and hire one of this new breed. But if you're looking for someone to help you make a qualitative decision about what software to use or how best to develop a system, detour widely around this genre.

My reasoning is quite logical. If you began to feel ill, you'd go to a doctor, wouldn't you? More than likely you wouldn't ask for a prescription from your next-door neighbor who has a hobby of reading health and medical books. How about fixing your car? When you hear that rattle, do you take the car to your mechanic or entrust it to the kid who likes to dabble with pistons? So why would you entrust your computer installation to somebody who has the same lack of credentials?

Civilians Turn Consultants

The following stories are about real people. I've just changed the names to protect the guilty.

Susan Rathskiller started her professional life as a teacher. When she could stand no more of her charges, she decided to go to work for the American Management Association putting seminars together. Somewhere along the line Susan learned about PCs. And she got really good at those pesky DOS commands. So when the AMA decided to run a course on DOS, Susan decided that she should be the one to teach it.

Generally speaking, people who take DOS courses don't know the difference between the delete key and the backspace key, so of course feedback is fairly meaningless. But Susan took her positive feedback as a great success, and her confidence grew.

And grew. By the time the AMA downsized her, Susan had already decided to become (what else?) a computer consultant. Hanging out her shingle, Susan concentrated on small businesses. After all, she most probably reasoned, they knew as little about computers as her DOS students did. Fortunately for the small businesses, Susan's lack of expertise was quite noticeable, and it wasn't too long before that shingle was dumped in the wastebasket. But what about the other Susans who hide their lack of experience better?

Harrold Renig started life as a science writer. Extremely smart, he decided to write about high-tech topics. His movement into this area piqued his interest, and it wasn't long before he had his first computer and was staying up into the wee hours learning Paradox, WordPerfect, and any other software package he could get his hands on. Then, like Susan, Harrold decided to hang out a shingle.

Today Harrold still has a shingle waving in the breeze—and an ad in the local business press. He too concentrates on small business, eking out a fairly good living installing PCs, networks, and software. But Harrold poses a great danger to businesses. He is small on talent and can't possibly see the big picture.

Obscuring the Big Picture

At one client/server conference, a debate raged over the best type of person to develop systems in this brave new world. Because client/server is predominately centered on workstations it would appear that developers with a solid PC or UNIX background would be the most suitable candidates for the job. But the general consensus at this conference was that developers with only PC-based or UNIX-based experience under their belts had a parochial view of the bigger issue. To these folks, all solutions are necessarily tied to the PC or UNIX. After all, that's their experience base.

Developers who start out on the mainframe and then migrate to the workstation are really twice blessed. It would be wise for organizations to take better advantage of their expertise, for these developers can truly see the broad picture. And they have options. Not all their solutions will be of the same flavor. They've already been trained to look at the problem and *pick the best solution, not just the solution they know best.*

Consultants spawned in the era of the PC seem to have just one solution. Their solution. If you've already gone through the process of researching your options and have chosen the PC avenue to transverse, then by all means the independent PC consultant is probably the biggest bargain around. On the other hand, if you're looking for a consultant who will study your business and make a decision that is the most effective for your shop, try someone else, please.

When one Dallas-based law firm decided to automate part and parcel of its business, it asked around for some advice on whom to hire for help. But the consultants who were recommended were considered far too expensive. So the firm turned to the Yellow Pages. Now picking a consultant from the Yellow Pages is about as effective as picking a doctor from the Yellow Pages.

But pick the law firm did. The consulting organization, one of a legion that provide PC assistance via a 900 number, came to the first meeting presolution in hand. Of course, the solution was PC-based, since that was the only experience the company ever had.

What the law firm ended up with was a bunch of PCs wired together with a LAN as well as word processing and database software. This, it seems, was the consulting firm's standard solution.

The law firm finally had its computers, but few of the real business issues were resolved. The consultants had no experience in the legal arena; nor did they do their homework to find out if prepackaged solutions were already on the market.

What the law firm wanted was a way for its lawyers to use the computer to bill their clients as well as do research. *Research* was the operative word here, but the consulting firm provided none of the interfaces between on-line services such as Lexis and the database and word-processing software they recommended. The consulting firm failed to see the big picture.

A small business owner wanted a computer for himself. But he knew nothing about computers. For some inexplicable reason, he contracted with a firm that not only delivered software solutions but built the hardware itself. Three things were delivered his way: the computer, Lotus-1-2-3, and WordPerfect.

The word-processing software was simple enough to use, but the consulting company delivered the spreadsheet software right out of the box. As easy as it's touted as being, Lotus is still quite a complex piece of software. And right from the box it didn't come close to doing what the small businessman thought it could do. So the businessman had to keep going back to the consultant to create the macros he needed to keep track of his business. The experience proved to be less than a success. The businessman has since sold his computer and gone back to doing things manually.

What to Look for in a Consultant

Of course, consultants can be mainframe bigots just as easily as PC freaks. With the rash of downsizings in corporate America, there is a whole crop of unemployed mainframe programmers out there who have decided to become consultants. Many of them have but one solution—the mainframe.

So whom do you hire?

It really depends on what it is that you're doing. As I've already mentioned, if you've already decided on what it is you're going to do and you merely need an extra set of hands, then by all means hire the best hackers you can find. On the other hand, if you're looking for someone to guide you to the right technological solution for your particular problem, then delve into the consultant's background much more carefully. This advice does not apply only to nontechnical business owners. It also applies to technical managers who might not be up on the particular brand of technology the consultant represents.

Much of the advice below is logical, and many of you may already follow it. But today's frenetic pace sometimes precludes careful scrutiny. Remember, a review of your human resources may mean the difference between success and failure. Here are the questions to ask.

1. *What are the consultant's credentials?*   Take a good, hard look at the consultant's résumé. What does it contain? Does the experience column indicate that he or she can do whatever it is you are asking? How many years of work experience does the consultant have in general? How many years in a particular subspecialty? What types of firms has he or she worked for? If yours is a large company, does the consultant have experience with large firms? Or with small firms if your company is small?

2. *What is the consultant's academic background?*   I firmly believe that the IT field is professional. A professional field warrants an advanced degree. You may not agree. Indeed, you may not even have an advanced degree yourself. But if you're in the position of hiring consultants, the rule of thumb is clear: The more education, the more bang for the buck. Of course, an advanced degree in horticulture is not what we're talking about here. But one in computer science or business can be quite valuable.

3. *Is the consultant a recognized expert in his or her field?*   Most bona fide experts work hard at being recognized. They do this by writing books (a plug here) and articles. They go out on the seminar circuit and get interviewed. Credits such as these invariably wind up on the

consultant's résumé. And if he or she is shrewd, copies of current articles or books wind up on your desk. Take some time to read what the consultant has to say and then make a decision as to whether this person can add value to your organization. Fair warning, though. Writing a book doesn't necessarily translate to expertise, so don't pick a consultant merely on the basis of some "hot" book. Being published is just one of the credentials that a consultant should have. The most important credential is "getting one's hands dirty." Does the consultant have actual, hands-on experience with a project such as yours?

4. *What references does the consultant offer?*   Get at least two references, preferably more. Find out if the consultant is as good as he or she claims.

5. *Is the consulting bark worse than the bite?*   There are some well-known speakers and published authors making major incomes out there. But as I've already discussed, notoriety does not necessarily beget excellence. The consultant might talk a good game, but can he or she do the job? Although the following saying is a bit unfair, it aptly explains what I mean: *"Those who can, do; those who can't, teach."*

Legitimizing the Field

I never thought I'd say this, but I'm beginning to see the wisdom of certifying just what IT people do for a living. There has been a group trying to achieve this for years—with limited success. Given the deluge of unqualifieds in the field, I would say that we really have no alternative.

Most of the professions have a certification requirement. Following suit would most definitely lend an aura of professionalism and legitimacy to our chosen profession. The problem is, critics maintain, there are so many programming languages, databases, and so on, that it is impossible to have a certifying procedure for each.

The current push toward certified data processor (CDP) certification tackles the problem from a bottom-up basis. I agree that we cannot possibly certify people in each and every software tool on the market. Instead, let's look at this from a top-down perspective. The people capable of causing the most damage are not the programmers but the system designers—the conceivers. Let's certify them. We need to test them, not on the vagaries of Sybase, but on the fundamentals of relational technology. We need to test them, not on Smalltalk, but on the principles of object orientation.

These are the folks who make the recommendations and design the systems, so it makes great sense that these are the people who must possess the credentials. This method has a sort of trickle-down effect as well. By seeing to it that our top-level people are indeed experts, we will ensure that the people they choose for the programming tasks will be expert as well. How often have managers hired programming duds who were less than qualified? So providing quality at the top level ensures quality at the bottom level.

I recommend that the certification procedure test applicants on their knowledge of the following areas (presented in no particular order except the way I thought of them):

Object theory

Database theory

Methodology

CASE

Telecommunications

Networks

Artificial intelligence

Programming techniques and languages

Multimedia

Productivity and quality theories

Metrics

Operating systems

Management of systems

Client/server

Downsizing methodologies

Cross-platform development (PC vs. mainframe vs. workstation)

A Money-Back Guarantee

If the field were certified, we wouldn't be running into the numbers of problems that we run into today. But, as of this writing, my ideas on certification are just words on a page.

Until certification arrives, if you must use consultants, try to frame the contract so that you have adequate protection concerning work inadequately or incompletely done. Don't fall into the trap of disregarding the contractual part of the process only to find that, when you need it, it offers little protection. You can also find yourself in quite a bind as to who actually owns what it is you're developing.

I'm a great believer in object theory—the art of the reusable. It makes for great efficiency. That's why I recycle some of my articles in columns and vice versa. I also do it with program code. Why reinvent the wheel?

Consultants tend to get possessive about the work that they've invested long, hard hours in. So when they move on, they may want to leave with some or all of the documentation as well as the program design specifications and code. If you let that happen, expect to find that same system up and running at one of your competitors sometime soon—very soon.

Izzy Sobkowski (this time a real person) is president of a small computer firm that sells expert system, neural net, and help desk products. When Izzy was building his first tool, he contracted the programming task to an outside consultant, who was later fired. Because of the vagaries of the contract, the consultant instituted a lawsuit over ownership of the program code. He contended that since he was the one who coded it, it rightfully belonged to him. Unfortunately, the law is very obscure in this regard. What Izzy should have done is to protect himself by carefully spelling out just who owned what in the consultant's contract. It could have saved him some big money and a nasty lawsuit which he ultimately won.

The bottom line is that the selection, care, and feeding of a consultant is risky business. Be prepared.

6

Peopleware

In the end, it's people who control whether there is a productivity paradox. And people in an organization consist of everyone from senior manager to junior clerk.

The art and science of working with people is often referred to as the real technology behind the organization. And motivating them, empowering them, liberating them—and all the other buzzwords that apply—make the difference between a successful organization and one that's not so successful.

In this chapter we'll peruse the good, the bad, and the ugly in the way of techniques for dealing with people. We'll also look into the effect of technology on people. Some of these stories will edify you, but many others will horrify you. Maybe you'll even see yourself (or your boss) in these pages.

To start this chapter off the right way, I offer up some legendary wisdom on the art of communication—perhaps the most important component of good peopleware:

> In the beginning there was the plan.
> And then came the assumptions.
> And the plan was without form.
> And the assumptions without any substance.
> And darkness was upon the face of all workers.
> And they spake unto their team leaders, saying,
> "Lo, this is a pail of dung, and none may abide the odor thereof."
> And the team leaders went unto the supervisors, saying, "This new thing, it is a container of excrement, and it is very strong, such that none may abide by it."
> And the supervisors went unto their manager, saying, "This is a vessel of fertilizer, and none may abide its strength."

And the manager went unto the vice president bearing this message: "Lo, this plan contains that which aids plant growth, and it is powerful."

And the vice president went unto the senior vice president, saying, "This new thing promoteth growth, and it is powerful."

And the senior vice president went unto the president and sayeth unto him, "This powerful new plan will actively promote the growth and efficiency of all units, even unto the uttermost parts of the organization."

And the president looked upon the plan and saw that it was good.

And "the plan" became "policy."

Liberate Rather Than Empower

There is more than one way to manage. There's the way most people do it. And then there's the right way.

If you think that managing means telling your people specifically what they can do and what they can't do, keeping tabs on their phone calls, and clocking the time they spend at lunch or at the watercooler, then give back your key to the executive washroom.

If you are like most managers, you aren't quite so monstrous. But you probably still worry that your staff may not be making the "right decision." What does the right decision mean, anyway? Is it the decision you would have made yourself if you were in your staff's position? Ultimately, the *right* decision may be different from the one you would have made. So giving your staff the impression that the right decision is the one you would make is a sure way to diminish motivation, creativity, accountability, and morale. As Xerox executive Barry Rand says, "If you've got a yes person working for you, then one of you is redundant!" Ultimately, since your decision may not be the "right" one anyway, having some real thinkers on your team could only help, not hurt, your own career.

A good manager is not a robotics cop overseeing clones. Instead, a good manager is one who creates an environment in which staff members take on the responsibility to work productively in self-managed, self-starting teams that identify and solve complex problems on their own. Think of the benefits of this modus operandi. You'll be freed to think about the bigger picture. Isn't this why you wanted to become a manager in the first place?

Every field has its buzzwords. The latest one among human resources people is *empowerment*. Perhaps you've even taken a course on "how to empower your staff." Back you go, full of new ideas. But the moment you get back, you call a meeting of everyone who *reports* to you. Presumably, these "empowered" people can't operate on their own for even a few days and need to report to momma or pappa every detail of every project they're working on. As management guru Peter Drucker maintains, "Much of what we call management is making it very difficult for people to do their jobs."

The monster in the corner office

The team was bright and well educated. Its total years of experience hovered around 50. But the firm still decided to "look outside" when it came time to replace the retiring senior vice president of technology planning and development.

After months of screening and interviewing, the corporate chieftains made their decision. Of course, the corporate chieftains knew little (if anything at all) about technology. So their interviews of candidates probably concentrated on what the candidates looked like, how they presented themselves, and the gobbledygook principles of leadership and management, which are hard to quantify and most certainly impossible to convey in an interview.

The team members, rankling from their collective rejection, figured that the new kid on the block was selected for his looks. In truth, he did look a bit like the lead on *L.A. Law*. Moreover, the main picker, an executive vice president (female), did seem quite taken by him (a definite politically incorrect statement here).

The situation was hardly conducive to productivity. But the potentially explosive atmosphere of the work environment could have been eased, maybe even eliminated, had the new "boss" been a good manager.

It turned out that he wasn't. Members of the team could never prove it, but they thought that, in spite of his interviews and résumé, his experience had been limited to managing lower-level staff—maybe even clerks. In other words, he hadn't the foggiest idea of how to manage a group of Ph.Ds.

But the manager plodded on, and so began the year that the team came to call "our time in hell." You see, the manager treated his staff like clerks. They weren't allowed to make decisions without his input; they couldn't make a presentation without his seeing it first. Worst of all, they spent their days in meetings.

First there was the weekly staff meeting. This took about 2 hours. Then each staff member had to attend a weekly "one-on-one" with the manager. Sometimes the one-on-ones were scheduled directly after the weekly staff meeting, so there was little more to talk about. But each meeting still took an hour. The manager loved to hear himself talk.

Then there was the weekly project meeting with the user department. Although each of the team members was intimately familiar with the users, and in fact was about as knowledgeable as the users and had long ago earned their respect and admiration, the manager wanted a formal meeting to discuss project progress. The problem was that everybody at the meeting already knew the progress. Again, the manager just wanted to hear himself talk.

Then there was the monthly meeting with the boss's manager. And a meeting with the user department's senior management. All told, each team member spent approximately 16 hours a month attending nonsubstantial meetings. Needless to say, little work got done. Instead of empowering his people, the manager depowered them.

Does this story seem familiar? It's a true one. All the examples in this book are. It happened at a Wall Street firm in the late 1980s, and I offer it as representative of the type of manager who seems so prevalent in the industry today. Of course, not all managers are as bad as this one was. Still, there are plenty of people out there who have a psychological need to justify their positions at their staff members' expense.

Liberating your staff

Oren Harari, a professor at the University of San Francisco and a management consultant, relates an interesting experience with one of his clients.[1] While he was waiting for an appointment with this particular client, he overheard two of the manager's clerical assistants calling customers and asking them how they liked the company's product. Professor Harari reflected that it was no wonder this manager had such a good reputation. When he finally met with her, he offered his congratulations on her ability to delegate the customer service task to her staff.

"What are you talking about?" she asked, bewildered.

"Why, your secretaries are calling up customers on their own," Harari replied.

"Oh, really? Is that what they're doing?" She laughed.

"You mean you didn't delegate that task to them?"

"No," she said. "I didn't even know they were doing it. Listen, Oren, my job is to get everyone on my team to think creatively in pursuit of the same goal. So what I do is talk to people regularly about why we exist as a company and as a team. That means we talk straight about our common purpose and the high standards we want to achieve. I call these our goal lines. Then we talk regularly about some broad constraints we have to work within, like budgets, ethics, policies, and legalities. Those are our sidelines.

"It's like a sport. Once we agree on the goal lines and sidelines, I leave it to my people to figure out how to best get from here to there. I am available and attentive when they need feedback. Sometimes I praise; sometimes I criticize—but always constructively, I hope. We get together periodically and talk about who's been trying what, and we all give constructive feedback to one another. I know that sounds overly simplistic, but I assure you that is my basic management philosophy.

"And that's why I don't know what my assistants are doing, because it's obviously something they decided to try for the first time this week. I happen to think it's a great idea, because it's within the playing field and it helps us keep high standards for being number one in our industry. I'll tell you something else: I don't even know what they intend to do with the data they're collecting, but I know they'll do the right thing.

"Here's my secret: I don't know what my people are doing, but because I work face to face with them as a coach, I know that whatever it is they're doing is exactly what I'd want them to be doing if I knew what they were doing!"

Technology and the Work Force

We must empower our developers to design systems that people can actually use. In all the hoopla surrounding the information highway and its spinoffs, we may just be forgetting the ultimate end user of the product. I'm sure you all remember a few years ago when home banking was all the rage. The bank sent you the software and you could do just about everything—save, get cash, make transfers. The problem was that the software was just too complicated for the nontechnical end user. I thought it was a snap, but my dad didn't. Nor did my husband. And how about those VCRs that forever blink 12:00?

A November 1992 survey of *Total Quality Newsletter* readers (see Table 6.1) gives credence to the idea that technology may be outpacing workers' ability to use it. Many respondents said that larger training investments could help narrow that skills gap. But most respondents felt that well-chosen technology could yield more responsive customer service, increased productivity, and improved information flows.

I hate to admit it, but I think that most IT professionals leave the end user out of the productivity equation. Even if a system is reliable and reusable, and even if it is implemented on or before schedule, and even if that system has a low maintenance-to-development ratio, unless that system makes the end user more productive, the system has failed.

So instead of implementing technology that far outpaces the worker's ability to use and master it, we must choose technology that better accommodates the work force. Because technology has been provider-driven, we've made all the efforts to accommodate to the technology without taking into account how to make the technology accommodate people.

Recently a major financial services company made the announcement that it was spending $150 million to upgrade its information-processing system. When asked why, the company responded that the

TABLE 6.1   Ability to use technology.

	Yes	No
Human/technology interaction is important to my company.	93%	7%
Our use of new technology has increased rapidly in the last 5 years.	93%	7%
Technology's role in my company will increase considerably this decade.	93%	7%
People have the literacy skills needed to deal with the technological aspects of their jobs.	40%	60%
People have the computer skills needed to deal with the technological aspects of their jobs.	28%	62%
People are comfortable dealing with the technological aspects of their jobs.	45%	55%
More training is needed if people are to make use of the technology available to them at my company.	86%	14%
We have a system for addressing concerns about human interaction with technology.	34%	66%
Technology is replacing workers at my company.	24%	76%

SOURCE: *Total Quality Newsletter.*

competition had done it. That is not the right reason. Spending $150 million has to radically improve service or quality for the company's customers. If it doesn't, then what's the point?

Alan Melville is the quality director and vice president of the loan management department at American Real Estate Group in Stockton, California. His view is that the secret to maximizing use of new technologies lies in matching innovations to customers' and employees' needs.

American Real Estate Group manages assets of savings and loans (S&Ls) taken over by the federal government. A staff of 300 is hard at work liquidating the assets of a $4 billion S&L portfolio. The work is very data-intensive, and productivity is measured by how "paperless" the environment can be made.

Melville says that simply asking why is key to any decisions regarding technology: "The goal is not just to automate tasks, but to change the way we do business." Melville doesn't want to just automate the stamping of a check. He wants to be able to ask, "Why do we have to stamp at all? Where does this check come from? Why do we even have to touch it?"

Budd Caitlin is vice president of quality management at Morgan Construction Co., in Worcester, Massachusetts. Like most manufacturing firms, Morgan has to keep pace with technology to maintain a competitive edge. So Caitlin's question is not whether to invest in technology, but how to prepare his people to use it. The first step is a hiring process that guarantees that the company will find the best people. The next task is training those people.

Hiring the Best People

Organizations that want to be competitive will simply have to hire the very best people they possibly can—both end users and technologists.

Of course, in these "politically correct" times, the concept of the best is being roundly criticized. The American Management Association publishes a newsletter geared to human resources personnel. A recent issue warned that anyone placing a help-wanted ad could be the defendant in a discrimination suit if the advertisement called for "recent graduates" or "college graduates" when the job didn't warrant such qualifications.

"Recent graduates" is highly discriminatory against anyone with a bit of mileage, and I agree with the AMA's warning. But I don't agree with the caution on requesting college graduates. The AMA's view is that proportionately fewer members of minority groups finish college than do members of nonminority groups. Therefore, indicating college grads only discriminates against minority candidates. I say, hogwash.

You can't help your age, but you can certainly help your educational status. Not all colleges cost $18,000 a year. There are many fine local colleges that are nearly free. The philosophy of my organization is to be the very best. This means that we have to hire the very best. This doesn't translate to recruiting at the best colleges (Harvard as opposed to Podunk), but it does translate to finding those people who persevere, who try to make themselves better than what they already are. That's what a college degree means to me.

In fact, a thorough reading of Dinesh D'Souza's fine book *Illiberal Education* might just sour you on graduates of some of the better colleges.[2] Basically the book argues that some of our leading universities have been mandated to "common denominate" students. In D'Souza's view, by charging universities with being

> structurally racist, sexist, and class-biased, a coalition of student activists, junior faculty, and compliant administrators have imposed

their own political ideals on admissions, hiring, curriculum, and even personal conduct, while eschewing the goals of liberal education.

Essentially, we can no longer be sure of why a student was accepted at a university or why he got the grades that he did. Given an education like the one D'Souza envisions, can we even be sure that future graduates will think on their own (recall the movie *Stepford Wives*) or work well in teams?

Organizations face rough competition every day of their corporate lives. To hobble them for social reasons is to make them lose that competitive edge. That, indeed, may be exactly the course if human resources departments are weighed down with impossible "equal opportunity" hiring requirements.

I believe firmly in equal opportunity. But only if the candidate has the skills I'm looking for. I won't hire a woman just because my quota dictates a woman. Unfortunately, many American companies have a mindset of "obeying quotas." As a result, instead of getting the very best staff money can buy, they wind up with the lowest common denominator. Hardly a competitive advantage.

Another interesting phenomenon in today's downsized economy is the sheer number of experienced, dedicated people who have been booted out the door. Many of them are finding it difficult to find new jobs. An acquaintance of mine, a secretary by trade, gets the same brush-off each and every time she goes for an interview: "You're overqualified." Now perhaps this is a euphemism for "You're too old," but think about it. Wouldn't you like to staff up with all overqualified people? I know I would. What benefits my company would reap from all that experience! Personally, I think organizations are shooting themselves in the foot competitively when they decide that Ms. Jones or Mr. Smith is "overqualified." The interesting thing is that, because of our wounded economy, all this experience is available on the cheap. A competitor's loss is my gain.

I belong to the New York Software Industry Association. This fledging group of New York City–based software vendors has a lot to grapple with, given the battered New York City economy and the sheer expense of doing business there.

However, there is no shortage of seasoned professionals in New York City, so I was aghast when one of the association's members spoke enthusiastically about a policy of hiring young programmers from abroad. The company's view was that excessed staffers were like so many bad tomatoes. They weren't worth salvaging.

I beg to differ. While it's true that many excessed IT professionals have rather worn skills, they most definitely can be salvaged with a little training. "Not so," said the marketing chief of this very well-known company. "Better to start from scratch." And the company's idea of starting from scratch was to hire someone young, PC-based, and from another country (cheap, cheap, cheap).

Let's examine the ramifications. Although it's true that a company following such a policy would get more modern skills for less money, it would also lose out in a number of ways. First of all, remaining personnel are not blind. That is, they are pretty cognizant of the firm's penchant for cutting staff at home and replacing it with what they consider to be "outsiders." Their feelings of firm disloyalty coupled with the fear of being a victim of downsizing in the next go-round, lead to lower motivation, dampened enthusiasm, and a marked decrease in productivity and product quality.

Second, for the most part, newly hired labor just does not "understand" the business. At a time when business and technology are moving closer together, is it wise to throw out all the accumulated business knowledge of the current IT staff?

Today, programmers with a COBOL background seem to be about as employable as chimney sweeps. What the industry tends to forget is that COBOL is merely an attribute of a far greater skill. That skill is being able to develop enterprise applications. Most COBOL folks have the title of programmer/analyst. The analyst is tacked on for a very good reason. Not only do these people know how to program; they can also look at the big picture and then apportion it into manageable components, each component becoming a program or a part of a system. This is a skill far too valuable to throw away. The key, then, is training.

To Train, or Not to Train

A recent report by an influential user and vendor cooperative concludes that organizations downsizing their computer operations underestimate the inherent training costs for personnel.

The report, published by the New York-based organization Open User Recommended Solutions (OURS) along with the market research Gartner Group (Stamford, Connecticut), suggests that businesses need to allocate greater sums of money to train users before the true cost advantages in downsizing to client/server can be realized.[3]

According to the study, entitled "Changing IS Organizations: The Effect of Client/Server Implementation on Job Skills Requirements," untrained users "spend three to six times the number of hours to reach the same functionality as trained users." The study model reveals that trained users will reach a level of proficiency at a cost of $35 per hour, whereas untrained users will drain corporate budgets to the tune of as much as $130 per hour to accomplish the same desired goals.

So lack of training costs. While the OURS study looked at the end-user equation, my company looked at the training equation through the eyes of the IT professional. What we found is that training makes workers 600 percent more productive. In other words, if you are tackling a move to Sybase from DB2, throwing a textbook over the cubicle wall just won't do it. The three best ways to get productivity are training, training, and training again.

Fortunately, there are many channels open. Most major software vendors offer off-site or on-site training. Resellers of computer equipment are another avenue. Independent trainers—that is, consultants who train—offer probably the best value of all, since they can tailor the course specifically to your organization and can train your end users as well.

A Better Work Force

Creating a better work force means understanding how to work with people. You'd be surprised (or maybe not) at how differently "bosses" look at things than do their "staff." Table 6.2 amply demonstrates this dichotomy. The object, clearly, is to narrow the gap. One way to do so is through motivating the work force. Now, this doesn't mean taking out the pom-poms and giving the old college cheer. It does mean taking some specific steps.

The first step is to understand your own motivations, your strengths as a manager, and your weaknesses. Probably the best approach is to ask your peers and employees to make an anonymous appraisal of your performance as a manager. Have them rate such traits as listening and communication skills, openness, and attitude. Painful as this process may be, it will actually make you seem heroic in your employees' eyes. At the same time, it will give you some food for thought on ways to improve your own performance.

The second step—one that many managers pay only lip service to—

TABLE 6.2   What employees want.

As rated by managers		As rated by employees
1	Good pay	5
2	Job security	4
3	Promotion/growth	6
4	Good working conditions	7
5	Interesting work	1
6	Tactful discipline	10
7	Loyalty to employees	8
8	Appreciation	2
9	Help with personal problems	9
10	Involvement	3

SOURCE: *Advanced Management Journal.*

can really make the difference between having a motivated employee and one who feels that he or she is just "another number." Take the time to learn about your employees and their families. What are their dreams? Then ask yourself how you as a manager can fulfill those dreams from a business perspective.

Perhaps the best way to learn about your employees is in a nonwork atmosphere—over lunch or on a company outing around Central Park. As you learn more about your employees' motives, you can help each one develop a personalized strategic plan and vision. Ultimately, you can convert those horrible yearly performance reviews into goal-setting sessions and progress reports.

Generating a positive attitude is the third step. Studies show that 87 percent of all management feedback is negative, and that traditional management theory has done little to correct this situation. Your goal should be to reverse the trend. Make 87 percent of all feedback good.

Respect for and sensitivity toward others remain essential in developing positive attitudes. Ask employees' opinions regarding problems on the job; treat their suggestions and ideas like priceless treasures.

The partner of positive attitudes in the motivational game is shared goals. A motivated work force needs well-defined objectives that address both individual and organizational goals. This means that you should include all your employees in the strategic-planning process. Getting them involved leads to increased motivation. It also acts as a quality check on whether or not you are doing the right thing. And you'll close the communication gap at the same time.

Just setting a goal is insufficient. You have to monitor progress. The goal-setting process should include preparing a detailed road map that shows the specific path each person is going to take to meet that goal. One of the things that IT professionals dislike the most is the feeling that they're left out of the business cycle. In essence, information technology simply puts one bullet on the grand strategic plan. IT staffers frequently complain that they rarely get to see the fruits of their labor. Distributing the IT function into the business unit mitigates this problem somewhat, but it is still up to the manager to "put technologists into the thick of things." Make them feel part of the entire organization.

Finally, recognizing employee or team achievement is the most powerful tool in the motivating manager's toolbox. Appreciation for a job well done consistently appears at the top of employee "want lists." So hire a band, have a party, send a card, or call in a clown—but thank that person or that team.

References

1. Oren Harari, "Stop Empowering Your People," *Management Review,* November 1993, pp. 26–29.

2. Dinesh D'Souza, *Illiberal Education,* Random House, New York, 1992.
3. "Changing IS Organizations: The Effect of Client/Server Implementation on Job Skills Requirements," white paper, New York City and Stanford Open User Recommended Solutions/Gartner Group Joint Study, July 1993.

7

Is Client/Server a Productivity Buster?

If one fact is a definite known in the computer world, it's that client/server is the fastest-growing segment of the industry. Publishers have dedicated new magazines to it, and promoters have all but inundated our mailboxes with conference notices.

But is client/server really good for us? That's the question this chapter poses. And along with the debate, I'll provide some concrete advice on how to downsize productively in this age of client/server.

The Hidden Costs

We've always had the power and security of the mainframe. So why "downsize" to a smaller, less powerful, and certainly more dangerous platform? A platform with few of the administration, backup, and recovery tools that we've grown accustomed to. There are probably two reasons that explain this massive movement downward. One is that downsizing is, presumably, much cheaper than running applications on the mainframe. This is especially true if the activity that end users want to perform is computer-intensive, such as graphically displaying and manipulating information. CPU cycles on the PC are much cheaper than on the mainframe. The other reason is that the graphical user interface (GUI) on the PC makes work, allegedly, just so much easier to perform. And so much easier to understand.

Let's quickly examine both of these reasons. When downsizing got its start, the majority of applications ported downtown were smallish and standalonish. It was easy to see an immediate decrease in the cost of these applications. The mainframe application was charged back to the user at an increasingly expensive rate, whereas the PC version of the application was free—except, of course, for the price of the PC.

To be sure, the idea that PC applications are free is an illusion. But it is an illusion that has staying power. Lately, there have been dissenting opinions about the true cost of client/server solutions (vis-à-vis the mainframe approach). What people are discovering is that client/server is not cheaper. In fact, in many cases it is far more expensive.

Once functionality is distributed out to hundreds of servers and thousands of PCs, the cost dynamic changes. In a centralized environment, you can dedicate a rather small staff to control a large environment. In a distributed environment, you need to have a distributed staff. What companies are finding is that even as their mainframe staff is dwindling, their distributed staff is growing ever larger.

For companies that were tied to a charge-back mechanism, the advent of the PC threw this nice orderly approach into chaos. They didn't quite know how to charge back the cost of maintaining the PC. And there is most definitely a cost. There's a maintenance cost per PC, a cost to keep the software up to date, and a training cost. After a bit of fumbling, organizations tailored these charge-back mechanisms to fit the world of the PC.

Then came the surprise. In many instances, the user departments found an *increase* in their costs rather than a decrease even as they downsized. Organizations that have not deployed a charge-back mechanism are only fooling themselves. The costs associated with PCs (in a client/server architecture) need to be accounted for somewhere. There is no such thing as corporate funny money. The piper must be paid somehow.

According to a report by Forrester Research of Cambridge, Massachusetts,[1] once an organization installs a LAN, the cost of supporting it adds up to several million dollars annually. For example, to keep 5000 LAN users up and running, a company will pay $6.4 million, or $1280 per user.

All this leads us to the next question: If client/server is not really a cost savings, then why do it? Obviously, the flexibility of the PC's graphical user interface has a lot to do with it. But the productivity of the GUI might be as much of as ruse as the cost-effectiveness of the PC.

Consider Doug's dilemma. He holds a high-ranking position with one of the leading computer manufacturers. A brilliant engineer, he is equally at home tinkering with the innards of a computer as speaking on the keynote podium. But Doug has one major failing. He's addicted to his PC.

Doug long ago advocated the paperless office. So he keeps everything on his laptop PC. The problem is it's hard to find anything, especially using those obscure 8-character file names that the DOS operating system is so good at.

But what really detracts from Doug's individual productivity is his presentation software. In the pre-PC days, when executives wanted memos written, they used a secretary or the typing pool. When they wanted 35mm slides for a presentation, they went to the graphics department.

All that's changed. Today's busy professional is spending hours glued to the PC, writing his or her own memos and pasting clip art into presentations. There goes the productivity curve.

There's a real trade-off here. On the one hand, literally hundreds of inexpensive PC products will enable you to do for yourself what, just a few short years ago, you used to pay for. But the flip side is that if you do everything yourself, you're far less productive than if you out-source part of the work to someone else.

But this conundrum has been largely ignored in the massive move to downsizing. I sincerely hope that in our mad dash to make things smaller, we don't forget to make things more productive as well.

Despair not. This chapter is not really about client/server bashing. It's merely a warning. A warning that, if you're not careful, client/server won't get you where you think you want to go. The chapter is also a guide to get you thinking about the right (translate that to productive and cost-effective) way to do client/server computing.

The Rush Toward Downsizing

Today, three synergistic forces are spurring the rush toward downsizing:

- Users, comfortable with their newly acquired PC skills, are demanding immediate and navigable access to their data.

- IT departments, mandated by their managements to cut costs and improve performance, are finding quick payback solutions from PC and workstation environments.

- The rapid pace of technological innovation has served to provide hundredfold *increases* in functionality with tenfold *decreases* in price (vis-à-vis performance).

As a result, downsizing has become a global euphemism for any one, or combination, of these three forces.

Originally, the term *downsizing* was quite clear in its meaning in the IT world. It simply meant moving applications from the mainframe down to hardware that was smaller in size. But it also meant looking to these smaller, but very powerful hardware platforms for completely new development, with the effect of essentially ignoring the mainframe.

Companies that followed this last strategy found that over time, and with increasing regularity, standalone PC-based development was not robust enough for all their requirements. Hence, a new term was intro-duced—*upsizing*. Organizations requiring increased power and capability solved their problem by using two variations of upsizing. One method saw these companies connect two or more PCs in a LAN. In effect, the network acted as a multiplier in providing approximately three times the power for each two PCs that were connected. The second upsizing method entailed replacing some of the PC hardware, usually the server, with either workstations or midrange computers.

Today, organizations should be carefully considering the best mix of hardware platforms to suit all their needs—in effect, *rightsizing* their computing strategy. But rightsizing concerns more than just hardware. And it concerns more than just software. Rightsizing also means seeing the solution in terms of the enterprise itself.

Organizations are a product of their parts. Although hardware and software play major roles, the dominant forces are the systems already in place. Although often ignored by downsizing zealots, these *legacy systems* are critical to the organization. They must be an equal partner to any downsizing strategy.

But are they?

Most downsizing strategies simply do not address the concerns of IT professionals. There is a simple reason for this. Since PCs entered the organization through the side door left open by end users, the enterprise and its attendant production systems were never originally part of the PC equation. As end users, and even "information center" subsidiaries of the IT department, began to network these PCs, they took a purely bottom-up approach.

But downsizing in a computing organization requires a top-down approach to achieve the synthesis between the two very different worlds of information technology and departmental computing.

Approaches to Downsizing

There are as many variations in the manner in which organizations approach downsizing as there are organizations that practice it. That downsizing is increasing in its popularity is not in dispute. In its study of the computing strategies of the Fortune 1000, Forrester Research found that downsizing is white hot. Of the Fortune 1000 companies interviewed, over 80 percent indicated a rise in downsizing in their organizations.[1]

How organizations tackle their downsizing strategy is perhaps more a function of when they decided to opt for downsizing than of why they decided to downsize. Early adopters of downsizing (1981–1986) were very much limited by the power of the newer, smaller PC platforms. As a result, their strategy was to ignore the mainframe and instead build standalone applications on the PC. These are the organizations that are today striving to upsize their computing capabilities.

The organizations that pushed ahead (1986–1990) are the ones we traditionally think of as downsizers. By the mid-1980s the power of the PC had improved considerably, and numerous advances were being unveiled in the software domain. But it was the ability to network that had the biggest impact.

Late adopters of downsizing (post-1990)are probably in the most advantageous position of all. Technology has improved to the point of providing downsized power equal to, if not greater than, that of the mainframe. This enhanced power comes from client/server computing. The world of client/server actually contains three components, not two: the client, the server, and the network.

The *client* is the device that sits atop the user's desk. The PC is clearly the most popular of clients, because of its combination of ease of use and local processing capabilities. But other types of hardware can function as clients as well. They include higher-powered workstations and dumb terminals.

The main function of the *server* is to act as a switch between the client workstation and organizational processing and information. Servers can either act as the repository of data or route an information request to the appropriate device in the network. Additionally, servers can either process a given request or route that request to another device on the network.

Any type of equipment can be designated as a server, with a corollary increase in functionality as server size increases. Although the workstation or midrange computer is, by far, the most popular hardware server platform, with plummeting prices there is a growing trend today to salvaging the mainframe and putting it into service as a server. Given the possible power of the server, it is no wonder that organizations use them in intriguing ways:

Electronic mail, including voice

Gateways to outside services

Batch processing

File sharing

Bulletin board

Facsimile sending and receiving

Videotext

The *network* is the component that links the client and server together. The typical configuration is to connect work groups and/or departments with a local area network. Ultimately, these separate LANs are connected into an enterprisewide wide area network (WAN).

The Business Research Group (BRG) of Newton, Massachusetts,

offers this definition of client/server: "a system in which application processing is shared between a desktop 'client' and one or more network-attached 'servers.'"[2] In BRG's study of organizations that are either adopting or working to adopt client/server solutions, it was found that 31 percent considered mission-critical applications as important to their client/server plans while another 23 percent considered these applications as critical.

Organizations with mission-critical applications must carefully develop a set of critical success factors prior to implementing a downsizing (or rightsizing, or upsizing) strategy in a client/server environment. Part of BRG's study is to fully understand approaches to downsizing.

Separate but equal

As mentioned, early adopters of downsizing primarily implemented two separate computing practices—one for PCs and one for mainframes. Initially, the reasoning for the strategy was the inability of the PC platform to perform enterprise functionality. But even as the PC matured, with attendant increases in the power and sophistication of the hardware and software that ran on it, the PC and the mainframe remained two separate and distinct environments. To some degree, this attitude still exists today, especially in organizations with heavily decentralized and distributed end-user departments.

Buy and unplug

When the idea of downsizing was conceptualized, it was projected that in time the downsized hardware would become so powerful, and the software so sophisticated, that the organization would be able to simply unplug the mainframe. Smaller organizations have certainly been able to achieve this feat. In the great preponderance of organizations, however, complex applications running on the mainframe simply cannot be downsized easily.

The turnkey system is not a new idea. Even before downsizing became part of the vocabulary, hardware vendors were packaging their low-end hardware with industry-specific software. The banking industry is a case in point. Few banking institutions today run their check-processing applications on the mainframe. Rather, since the 1970s banks have been running these applications on specialized midrange hardware with specialized, or "off the shelf" software.

In spite of an inability to simply "unplug" their mainframes, most organizations are actively planning to curtail mainframe purchases and/or upgrades. Forrester Research reports that of the Fortune 1000 companies interviewed, 48 percent will upgrade their mainframe every 5–7 years, 33 percent will never buy a mainframe again, and 5 percent will upgrade their mainframe only every 1–3 years.

The decision-support paradigm

Because few analytically oriented systems require access to real-time data, an opportunity arises to asynchronously download corporate information to an analyst's workstation. Armed with a plethora of graphical tools—such as spreadsheets, statistical software, and databases—the corporate analyst gains immeasurable productivity in the area of decision support. In some cases, it was just this reason that precipitated the rapid acceleration of the downsizing movement. As mentioned, users saw the possibilities that PCs had to offer as early as 1981. Armed with low-end PCs and VisiCalc (the precursor to Lotus 1-2-3), users had a hundredfold more flexibility than they did on the mainframe—if they had access to the mainframe at all.

To this day, a distributed approach to decision support is popular. Under this strategy, the mainframe both continues its role of running production applications and takes on a new role of acting as a centralized data repository for asynchronously distributed systems.

Each system must be independently evaluated to determine the need for a PC-platformed decision-support environment. If one is required, a second decision is made as to frequency of download.

For systems in this mode, an additional jobstream is added to the nightly (weekly, monthly) production schedule which extracts information from the system(s), formats it for download, and then either downloads it to a server (one or more PCs) or sits in a queue waiting for the user to access the mainframe for a manual download.

Some organizations enhance this strategy by providing a duplex asynchronous sharing of mainframe data. Here, data is periodically downloaded to the PC or server and then periodically updated back to the mainframe, with attendant updates. Although this is the methodology that has long been popularized by industry experts, it is also the strategy that contains the most pitfalls.

Because both mainframe production systems and workstation-based analytical systems are maintained in parallel, there is no decrease in cost expenditure. Although the availability of sophisticated PC software produces a marked rise in productivity and service, maintaining asynchronous links between the mainframe and PC compromises computing integrity. Essentially, what has been created here is a discrete client and a discrete server without the networked benefits of client/server computing.

The RDBMS approach

Relational database management systems (RDBMS) may have been the first to really take advantage of the capabilities of client/server. With the introduction of UNIX workstations into the picture, it became important that an organization be able to process in a three-level architecture: PC, workstation, and mainframe.

To do so, the organization needed software that exhibited four extremely important traits: scalability, interoperability, reliability, and controllability. Essentially, this is the definition of an open system.

Ever since the relational database format was introduced in the early 1980s, database vendors have been working diligently to port their version of the relational model to the many platforms that can be found in an enterprise computing environment. What enables this portability is relational's reliance on the standard query language (SQL) standard. Essentially, all vendors were developing and selling the very same product. With one caveat though: extensions.

Probably one of the most widely used standards today, SQL permits the existence of extensions to the standard. Vendors, in their zeal to add enhanced functionality to their products, greatly reduced the one advantage that SQL offered: compatibility.

Today's relational databases offer much more than the database itself. Many offer complete environments enabling organizations to tie together relational systems residing on distributed and heterogeneous platforms.

Using the RDBMS to simultaneously distribute and integrate the enterprise's databases requires consideration of the following questions:

1. *Does the organization utilize only relational databases?*   If so, there is a definite, and immediate, payback to the RDBMS approach. However, since most legacy systems are not relational, the organization must either exclude these systems from the network or plan an extensive and expensive conversion effort. In instances when the relational database package can read the legacy data (VSAM, hierarchical, or network), can it write to it as well?

2. *How many forms of the relational model are being used in the organization?*   It is not surprising that many firms use more than one database package. For example, they may have IBM's DB2 on the mainframe, Sybase on the server, and Oracle on the PC. Given the propensity to use proprietary features, a key question arises: Will these diverse relational databases be able to communicate? A corollary to this question is: Will the organization be migrating to object-oriented DBMS (OODBMS) sometime in the not-too-distant future?

3. *What is the transaction throughput of a network based on a meta-database model?* Bread-and-butter applications are notoriously transaction-bound. Will the RDBMS perform as robustly as the transaction-processing (TP) monitor that the organization is now using?

Although the relational model is the standard for databases, the same cannot be said for the relational model vis-à-vis TP systems. In fact, to create the sophisticated functionality of a TP system, the proprietary features of the RDBMS must often be employed. Use of these proprietary features will put organizations back in the same boat in which they started. They'll be locked into one vendor, using one database.

The integrated approach

Of all the approaches to downsizing, integration holds the most promise for enterprise organizations. It's also the approach, according to the Seybold Group report on open information systems,[3] that users are demanding. As Patricia Seybold puts it, "Users seek virtual integration: tightly wired functions, no strings attached."

To achieve this end, the organization must take a long, hard look at the different platforms—what they're being used for today, what they could be used for tomorrow—and the advantages and disadvantages of each.

In a client/server architecture, it is possible to distribute applications in any number of ways. Over the past few years, trial and error in many organizations has produced consensus on the following issues.

The PC.   The graphical powers of the PC combined with its ease of use make it a natural for user interface. Since the introduction of desktop managers such as Microsoft's Windows and IBM's Presentation Manager, applications—whether they be word processing, spreadsheeting, or database—take on a familiar look and feel. Because these vendors have had the presence of mind to offer developer toolsets, even enterprise organizations can create in-house applications that look remarkably similar to the off-the-shelf software that users have worked with for years.

In addition, there is perhaps no other hardware platform today that has had such a plethora of software developed for it. The value of the PC has not diminished since its introduction more than a decade ago. And used in conjunction with other hardware and software, the PC definitely provides immediate productivity gains.

The Server.   The key component of the client/server model is the server. The server acts as a switch or gateway, enabling resources such as databases and processing power to be shared in an efficient and cost-effective manner.

In the early days of PC computing, the server was connected to the PC through a local area network. In most cases, the PC-oriented network took its cue from the PC's DOS operating system. Although currently compatible with operating systems such as Windows, the PC-to-PC orientation of these networks remains the same.

Trilevel client/server architectures require a robustness several magnitudes higher. The future truly belongs to the multiprocessing capabilities of OS/2, UNIX, or Windows/NT. Only time will tell which will be the ultimate winner.

The operating system with the biggest lead is UNIX. Preeminently popular within the academic, scientific, and engineering communities, UNIX entered into the commercial arena through applications that needed strong networks coupled with robust workstation processing capabilities. This combination was singlehandedly responsible for the popularity of the workstation in the financial services community. There is nary a trader without a powerful workstation hooked to an even more powerful mainframe or supercomputer.

Of the three competing operating systems, only UNIX fits the basic requirements of an open system: scalability, interoperability, reliability, and controllability. In addition, only UNIX has the advantage of being a mature operating environment.

The mainframe.   Of those Fortune 1000 companies interviewed in the Forrester Research survey, 51 percent indicated that they would soon be deinstalling at least one computer. Even so, the vast majority of enterprise organizations will maintain as many mainframes as needed to run their legacy systems.

Interestingly, these same organizations also found that the mainframe still has enormous value when it is called into service as a sort of superserver. Whether the mainframe becomes part of the overall schema because it runs legacy systems or acts as a superserver, it will not be departing from the enterprise organization any time in the near future.

More About Legacy Systems

The Forrester study estimated that by the end of 1994 only 45 percent of mission-critical applications would be run on the mainframe, as opposed to 77 percent today. At that rate, it will be well into the twenty-first century before the mainframe is relegated to the computing junk pile.

There are some very good reasons for the slow transition from mainframe to server. The majority of legacy systems are at least 5 years old. Many, in fact, predate the migration to relational databases. As a result, legacy databases can be any combination of hierarchical, network, and relational. Additionally, many earlier systems were implemented on flat or indexed files (VSAM and ISAM in the IBM arena). As a result, the organization often finds itself in a dilemma. It is simply not possible to port these databases from the mainframe to the server or PC gracefully. For the most part, legacy databases, and the applications that use them, must be rewritten—a very tall and expensive order for an organization.

Legacy application programs present difficulties as well, but they are usually easier to downsize than are databases. Most applications were generated by outmoded and outdated software development methodologies. As a result, organizations found themselves saddled with monolithic monstrosities as opposed to the more efficient and compact type of code that characterized later systems. To achieve downsizing, then, application programs would need to be entirely rewritten.

There's some $80 billion worth of Cobol, the predominant legacy programming language, in tens of thousands of organizations. There are also well over a million Cobol programmers out in the field. Although much maligned as over the hill by the computer press, these people have the very background that makes for a successful client/server environment.

Cobol developers don't just know Cobol. They are also possessed of a set of essential skills that savvy organizations, and industry gurus, are just beginning to appreciate. It is just these people who understand how to develop systems with adequate reliability, backup, security, and control—some of the most important attributes of a mission-critical system.

Integration—The Right Choice

Organizations with mission-critical mainframe systems have one goal—to phase out the mainframe gently. The existence of these systems simply cannot be ignored. But whereas enhancements to such systems formerly were done at the mainframe level, organizations pursuing a downsizing strategy are now mixing PC, server, and mainframe to achieve their goals. Their key strategy? To acknowledge and address their legacy systems problem.

A legacy system can be downsized in a variety of ways. But the method should be preceded by a decision which answers this key question: Do you expect to change the role of the mainframe to a large data server and move application processing to distributed platforms (surround), or do you want to get fully off the mainframe (transition)?

Early adopters of downsizing chose to deal with the limitations of the hardware and network by retrofitting a windows-based GUI to an existing application on one or more remote hosts. Known as *facelifting*, this method entails little more than loading PC-based software and "informing" it of where accessible data is located. Fundamentally, facelifting tools do exactly what they are named after. They are neither robust enough nor sophisticated enough to be a real answer to the mission-critical requirement. Ultimately, they are merely a temporary, cosmetic improvement.

Few enterprise organizations see facelifting as a real solution and even fewer have the ability to totally "unplug" their mainframes. But the majority of organizations do have the ability to solve their problems using either a surround or transition strategy.

The surround strategy

By now the term *surround* is probably familiar to most, if not all, IT managers. Coined by a mainframe vendor as a marketing strategy to keep the mainframe in the picture in an increasingly downsized world, surround simply means "surrounding" (legacy) mainframe-based systems with newer PC-based or workstation-based systems.

While many mainframe vendors saw the surround strategy as an opportunity to maintain their customer base, their customers saw it as an opportunity to leverage their existing computers and employees against a new set of computers and skill. Predominately the strategy of large sites, a surround architecture has the ultimate goal of using computers strategically. That is, it seeks to employ each type of computer in a heterogeneous environment in the most effective manner.

Surround strategists make some financial decisions as well. Here, a conscious decision is made that the mainframe budget will no longer increase, but stay flat, in spite of the fact that the budget as a whole will be increased.

While expenditures need no longer be made to upgrade the existing mainframes (new processor, more disk, and so on), additional budget dollars are needed to architect, purchase, and then implement the many surround subsystems that are part of the strategic plan.

Strategy, in the case of surround, calls (whenever possible) for new development to be done in a downsized mode. A good example of this is the creation of a new sales division. Prior to the introduction of the three-layer architecture, organizations had little choice but to develop the bulk of sales applications on the mainframe. But today, the logical as well as practical route is to employ all three layers to develop the system. The PC is utilized as a graphical front end, the workstation acts as a server as well as the analytical engine, and the mainframe becomes the repository of corporate data and the link to existing sales, payroll, and inventory applications.

It should be noted, however, that smart organizations often vary from this simple scenario. They might opt to do some processing on the client as well as the server, thereby minimizing the change of server bottlenecks. In essence, the organization is "surrounding" legacy systems on the mainframe with newer PC/workstation-based systems.

The transition strategy

Whereas the goal of surround organizations is to have mainframe, workstation, and PC all live in harmony, the goal of the *transition* strategy is to move off the mainframe as quickly as possible. Although this approach is quite similar in practice to the surround strategy, an organization in a transition mode is actually more aggressive in migrating from the mainframe. Unlike the surround model, in which the mainframe budget stays flat, here the mainframe budget actually decreases while the overall budget remains flat. In other words, no additional monies are allocated to downsizing. The downsizing budget is obtained by using the savings achieved through aggressive cutting of the mainframe budget.

The strategy is typical of medium-size sites that have never had as large a stake invested in the mainframe as surround organizations. Nonetheless, transition organizations have enough mainframe mission-critical applications to necessitate treading carefully.

In a major study performed by Software Productivity Research of Burlington, Massachusetts,[4] computing was split into three components: new development (41 percent), enhancements (45 percent), and maintenance (14 percent). Of the work performed in these three areas, the portions done in a client/server environment were 55 percent, 20 percent and 25 percent respectively.

Unfortunately, these statistics underscore quite a serious problem. That is, the majority of organizations have no formal plan, or strategy, for downsizing. For downsizing to be effective, especially when an integrated approach is used, a formal plan must be developed.

Select an architecture.   This chapter has carefully reviewed each of the three components of the trilevel architecture. Since there is no generic solution that will solve all problems, the organization should decide what combination of components is most suitable for its unique circumstances. The objective for most organizations is to move as much of the processing as possible to the servers while remembering that legacy applications are far easier to downsize than legacy databases. The most popular choice, however, encompasses PC clients, distributed servers, and mainframes maintaining legacy systems.

Create a time line.   The order in which applications are to be downsized should not be randomly decided. Organizations should find the optimum order for migration. It will be different for each company.

However, some of the time line can be automatically filled in from the organization's project plan. A rule of thumb is that projects already in the plan should be studied first to determine whether they are candidates, using either a transitional or surround approach. Additionally, the organization should take a long, hard look at the usage level of its current systems. Less advantage will accrue to downsizing systems that are used but once a month than to those used daily.

Since databases affect multiple systems, those that affect the fewest systems should be downsized earlier rather than later. Databases with tentacles out to a vast number of applications, or databases that are extraordinarily large or that use nonrelational technologies, should be placed at the bottom of the list.

Choose your technology.   Once the number of levels in the architecture is decided, it is time to select the software that will be running on the system. Since the mainframe topology has already been selected, careful consideration should be paid to the remaining two levels.

On the PC level, three questions need to be answered:

- Will the PC merely serve as a front end or will there be local processing?

- What type of front-end software will be used?

- What operating system will be used (e.g., DOS, OS/2, Windows)?

A recent study performed by Cowen & Co., New York, found an increasing interest in UNIX-like capabilities for PCs as organizations develop multiuser, multitasking client/server systems of greater and greater power.[5]

The server question presents an interesting dilemma. As attested to by the Cowen survey, more and more organizations desire to use UNIX on their PCs. The question then becomes: What type of hardware should be utilized for the server—PC or workstation?

With the introduction of the Pentium chip by Intel, a high-end PC loaded with UNIX could prove to be every bit as powerful as a high-end workstation, but at a much lower cost. Ultimately, the choices are:

- Is the server a PC, workstation, midrange computer, or mainframe?

- Is the server's operating system OS/2, NT, UNIX, or something else?

Pick an application development technology.   There are dozens of technologies to choose from. Everything from third-generation programming languages, utilities, and compilers to completely unfamiliar (to many enterprise programmers) object-oriented technologies. The best path is the one that seems the most familiar but that also makes developers more productive than they've been in the past. Be wary, though. Many client/server technologies completely ignore the existence of legacy systems and databases. The only tool the organization picks should be able to work with these as well.

What the Experts Recommend

How many of us really understand the ramifications of making the transition from today's entrenched centralized processing architecture to client/server's more distributed mode? And do we really understand that this migration alters more than an architecture? It just might alter the function of systems development itself.

In order to appreciate the magnitude of these differences, we first need to understand specifically what components make up the client/server architecture. Berl Hartman is director of product marketing at the venerable Sybase. Located in Emeryville, California, Sybase is one of the leading, and earliest, vendors of client/server software tools. Given Sybase's experience in this arena, Hartman's perspective on the client/server equation is to the point. Her feeling is that client/server, or cooperative processing, is any form of computer program that divides processing into two sets of entities—usually a front end that deals with the user interface and a back end that deals with data processing.

Client/server is not a black-or-white issue. There are gradations. In a host of trade magazines, journals, and industry newspapers, we read, with increasing frequency, about products that sit in the client/server arena. A careful review of these products permits us to categorize at least four models, or market definitions, of client/server architecture.

At the lowest level is the model that deals specifically with graphical user interfaces. In this GUI arena, the goal is to front-end a mainframe system with a more user-friendly interface. Here developers concern themselves with cut and paste, windows, and other issues at the new frontier of graphical interfaces. A second paradigm of client/server concerns itself with presentation logic—an extension of the first model. Here the developers must concern themselves with the rules of logic concerning placement of data on the display screen. For example: "If field A is turned on, then field B must be turned off."

A third paradigm involves what Hartman calls integrity or transaction logic. In this paradigm, client/server architecture, in addition to the user interface and presentation capabilities, also has the advanced capability to deal with transaction-oriented rules. For example: "Don't give credit to people who have bills that are more than 90 days past due." In other words, Hartman's transaction paradigm closely parallels the actual business transaction. The fourth, most robust, and thus most complete, model of client/server architecture permits actual update of data from distributed locations.

There are major differences among the four paradigms presented here, and a thorough understanding of these differences should give the developer the insight to match up specific business needs to a specific client/server environment. The key here is business needs. Even in the era of the robust client/server model, it is worthwhile to note that some organizations need only add what Sybase's Hartman refers to as *frontware*. This concept relates to Hartman's first paradigm of graphical user interfaces. If all you do is put the user interface piece on the client, you have something called frontware. Essentially all you do is make the user interface prettier. It can blink or do pulldowns—but the fundamental application doesn't change. Mozart and Easel are examples of toolsets that improve the user interface without adding much functionality.

Hartman's frontware is the client/server model that most developers in the mainframe world cut their teeth on. In this arena all logic, from presentation to data processing, takes place on the mainframe. PCs, used as terminal emulators, are brought in to "liven up" the user interface. With this successful first implementation of client/server under their belts, developers typically want to race to the deep end of the pool and dive in. In their rush, many fail to realize that the pool is a lot deeper than they first suspected.

A deep pool is indeed an apt metaphor to describe the many complex issues that must be addressed if developers are to successfully navigate the rather murky waters of client/server development.

Once and always a distributed environment

In all the hubbub surrounding the rather sexy term *client/server,* we tend to forget that today's client/server environments are actually yesterday's distributed environments. At least one person in Palo Alto is here, though, to remind us of our roots. Brian Szabo is a principal with Network Intelligence Inc. A network management consultant, Szabo has been part of literally hundreds of migrations to the client/server environment. As a result, he can offer up some interesting insight into the roadblocks that developers are running into.

First and foremost, Szabo reminds us that history does repeat itself. He indicates that, from a technology point of view, when we migrate to distributed client/server environments what we're really moving into is the old concept of distributed computing. Szabo then proceeds to remind us that the fault-tolerant machines of the late 1970s relied on a requestor/server relationship, which is essentially the same as today's client/server architecture.

For Szabo, the important point to remember is not that client/server is a spinoff of yesterday's distributed processing, but that today's client/servers are essential distributed. The main consideration is what should run in which environment. For example, should the database be on the mainframe? Should it run on the PC? Or should it be a true distributed database?

Perhaps the most important issue for Szabo is the mechanics of distribution. Underlying any distributed, or client/server system is the ability to communicate discrete commands in order to "get or put" data across numerous network nodes. In essence, then, it is the network that forms the heart of client/server systems. And the network is the one thing that developers rarely had to contend with in a mainframe environment.

Mark Wich is a principal at Los Angeles–based Logicon/Ultra Systems. He sees the network as the pivotal issue for those organizations making the move off the mainframe to client/server. In his view, the problem with mainframe developers is that they have very seldom dealt with networks in general. They have never had to deal with Ethernet or the OSI protocol. For Wich, this concern translates into the primary question that client/server network developers must ask themselves during the planning stages: "The biggest issue is how many clients you're going to have. Or how many client processes can be running on the platform you're trying to deal with."

Wich's analysis aligns itself nicely with Szabo's suggestion that it is necessary to plan in advance exactly where the processes will be run. Will they run on a server, on a mainframe, or on a PC? For the first time, developers need to be very cognizant of the location of a process and the underlying network traffic competing for shared resources on the platform that the process is contending for.

According to Wich, one of the big problems encountered in client/server systems is that the machine acting as a server starts to hit the upper bounds of its processing capabilities. Let's say you have a network of powerful computers and X-terminals. Each one of those X-terminals is going to be using processing resources from the server computer. Suppose that each X-terminal wants to run a copy of Framemaker. But the server was designed to run only one, maybe two, copies of Framemaker. So you start to hit the bounds of that processor. In addition, you need to deal with network bandwidth problems at that point—because all the display and updating is being handled by the network as well.

As anyone who has ever run a network can attest to, network considerations are major. Wich and Szabo emphasize the importance of carefully planning for the distribution of functionality in such a way as to minimize network traffic.

Some would say that minimizing network traffic is not an appropriate domain for the system developer. Developers are specialists, after all, who deal in program logic. This may have been true in the past, and it is still true for centralized environments. But today, Szabo asserts, developers can no longer be specialists and Cobol programmers. New-age developers need an expertise in the design portion, an appreciation for the number of things happening simultaneously, and an understanding of the limitations of the network.

The issue of security

Distributing applications to run cooperatively on multiple platforms raises issues other than networking. One is the thorny specter of decreased security and integrity. At a recent Unisys press conference, the Gartner Group's James Cassell, vice president of large computer strategies, broached the topic of "consolidation" of diverse mainframe processes as an enabler of client/server architectures. Cassell lamented the common problem of uncontrolled downloading and subsequent changing of mission-critical corporate data to the PC level, perhaps to a spreadsheet. The result is a plethora of redundant and dissimilar files.

Cassell's point, and one echoed by many in corporate America, is that distributed data runs the risk of losing its integrity and, worse, becoming a security risk.

John Kish is vice president of desktop products for Oracle, based in Redwood Shores, California. Kish agrees with Cassell that one of the most important issues in client/server architecture is the security of the data. Too often, people forget that security in these networks is only as strong as the weakest link.

As the concept of client/server becomes more and more of a factor in corporate America, organizations need to take a step back and reassess their security requirements. Kish recommends that developers at least look at the following four issues:

- What sort of data integrity is guaranteed by the software selected?
- What level of data security is required by the installation?
- How will actions taken on behalf of security and integrity affect performance?
- What happens if another machine needs to be added in the middle of the network?

The final question is one that should be asked by all developers embarking on a client/server path: Is there a way to integrate all these elements together with little or no work? This question has no easy answer. The amount of work required to build a client/server system is dependent upon the actual application or set of applications that will ultimately be distributed to the client/server model.

Con Edison's client/server environment

Earlier in this chapter, we looked at systems that were gussied up with frontware. Although this is one of the four client/server paradigms (PC as client and mainframe as server) described by Sybase's Hartman, it is the least robust and least functional.

At the other end of the complexity spectrum is New York-based Con Edison's VISION project. Izzy Sobkowski, president of Knowledge Associates in Stamford, Connecticut, was recently on assignment at this giant electric utility. He describes VISION as a major implementation of client/server architecture. The goal behind the project is to take the 30,000-odd maps that Con Ed maintains and store them on a server. An example is the map known as C and DO, the acronym for cable and duct occupancy. C and DO describes the various cables and ducts underground—specifically, what cables are in what ducts—in terms of a distribution network.

According to Sobkowski, the process of tying systems into a client/server environment makes a whole lot of sense. Using an IBM mainframe as a central server and UNIX-based Intergraph workstations as clients, Con Ed has designed a proprietary approach to a very specific and unique business problem. And it is because of this very uniqueness that Con Edison has opted to go the route of building much of the software from scratch.

In this environment—a combination of UNIX, Prolog, and C, as well as a computer-assisted design (CAD) software package—the level of complexity is extreme and requires much expertise on the part of the programming team. Sobkowski's experience makes him an excellent source for clarifying the differences between developing systems in a mainframe versus client/server environment.

In a mainframe environment the cycle is plan, code, and pray. That's very different from a distributed system, in which the designer as well as the coders have more intimate access to machines. The cycle here is plan, code, test, plan, code, test. It's more iterative.

Con Ed, in its "from scratch" approach, was faced with the problem of developing a system that would enable the programming team to face down the myriad issues mentioned so far. The team had to contend with network issues, diverse communication protocols, and even data distribution issues. Grounded in a typically mainframe environment, Con Edison did not have experience in dealing with these issues. The hiring of Sobkowski has paved the way to a wholesale use of client/server within the company.

To this end, a number of Con Ed staff members have been assigned to Sobkowski's project. Sobkowski, as mentor, takes very seriously his role of training Con Ed employees to carry on without him. His approach is to first assign a small task. When the employees come to a roadblock, rather than showing them what to do, Sobkowski moves into the conference room and does some ad hoc training with the group as a whole.

A people issue

Although Con Edison's ground-up approach to development of a client/server system is atypical, it is typical in that it raises the issue of migrating not only systems to this architecture but people as well.

Andersen Consulting, as a system integrator, is perhaps one of the most experienced firms around in dealing with this issue. Hugh Ryan, director of new-age systems at Andersen's Chicago headquarters, describes the significant learning curve for both MIS and end users alike.

According to Ryan, MIS is threatened by the move to a client/server architecture. The technology is very different. A whole host of questions and issues need to be explored that were "automatically handled" on the mainframe. Some developers find it difficult to move from what Ryan terms a "stabilized mainframe environment" to an unstable environment in which it is up to the developer to pick the database. Or the operating system. Or the LAN. Or the fourth-generation language (4GL).

People are surprised at the number of decisions that have to be made in terms of hardware and software. But, according to Ryan, perhaps the most pronounced change is the way programs are structured in this environment. The move to distributed data is fundamentally different in terms of programming.

Con Ed's Sobkowski provided us with an example of the tack some firms are taking in building from scratch. Then again, Con Ed is unique in that its applications, and therefore requirements, can't easily be satisfied with off-the-shelf software. But the vast majority of corporate applications can.

Recall the question posed earlier: Is there a way to integrate all these elements together with little or no work? The answer, according to those involved in client/server computing, is a resounding yes!

Kay Arnold, manager of software development at the Austin-based Texas Rehabilitation Commission, is currently involved in a prototype project that relies on a set of off-the-shelf tools to deal with the issues raised. Arnold's task is to build a client/server environment that stores everything that's mission-critical on the mainframe but off-loads to a workstation anything that can possibly be done on a local level. Basically, the Texas Rehab project concerns itself with investigations into social security disability claims. Data that must be reported to the government is stored on the mainframe, while examiner investigative data is stored at the local level.

Texas Rehab, a long-time Unisys user, chose a suite of Unisys tools to achieve its client/server goal. The Unisys relational database was used on the host, while the Informix database was used on a midrange computer—an arrangement that required some fancy communications between the three levels of mainframe, midrange, and PC. All is being accomplished through UniAccess, the Unisys communications package.

According to Arnold, the move to client/server was prompted by more than just the need to communicate on several platform levels. It was also spurred by the fact that people in the real world want slick stuff. In other words, Arnold's users, like users everywhere in the 1990s, want full access to data as well as a presentation style that outclasses mainframe textual displays. For this project, the "user responsive" goal is being satisfied by another Unisys product. Ally is a 4GL that permits Arnold's staff to develop full-featured systems across a distributed environment.

Brush Wellman, a Cleveland-based firm specializing in the metals mining field, also had a real need to develop systems across distributed platforms. Mark Jasany, Brush Wellman's database administrator, describes his shop as a heavy-duty IBM mainframe facility (using a 9000 series) that is just now moving into client/server architecture. Like most of the companies described in this chapter, Brush Wellman was prompted by the need to be more responsive to users. So many people were vying for resources on Brush Wellman's one box that the box kept getting bigger and bigger. The goal here was to put power on people's desks and thereby use minimum resources on the mainframe, with the net result of freeing up resources so that performance could increase for the more important tasks.

As Jasany describes it, Brush Wellman's ultimate plan was for nothing less than complete distribution of the database to three different platforms: mainframe, midrange DEC VAX, and PCs. Already a user of Computer Associates' IDMS database on the mainframe, Brush Wellman was nonetheless shopping for PC and VAX databases that could interact with the IBM mainframe.

For the PC platform, the ultimate winner of the Brush Wellman account was again Computer Associates' IDMS. IDMS for the PC permits the company to develop cooperating databases between the mainframe and the PC in a network mode.

The real challenge for Jasany's group was the VAX platform. For Brush Wellman, the all-important application was inventory. The inventory database ran on the VAX and required a link to the customer and order databases, which resided on the IBM mainframe. The missing link, then, was the VAX.

The answer to the problem came when Brush Wellman asked to become a beta test site for Computer Associates' version of IDMS which runs on the VAX. Finally, Brush Wellman had three cooperating databases.

The toolset

As these descriptions of applications of client/server technology to real business problems suggest, there are as many ways to approach the building of these systems as there are numbers of systems needing to be built. Con Ed's Sobkowski, in his "build your own" approach, needed to be very cognizant of the intricacies of the network and how to send and receive data across the different nodes. On the other hand, Brush Wellman's Jasany relied on IDMS software to handle communications among the discrete components of the distributed databases.

It should, by now, be quite apparent that client/server systems do much more than handle database inquiries. They are in a large measure responsible for the communications aspect as well. David Litwack, senior vice president and general manager of systems products for Powersoft Corporation in Burlington, Massachusetts, has been in the database field for over 20 years. He, too, has noted an evolution in the database concept. According to Litwack, the definition of a database keeps changing. A modern database is not only SQL, but also has a client side piece with built-in communications. So you speak SQL, and the underlying database takes care of getting that data transparently to you.

The database of choice in a client/server architecture is most often a relational model. But despite all the press about relational databases, there are an awful lot of people who have yet to program in a relational database.

As noted, the key attributes of a client/server system are a distributed database and a graphics orientation. Litwack has seen many a case in which the team assigned to design this sort of system has prior experience in Cobol and encounters problems in conceptualizing how to use the power of the desktop machine and how to design applications.

That's where tools such as Powersoft's PowerBuilder can come in handy. The differences between mainframe and client/server development are quite tangible. In the old days, mainframe applications were self-contained. The mainframe lived in its own world. The user couldn't touch anything unless the programmer included it. When an application is developed today, the designer has to think about how that application ties into other applications.

Litwack gives an example of a customer who used PowerBuilder to easily connect mainframe textual documents to Microsoft Word on the PC. Today's application designers would never think of developing a text processor. They would just integrate a word-processing package. In a windows environment, it looks just like another part of the application.

Along with PowerBuilder are a whole host of vendor application packages that give developers the luxury of "painting" graphic and/or SQL-based applications without going through the same pain as Con Ed's

Sobkowski. SYSCORP International of Austin, Texas, provides such a tool in its MicroSTEP product. 3M's Dynatel Systems Division made good use of it in building a system to work in conjunction with a real-time test controller which monitored the quality of telephone lines. Intelligent Environment has another popular software package that provides everything from presentation management in the OS/2 environment to a SQL workbench. From this suite of tools, the Texas Department of Mental Health and Mental Retardation chose Applications Manager as a front end to an important system geared to placing on-line the mountain of paperwork that constitutes client/caregiver interactions.

Gupta Technologies of Menlo Park, California, is fast becoming a leader in providing solutions for client/server computing in the SQL environment. Its suite of tools includes:

- Quest, a Windows 3.0 data access, query, and reporting tool for SQL databases

- SQL Windows, a powerful application development system

- SQLBase Server, a SOL database server that runs under DOS, OS/2, and UNIX

- SQLNetwork, a line of connectivity software that allows Quest and SQLWindows to access data in the SQLBase server, DB2, Oracle, and others

So impressive is this cadre of SQL-based tools that banking giant Citibank, under Gail Port, has standardized on this product line in creating what the company refers to as "the credit workstation." The objectives of the credit workstation are to standardize the credit process, improve efficiency, establish a single point of entry for all credit-related systems, create a single database for all credit information, and reduce costs.

Citibank's mainframe host stores central liability and portfolio management data in a DB2 database. Gupta's mainframe SQLHost software makes an LU6.2/APPC link to the SQLGateway to connect mainframe data with SQL data resident on a PC LAN. Running on the LAN are SQLBase, Quest, SQLWindows, and the SQLBaseserver—making the Citibank credit workstation an extremely robust example of client/server architecture.

Making the move to client/server

If this chapter has accomplished anything thus far, it is to make the reader aware of the many considerations involved in moving from a centralized mainframe to a client/server environment. This environment—already termed the MIS environment of the 1990s by many—is characterized by increasingly complex, but necessarily distributed applications; databases that may be componentized across diverse hardware platforms but that need to fully cooperate to achieve integrity of data; more graphical presentations to users; and a ready ability to link diverse database servers as well as off-the-shelf application packages such as spreadsheets and graphics.

The size of this market is enormous. According to Powersoft, it will grow to $6 billion by 1995. Oracle, Sybase, Computer Associates, and other vendors will divvy up part of this market with extended versions of their database products. Already taking on the responsibility for communications as well as database functionality, these database vendors are positioning integration to diverse corporate databases—somewhat echoing IBM's *information warehouse* concept. In its approach, IBM aims to provide the corporate user with seamless access to all corporate data regardless of its location and regardless of whether it's in a relational format.

Along these same lines is Sybase's *open interface* concept. Open interface is an intermediary between the data source and what the client expects. Let's say you have a flat file and want to use it with a spreadsheet. You put the open server there and it takes care of pulling the data from the flat file and making it look like it came from a relational database.

With all these issues and a plethora of vendor tools to choose from, just how should a company get started? According to Michael Hawotte, director of systems integration with the Chicago-based consulting firm of A.T. Kearney, the company should first ask itself a few questions. Unless the entire organization is committed to client/server, and that's down to the end user, it won't work. Here are the questions to ask:

- Are we capable of doing it?
- Are we capable of using the system properly so that we get what we need?
- Will it be accepted?

Hawotte's advice to those with no experience in client/server architecture is to start early with someone who knows how to install the system and address technology and organizational issues. The key is to be able to understand business issues up front.

There are four good reasons for calling in a systems integrator such as A.T. Kearney or Andersen Consulting:

1. The consultant has done it before so there's tangible expertise.
2. Using external resources precludes your company from pulling off resources from other projects to do the job.

3. Even though the cost of these consultants is high, it actually might be less expensive than stumbling around on your own.

4. The move to client/server requires a mindset that the organization more than likely doesn't have.

One of the more interesting case histories of the move to client/server involves NCR of Dayton, Ohio, now AT&T Global Information Solutions. In late 1990, NCR announced its new Cooperation software. At the time, NCR chairman and CEO Charles E. Exley, Jr. said that Cooperation puts the most modern services and tools together into an integrated software environment, just as operating systems put lower-level, hardware-oriented services together. Cooperation is an enterprisewide environment that integrates users, applications, information, and networks via three underlying concepts: object-oriented technology, the client/server model, and open systems.

What few know is that this 1990 offering was a direct result of NCR's own need to get into client/server as far back as 1986. Ed Jebber, assistant vice president of information systems and services for NCR's U.S. group, like many data-processing managers, gained the majority of his experience in a centralized, mainframe environment. With little precedent or advice available back in 1986, Jebber made the migration from centralized mainframe to client/server in two discrete steps.

The first step saw the distribution of processors and databases out into the field. At the same time, Jebber began to migrate away from Cobol to Progress 4GL (from Progress Corp., of Boston). One of the problems with the desire to migrate away from mainframe boxes is what to do with the legacy data. In Cobol shops, legacy data is controlled by older Cobol programs which the company has no desire to upgrade but is required to maintain. No shop can move to a fully client/server architecture until the questions surrounding the disposition of this legacy data is resolved.

Understanding this, NCR's Jebber worked with MIT's Dr. Donovan, whose surround theory has gone a long way in resolving the dilemma. The object of surround is to reduce and eliminate maintenance on the mainframe. According to Jebber, it does this by "surrounding" the mainframe with UNIX and PC boxes and adding functionality there instead of in the mainframe. Development on these more productive platforms has reduced maintenance to a bare minimum on NCR's mainframes under Cobol.

Once Jebber successfully distributed his databases off the mainframe, his (now) 4GL development team was able to garner much experience in the downloading of files and maintaining exposure at the user site. As a result, Jebber's team gained the experience it needed to operate remote databases and migrate to a fully functional client/server environment. In this environment, data is distributed across platforms accessed by programs written in Progress 4GL. Users use a combination of Progress-written application programs as well as off-the-shelf software on a day-to-day basis.

Ultimately, the move to client/server requires some fundamental changes in the way system development is done. But the company must change fundamentally as well. Instead of merely making an *active* use of data, today's end-user departments need to make a more dynamic and *proactive* use of data. So perhaps the real key to successful development of client/server applications is to worry less about networking and database issues and more about business issues. Ed Liebing, a principal of Network Technical Services in Provo, Utah, puts it this way: "Look at the company's needs and the assets of the divisions, and then tie it all together."

Critical Issues in the Move to Client/Server

In any downsizing effort, it is wise to ask a series of questions whose responses will help crystallize the path of the data, the programs, and the people in this new heterogeneous environment.

1. *Will you truly be meeting the needs of the users in the new environment?*   This issue may be obvious, but it's surprising how many organizations fix things that are not broken. If it works and it's not excessively costly and if users are not clamoring for increased functionality, then by all means leave it where it is. Downsizing is not a trendy event; it's a difficult and complex process that should be undertaken only after much analysis and soul searching.

2. *Is your data monolithic, or can it be easily pulled apart?*   If the organization followed the programming tenets of the 1970s and early 1980s, it is most surely a victim of large, unwieldy corporate databases. Unfortunately, these databases are impossible to downsize as a monolith. Instead, they must be restructured and ported to a server environment—or the host itself must act as a server. In the latter case, the database remains on the mainframe forever, precluding a transition strategy.

3. *Is your mainframe database relational?*   Although relational is today's standard, yesterday's systems made full use of networked and hierarchical databases. If this is the case, the organization must either bite the bullet and restructure the database or, as in the case above, maintain the data on the mainframe indefinitely. If the decision is made to port to a relational database, careful consideration must be given to the difficulty of such a task. Migrating to new hardware, new

software, and then a new database format may be the straw that broke the camel's back.

4. *What are the skills of your staff?*   Most enterprise computing organizations are top-heavy in Cobol skills. But, as already discussed, this is hardly a negative. It is just this Cobol orientation that provides the discipline needed for building industrial-strength applications in a downsized environment. Unfortunately, many organizations that don't fully understand the ramifications of building this type of application presume that the best skill sets are those of the PC or workstation programmer. This is simply not the case.

Successful examples of workstation-based or PC-based development abound, and these types of programmers are much in demand today. However, a careful analysis finds that the majority of these systems are standalone. Such applications simply are not industrial-strength. It is the juncture where the mainframe developer meets the PC/workstation developer that is desirable. But the manner in which these skills are obtained should be top-down. That is, mainframe discipline should be leveraged with PC/workstation skills and not the other way around.

5. *Are there commercial packages available that fit the organization's needs?*   Living in a mainframe-centric world, most organizations have never researched the literally thousands of commercially available application packages. A scant 10 years ago there were but few commercially available packages, but today there are probably few niches without a dozen or more choices. A good downsizing plan reflects an intensive R&D phase to search out the possibilities. The latest hot technologies being touted by the press and some industry analysts include Dynasty, built by Dynasty Technologies, Inc. of Naperville, Illinois, and Forte Software of Oakland, California.

This new breed of object-oriented (OD) client/server tool lets developers slice up their applications and run the pieces on the most appropriate clients and/or servers. It's object-oriented without the pain of object-oriented. Of course, some will argue, object-oriented is the greatest thing since sliced bread. Actually, I'm an OO bigot myself. However, the current generation of OO toolsets, while powerful, is anything but user-friendly. Cryptic is more like it—hence, the pain of object-oriented. Chapter 10 unveils a new application methodology called Development Before the Fact. The methodology, and the tool suite that revolves around it, is a must review for readers heavy into developing productive and reliable client/server systems.

6. *Is transaction processing (TP) a significant part of the IT schema?*   There are few enterprise computing organizations that don't rely heavily on transaction processing. In the IBM environment, CICS teleprocessing applications account for a major percentage of all applications. Undoubtedly, then, the majority of organizations will

require TP services in the chosen downsized environment. But it will be TP of a different flavor. In mainframe-centric organizations, TP, database, and application are all centrally located on one platform. But in downsizing organizations, questions need to be asked and answered about the location of the data, the origin of the TP request, the location of the TP response, and the availability of TP-to-TP communications (cooperative TP) across platforms.

7. *What type of enterprise functionalities must be available in the downsized environment?*   Mainframe-centric organizations have come to take certain mainframe features for granted. These include facilities for backup, audit, and reorganization. Downsizing organizations would do well to question the availability of these facilities on their chosen platform. If such features are not available, or not sufficiently robust, the organization must make a choice between writing its own or reconfiguring its downsizing strategy to maintain mission-critical applications on the mainframe.

8. *What type of development tools are available?*   Over the 30 years of its commercial existence, the mainframe has honed its developmental capabilities to a precision level. In moving staff from a mainframe developmental mode to a PC/workstation developmental environment, the downsizing strategist would do well to ensure that the toolset chosen is just as robust (if not more) as mainframe developmental toolsets.

9. *Will the complexity level of the new developmental toolset exceed that of the toolset most developers are familiar with?*   Although downsizing seeks either to reduce costs or to increase competitive advantage, neither goal will be realized if the complexity level of the new solution greatly exceeds that of the old solution. If it's harder to work with the new hardware and harder to work with the new software, costs will rise *and* projects will not get done on time.

10. *Is it necessary for the application to be scalable?*   *Scalability* is one of the newer buzzwords in the enterprise computing organization, but it's long been familiar in the workstation community. In workstation terms, scalability means that a given application has the ability to run on different processors, some larger and some smaller. For enterprise computing organizations, the question of scalability becomes even broader. It might well mean that the application should be developed in such a way that it can be ported from a workstation to the mainframe and back again. A warning here is that with scalability comes additional programming complexity.

11. *Who will be responsible for maintaining this diversity of hardware and software?*   In the age of the mainframe, it was a simple matter to assess responsibility if some piece of hardware or software broke down. It's not as simple in the world of the downsizer. Unfortunately,

the more vendors, the more problems—and in all likelihood the longer it will take to fix the problems.

An Intelligent Architecture for Client/Server

The central challenge behind the move to client/server becomes how to best build the enterprise's information technology systems architecture (ITSA) in an environment of proliferating workstations, APIs, standards, and software tools. And how to do so in a manner that promotes enterprise integration and reusability of existing databases and applications.

There is probably no better business model for the enterprise than client/server. It uniquely characterizes the way an organization manages its work flow. At the very lowest (atomic) level, work consists of a series of tasks. These tasks naturally integrate to form basic (molecular) units of work. The bidirectional give-and-take between the tasks is the very essence of the way client/server operates.

Unfortunately, the way most software vendors implement their client/server solutions does not exploit this natural affinity between the business model of client/server and the technological model. To do so requires expanding the current definition of client/server. Instead of systems that are merely technology-based, an enterprise-integrated version of client/server would be business-focused—and industrial-strength. That is, this breed of client/server must have the attributes of availability, reliability, recoverability, resilience, and serviceability.

One of the more interesting solutions to the client/server dilemma comes from Unisys. Now Unisys, like IBM, is primarily a mainframe vendor. But the company has thought long and hard about the subject and has put together what I consider to be a top-notch architectural schematic of high-performance, distributed client/server. You might not be a Unisys fan, and you might not want to buy Unisys products, but a review of the company's ideas will provide you with an interesting perspective on the subject.

SolutionVision by Unisys

SolutionVision uniquely combines the business and technology focus to produce a single view of the enterprise from the workstation while masking the technological complexity of its navigation path. Wherever and however an organization's information assets are distributed, SolutionVision steers the end user, the developer, and the project manager to one or more desired resources.

For this task, Unisys is uniquely qualified. With decade-long commitments to customers in a diversity of industries, including banking and air transport, Unisys has long been required to support heterogeneous, distributed business-focused environments. Unisys well understands that it takes more than just software development tools to support this type of environment. Also required are robust tools to both run and then manage the systems that the organization builds.

SolutionVision consists of three software components:

Build. Integrated development environment (IDE) is a workstation software development environment tailored to the specific needs of the organization. Whereas most organizations are victimized by a lack of integration between the diverse toolsets they use for software development, the Unisys approach provides "solution sets" of integrated life-cycle tools. Whereas most organizations suffer from a wide divergence between their software environment and their business environment, the Unisys "solution sets" are actually assembled around a specific set of business objectives—complete with the professional services needed to ensure their success.

Run. Integrated deployment services (IDS) provide the integrative framework that enables the "solution set" chosen by the organization to freely navigate its heterogeneous, distributed information network of hardware platforms, databases, and applications. IDS, then, is the invisible glue that binds the business to the technology.

Manage. Systems management services (SMS) create a workstation management environment that enables monitoring, control, and administration of open, multivendor systems and networks.

Of the three components, IDS epitomizes the best solution I've yet found for the serious problem of the disconnectedness of client/server. The remainder of this section examines the Unisys solution in a bit more detail.

Integrated deployment services

Information technology is a sea of systems. And it's not usually calm sailing. Confronted with a host of user demands to support existing systems as well as to build often mission-critical new ones, IT departments find themselves in the position of having to do the impossible. How is it possible to simultaneously foster competitive advantage through newer and more advanced forms of technology while at the same time minimizing the risk? How is it possible to leverage legacy systems while at the same time invest in the newer, open architectures? Just how is it possible to provide seamless, and effortless, integration of all an organization's information assets in the form of databases distributed across far-flung networks that employ heterogeneous hardware running an amalgamation of both newer and legacy application software?

The component of SolutionVision that achieves all these objectives is the Unisys run-time environment. The IDS strategy provides the software infrastructure to integrate and distribute information throughout the enterprise. IDS enables workstation access to *any database* and *any application* for *any network* on *any platform* in the enterprise.

The key to the Unisys IDS strategy is its business-services view of the enterprise. Solutions architected solely from a technology perspective severely constrain the user's ability to obtain information crucial to the task at hand. Solutions architected from a business-only perspective, on the other hand, usually fail to employ the best technology for the job. IDS uses the concept of "solution sets" to achieve a careful balance between business and technology.

The benefits are many and tangible. The IDS approach:

- Enables a user-centric, heterogeneous workstation environment
- Promotes a "hide from view" version of interoperability
- Presents an enterprise view of the organization's information assets
- Provides an integrated communications strategy
- Enables database diversity
- Seamlessly integrates new and legacy applications
- Provides industrial-strength distributed transaction processing (DTP)

The workstation environment (INFOConnect)

While all organizations strive to achieve seamless connectivity to business services through a single workstation, none actually achieve this goal. The reason? Conflicting standards and formats among the organization's databases, applications, networks, and hardware make the single full-function workstation unobtainable.

Yet this is exactly what the Unisys IDS strategy provides. IDS manages system, database, network, and hardware conflicts transparently, providing end users with the integrated view of the enterprise that will make them a hundredfold more productive. Where end users are shielded from the complexity, so too are the organization's system developers eliminating the most difficult obstacle to building a single, secure, manageable environment.

IDS' INFOConnect is smart enough to manage both individual users as well as the work group while drawing together the organization's widely distributed information assets into a user-centric, integrated enterprise view. IDS turns today's "islands of information" caused by lack of workstation integration into a navigable sea of knowledge.

Transparent interoperability (distributed cooperative computing)

Whereas organizations in the 1970s and early 1980s were characterized by single-platform, single-vendor solutions, today's organizations are characterized by heterogeneity. Yet achieving interoperability is much discussed but seldom achieved. When it is achieved it is often plagued by unreliability, lack of availability, inflexibility, and unrecoverability. IDS succeeds where others have failed. It empowers workstations to access any database and any application function, over any network. It does this regardless of the platform type of the workstation or server system. And it does this without encumbering "gateways." The client/server architecture gets its power from its two-tier architecture. Introducing a third level to this architecture, that of the gateway, seriously reduces the power of the client/server model. IDS enables the client/server model to remain a two-tier, and therefore more efficient, architecture.

The enterprise view

Organizations can lose their competitive edge by providing too narrow a view of their information assets. Distributed databases across distributed networks suffer from a disjointedness that precludes a unified view of the organization. Because it provides seamless integration of all an organization's business services, IDS supplies the perfect enterprise view of the organization itself.

Integrated communications strategy (distributed system services)

Heterogeneous hardware environments require the support of heterogeneous communications standards. Toward this end, the networking communications component of IDS, distributed system services (DSS), supports the open ISO OSI model as well as industry standards TCP/IP, SNA, DCA, and BNA. Providing protocol transparency, the Unisys communications strategy is naturally integrated with the Unisys workstation strategy.

Database diversity

A business services approach to client/server recognizes that no one database is sufficient to satisfy all the needs of the organization. The difficulty lies in the fact that database vendors take a database-centric view of the world, making cross-database and multidatabase access difficult, if not impossible. A business services approach cares not where the data resides, or what database format it is in. A business services approach sees independent databases as atoms which together make up the molecular structure of the organization's information resource management (IRM) function.

IDS enables the access and use of enterprise information for business analysis and management support systems through an open, transport-independent, database-access strategy. While supporting industry standard architectures and services for remote database access (RDA), the Unisys database-access strategy focuses more on the architectures with superior open attributes.

Integration of new and legacy applications

Most proponents of client/server architecture advocate a complete re-engineering of the organization's stock of legacy systems. But rewriting these systems is risky, time-consuming, and costly.

For the most part, an organization's legacy systems are its most valuable asset. They represent often thousands of labor-years of effort in encoding the logic of the many and varied business processes which comprise the organization.

Although re-engineering is a viable solution for those systems that require massive changes in business logic, it would be strategically disadvantageous to rewrite legacy systems which require minimal change. Because current models of client/server afford no effective way to deal with these older, but still valuable legacy systems, vendors often advocate a "trash and burn" solution. That is, rewrite the entire system on the new platform.

As mentioned, this is risky. And foolish, if there is some way to integrate legacy systems "as is" into client/server.

The Unisys approach provides such a way. Relying on the principle of reusability, IDS enables the organization to incorporate—in object-oriented terminology, *encapsulate*—the legacy system into the client/server system as a named service. The benefits of this approach are enormous. Legacy systems become fully interoperable with the newer, open client/server systems. Thousands of labor-hours are saved and, more important, the risk of rewriting or re-engineering is averted.

Ultimately, this approach permits organizations to take advantage of new technology when and if they choose. Instead of revolutionary change increasing risk, organizations can opt for evolutionary change, thereby minimizing risk.

Industrial-strength distributed transaction processing

The business services model is inherently transaction-based. Whether corporation databases are updated through a formal process or ad hoc, the very nature of business implies that it is transactional.

The failure of the legacy model to understand transaction-based systems is its major flaw. IDS corrects this omission and enables business process automation through distributed transaction processing (DTP).

Based upon the X/Open standard, DTP provides the robust transaction-based infrastructure that a business services organization requires. This infrastructure includes the support of multivendor platforms, interoperability, and transport independence, as well as the reliability-enhancing two-phase commit, rapid recovery, reduction of network traffic, and global transaction synchronization.

Using X/Open DTP as a strategic part of the Unisys IDS allows the organization to easily grow and adapt. In essence, X/Open DTP enables a multifaceted deployment of client/server. Most organizations enter the client/server arena through screen scraping (i.e., GUI front ends). Other approaches include the remote-presentation view, the distributed-function view, and the database view. What's common among these views is that they are mutually exclusive. X/Open DTP enables the organization to easily adopt one or more of these lower-level client/server models into its infrastructure. As a result, the organization can choose a solution appropriate to the problem, rather than forcing the problem to fit the solution.

Perhaps the most interesting advantage of the X/Open DTP strategy is that it lays the groundwork for the organization to migrate to an object-oriented technology. Essentially, this is the avenue that IDS utilizes to integrate legacy systems transparently and easily.

The Scuttlebutt

In the end, client/server can yield a big productivity windfall for many organizations, but it can also hamper productivity if it is not done correctly. That's because organizations often fall for the advertising hype of the client/server industry at large, or of one vendor in particular, and deploy a strategy that doesn't exactly fit the firm. Like a good shoe, it's got to fit well to be able to walk in it.

Although it's true that any access to information is better than no access from a user's perspective, management needs to step back and take a long view of just how much it's costing to provide that particular resource to that particular user. If the "under the covers" work being done by the system department to deliver that data is painful and excessively costly, the client/server strategy needs to be re-examined. And if the end user winds up with more information but little of it that is value-added—or is saddled with a heck of a lot of extra work but little payback—the organization needs to think long and hard about its client/server approach.

Client/server is not a panacea. In spite of the hoopla by the press, it's just another idea. It's how you implement the idea that really counts.

References

1. Forrester Research, Inc., "The Mainframe Voyage," *The Computing Strategy Report,* vol. 9, no. 4.
2. Business Research Group, Newton, White Paper, Fall 1992, Newton, Massachusetts.
3. Patricia Seybold Group, "Integrating Applications in the Real World," *Open Information Systems,* vol. 7, no. 7.
4. Software Productivity Research, Inc., *U.S. National Averages for Software Quality and Productivity and Client/Server Applications,* Burlington, Massachusetts, from a presentation delivered November 1992.
5. Cowen & Co. Institutional Services Division study, New York, 1990.

Sampler Solutions to Productivity Problems

Chapter

8

Re-engineering Your Way to Smart Systems Through Object Orientation

Perhaps the biggest bane of an IT department is its legacy code. In fact, if there is one thing that most organizations agree on, it is that if all this legacy code could somehow be re-engineered, the organization and its IT department would be a heck of a lot more productive.

Elizabeth Ash and Richard Cullom faced this very problem. Their IT department at First Union National Bank develops systems for some 24,000 workers. Object-oriented development seemed like a sure route to enhanced productivity. But then there was all that legacy Cobol code. In most organizations Cobol is everywhere, and rewriting any of these application programs is a major process.

Cullom and Ash's immediate goal was to extend the life of First Union's legacy systems by front-ending these systems with fancy object-oriented and graphical interfaces. First Union's problem is one that many IT shops face. They (think they) can't solve the legacy code problem right now. And while they're waiting, all they can do is provide the data in a format that folks can use.

Cullom and Ash's 350-person IT department uses two distinct technologies. On the mainframe, they are working to bring in computer-assisted systems engineering (CASE) technology to reorganize and go forward. And on the PC, they are very much into object-oriented programming. For now, Cullom and Ash are waiting for the fallout in the industry to determine the best way to approach their Cobol systems on the mainframe.

This chapter offers some real-life solutions to the legacy code problems that IT managers like Cullom and Ash face.

Re-engineering Legacy Systems from the Bottom-Up

One of the brightest new ways to handle the legacy code productivity problem is to re-engineer it down to the PC. Perhaps the most precise definition of re-engineering comes from Elliot Chikofsky and James Cross.[1] They define *re-engineering* as the examination and alteration of existing code for the purpose of recasting it into a new form. This is one case in which the task is actually much harder than it sounds. Most of the literature on re-engineering tools overlooks one crucial fact. The majority of legacy systems are undocumented. Finding the appropriate line of code, in the appropriate module and in the appropriate program, is akin to finding a needle in the proverbial haystack.

A recent effort to re-engineer several large legacy systems at AT&T is a case in point. The bottom-up re-engineering technique employed by the prime architect of the re-engineering effort, Frank Doscher, is of particular interest.

Troubleshooting the troubleshooting system

TTS is the name given to each of the six strategically important trouble-tracking systems at AT&T. Each TTS is a true megalith, consisting of over 200 programs (on-line and batch) in addition to copybooks that contain over 5000 elements and multiple files. TTS tracks the 75 or so components (CPUs, circuits, private lines, and so on) that make up a telephone network as well as the network itself. Maintaining some 250,000 records per quarter, TTS is one system that will remain mainframe-based for quite some time. So when it was decided that the system needed a tune-up, the green flag went up for the idea of re-engineering.

TTS was written over 8 years ago by programmers who are no longer at the company, and like many legacy systems its documentation was out of date. As a result, in a system of this size, complexity, and significance, re-engineering in the traditional sense was all but precluded.

Most re-engineering efforts are of the top-down variety. That is, the process is performed by analysts and end users attempting to retrofit old code to new business requirements. In the case of the TTS system, Frank Doscher attempted a bottom-up approach. In other words, he used a programmer's perspective on re-engineering. He looked at the code the way a fortune teller looks at tea leaves in order to uncover the truth. Uncovering the truth for the TTS system meant that Doscher had to answer one overriding question: "Given the changed business requirements, which of the hundreds of programs contained the files, fields, and copybooks that required modification?" Needless to say, the task was also to be accomplished in the minimum amount of time and at a minimum cost.

Navigating the solution

Looking at the problem through the eyes of a programmer usually leads to some pretty practical solutions. In Doscher's case, he viewed the problem as a series of challenges. To solve the challenge of time, he knew he had to automate the task as much as possible. Although the usual tack is to select one tool and surround that with intensive manual labor, Doscher's solution was to choose a series of tools and try to weave them together.

Since downsizing the TTS application from the mainframe was out of the question, Doscher decided to dispense with mainframe tools and mainframe budgets and downsize the re-engineering solution, thereby solving the budget problem to a large degree. Ultimately, he chose a combination of PC-based tools, in effect creating the definitive re-engineering workbench for his needs. The various components are shown in Figure 8.1 and Table 8.1.

If there is one best place to start the bottom-up re-engineering process it is with *job control language* (JCL). Even though most organizations consider JCL little more than a necessary evil, it is actually a veritable gold mine of information about the batch system process.

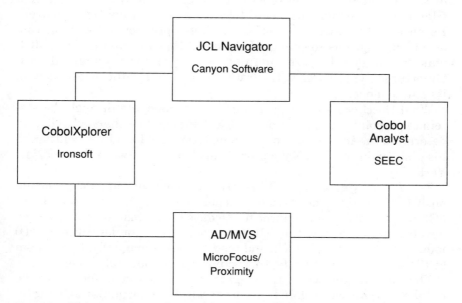

Figure 8.1   Main components of a re-engineering workbench.

TABLE 8.1 The re-engineering workbench

Re-engineering Workbench	
JCL Navigator	Canyon Software Corp.
AD/MVS	Microfocus & Proximity
Cobol Analyst	SEEC
CobolXplorer	Ironsoft
Other Toolsets/Utilities	Microfocus
VS Cobol Workbench	Microfocus
CICS Option	Microfocus
Assembler 370	Microfocus
Host Compatibility Option	Microfocus
EBCDIC to ASCII Translator	Microfocus
File Tool	Microfocus
Data Editor Facility	Microfocus

JCL is a road map to a system's data flows. Virtually everything from files used, to programs used, to parameters is neatly captured. Because part of Doscher's task was to find a productive way to discover which programs to change, he decided that examining TTS's JCL was the most effective means to accomplish the desired end. Unfortunately, though, JCL is rather obtuse and difficult to follow in its native mode.

What Doscher needed was a quick way to navigate through the system to pinpoint the specific programs that had to be changed and then determine the impact of those changes. Doscher found the solution to his problem in the JCL Navigator, from Canyon Software Corp. of New York City.

The JCL Navigator is an OS/2-based tool for analyzing and reporting on JCL. Using this tool, Doscher was able to automatically import TTS's JCL in about 20 minutes. Prior to the days of automated analysis tools, developers had to sort the JCL to uncover the data description (DD) names, or even print the JCL and read the pages manually. In a system of TTS's size and complexity, this activity alone could take weeks.

The Smalltalk-based JCL Navigator creates a visual and navigable database from scanned JCL. In other words, it turns flat JCL statements like

```
//TTS0001 DD DSN = &&TTS7U, DISP = (NEW,PASS),
// UNIT = SYSDA, SPACE = (TRK,(10,2),RLSE),
```

into a series of objects in the guise of a flowchart. The engineer can
then use a mouse to point and click the way through the system. Each
JCL Navigator object has the ability to describe many things about
itself—such as where it is used, what its attributes are, and even what
text has been entered about it.

To pinpoint the TTS programs that needed servicing, Doscher relied
heavily on the JCL Navigator's impact analysis, program and file
cross-referencing, and "find" capabilities. But first, Doscher decided to
eliminate some of that "information anxiety" that JCL is known for.
Many of the statements in a JCL stream are extraneous to research
such as Doscher's. (For example, SYSUDUMP is a system file which
will produce a report of the program abends.) Rather than clutter up
the on-line flowchart, he decided to customize the flowcharts for the
project's particular needs. This meant eliminating all extraneous files.

Once the flowcharts were customized, Doscher was able to determine which of the system's programs and/or files needed to be modified. Because some of the information in the JCL was ambiguous,
Doscher used the JCL Navigator's source-scanning facility to fill in
some of the missing pieces. Total elapsed time? Less than 2 hours, versus 3 weeks if done manually.

To the point

Once the JCL Navigator zeroed in on the targets, Doscher was able to
go to the specific programs that required change. But even then, he
stayed at the PC level. Using AD/MVS—a tool created jointly by
MicroFocus of Palo Alto, California, and Proximity Software of
Hanover, Maryland—Doscher downloaded all affected source code,
maps, and copybooks to the PC.

Historically, one of the biggest problems that organizations face in
downsizing their development and maintenance activities has been
the lack of available mainframe-ready tools. AD/MVS essentially over-
comes this hurdle. With an AD/MVS-configured PC, a mainframe programmer need never know what he or she is actually running on.
Mainframe programmers are used to seeing the world in a certain
way. Although there are many tools on the PC which mimic the "look
and feel" of mainframe (MVS) editors, programmers are still thrown
off balance by the necessity of storing files in PC formats. Where
MicroFocus provides the workbench application development environment, Proximity provides the ability to store files in a simulated PDS
(partitioned data set). Add to this MicroFocus's VS/Cobol workbench
and you end up with a mainframe on a PC. The effect of this combina-

tion of tools is to reduce the learning curve of the PC-transplanted mainframe programmer to nearly zero—an important factor for a time-critical project.

Once the TTS source was installed in a replica of the mainframe environment, Doscher utilized two Cobol source code analytical tools: the JCL Navigator, which provides the ability to see a system through its JCL, and Cobol Analyst (from Pittsburgh-based SEEC, Inc.), which provides the ability to view a system through its source code.

Because Cobol source comes in as many flavors as there are file types, it was necessary to gain the ability to scan and interpret Cobol instructions for files such as VSAM, databases such as IMS and DB2, and the CICS transaction-processing monitor. SEEC's Cobol Analyst enabled Doscher to scan the system in search of a particular data name.

Like the JCL Navigator, Cobol Analyst stores all downloaded information in a repository. Because of this feature, robust impact analysis can be performed. Where the JCL Navigator's impact analyzer determined which *program* had to be changed, the Cobol Analyst's impact analyzer allowed Doscher to determine the specific *source* to be modified.

Because Cobol source can be just as difficult to follow as JCL, Doscher needed to have a navigator for the source code as well. CobolXplorer, from Ironsoft Inc. of Madison, Wisconsin, offered this capability. Using CobolXplorer, Doscher was able to trace the flow of an individual TTS program in a stepped approach. In this way, he was able to easily follow the branching logic of some rather large programs.

Programmers familiar with CobolXplorer liken it to the old manual method of putting paper clips or pieces of paper in green and white listings. The reason is that CobolXplorer has the ability to "mark" the path that the programmer has. For Doscher, this accelerated the process of tracking the movement of the data through the system.

Using Cobol Analyst and CobolXplorer in tandem enabled Doscher to rapidly recover from the confusion of source code, determine what had to be changed, and then evaluate the impact of those changes. Where CobolXplorer provided auto navigation and path and data analysis, Cobol Analyst gave Doscher the ability to see the big picture. In effect, he got the benefit of seeing both the forest and the trees.

Once Doscher decided on the exact changes that had to be made, he went back to MicroFocus's AD/MVS workbench to implement the physical changes. AD/MVS workbench is much more interactive than mainframe compilers and editors and enabled Doscher to make changes quickly.

The bottom line

The remainder of the tools listed in Table 8.1 were used to handle the finer points of the re-engineering effort. Most legacy systems have one or more modules written in Assembler, and Doscher's system was no different. Assembler 370, which runs on the PC, was just the tool to handle his problem. Because the TTS is CICS- and DB2-based, Doscher needed some PC features to handle both requirements so he could test as well as develop on the PC.

Perhaps the biggest problem in this whole effort was the data itself. Because Doscher's goal was to perform the entire re-engineering task on the PC, with no mainframe resources whatsoever, he needed to be able to handle mainframe data on the PC level. Since numeric mainframe data is traditionally stored as either packed or binary, a new set of tools to handle this problem was needed. Converting between EBCDIC and ASCII was one half of the equation, and the ability to edit these types of files was the other half.

The bottom line? The original estimate for a mainframe-based approach was two people for a period of 5 labor-months. With the jury-rigged bottom-up re-engineering workbench, Doscher was able to scale back to a one-person, 1 labor-month project. But the biggest benefit was that he was able to do so accurately. Not long ago AT&T had to spend hours poring over paper listings to determine what the system was doing. Today AT&T can reliably navigate its way through TTS using automated tools.

Trapped Between Two Worlds

AT&T's approach to its legacy system problem was unique. But note that it took some help from object-oriented toolsets like the JCL Navigator.

Today, most firms find that they are trapped between two different worlds. Momentum is now moving toward programming languages that provide reusability benefits. Unfortunately, these object-oriented languages, such as C++ and Smalltalk, sit squarely in the center of the workstation world—far from the mainframe legacy systems that need them the most.

For the most part, companies can only "wrap" the flavor of object orientation around tired and worn legacy systems by providing GUI front ends. Like prisoners who can see but cannot reach what is beyond their bars, these companies must wait for the key that unlocks the door to this other world. The question therefore arises as to when mainframe legacy systems will be able to take advantage of object-oriented technology.

Some take exception to the notion that simply moving from one technology (Cobol) to another (object-oriented languages) will, by itself, solve the problem. These observers include Clive Finkelstein and James Martin, developers of *information engineering* (IE) methodologies. Others warn that concentrating on technology at the expense of methodology is dangerous.

In 1993, Sentry Market Research, Westborough, Massachusetts, surveyed software managers to determine which languages were being used for re-engineering. As you can see from Figure 8.2, a preponderance of organizations are still using Cobol to both maintain existing systems as well as re-engineer critical systems. The 300 responding managers, therefore, seem to agree that moving to an object-oriented language (e.g., C++ and Ada) does not solve the problem.

Finkelstein and Martin make a strong case for a business to concentrate first on its goals and strategies, and then to translate those goals and strategies into business rules. Only then should a business begin to select a technology to automate those rules.

Many believe that the rule-based IE approach is a key component in the legacy system equation. Organizations are in constant flux today. They need to be able to change rapidly to survive. Many of the existing systems have not been designed for this rapid change. To move to object orientation under these circumstances might well be dangerous.

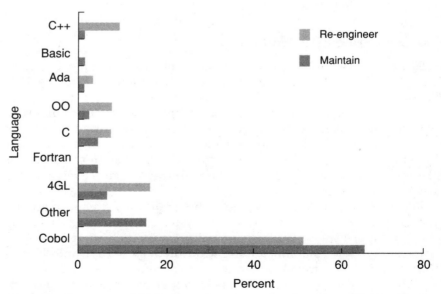

Figure 8.2 Languages used for re-engineering and maintenance. (*Source: Sentry Market Research.*)

Legacy code contains the business rules of the organization at a particular time. Simply to convert this code is to lose sight of the fact that the business organization is in a state of flux. And as the business changes, its rules should be changing accordingly. Therefore, the move to object orientation should be done only in conjunction with what the business needs for the future.

The key point is to understand what the organization seeks to achieve. With goals and objectives firmly established, appropriate strategies can be developed. This business point of view leads to establishment of functions and processes, which ultimately lead to systems.

Since change and flux are constants, the only organizations that will be successful in the 1990s are those that develop the capability to change their businesses very rapidly. At the same time, they must ensure that their systems can change at the same rate.

The key to good systems is in being able to create a business model. The technology that automates this model is theoretically secondary; therefore, object tools should be able to automate any model the business uses. The organization can capture that level of knowledge in the business model and then translate it into cohesive logic "Lego" building blocks, which can be clicked together in every different way and which can change each time the model is used.

Having these higher-level representations means that systems can be maintained at a higher level, and ultimately be more flexible and less expensive. Exponential improvements will come from tying business systems into business strategies and thereby developing a business architecture on which everything else can be built.

The organization should focus first on what it needs in the future. Then the organization should think through the various alternatives before choosing a solution.

Ready for change

There is an immense investment of intellectual capital tied up in legacy systems. An organization would be much better off if its code were in object-oriented form, which permits better redesign. However, getting from legacy code to object-oriented code is not an easy process. One problem is that there are virtually no available tools to help make this great leap.

Only now are the necessary tools emerging—including Easel from Easel Corp. of Burlington, Massachusetts, and Mozart from Mozart Systems of Burlingame, California—that will enable an organization to shrink-wrap a legacy application, such as a mainframe application, and then build a GUI front end to it. Then the business can go outside the legacy system—for example, by building add-on modules directly on the PC.

Since the tools are not quite here, how does the organization prepare for change? Most organizations today are using models that adhere to conventional structured techniques, with conventional data administration and normalization of data. More advanced organizations are modeling their enterprise in terms of objects. By the year 2000, the advanced corporation is going to have a very thorough object-oriented model.

The practical question, then, is when and how fast organizations should move. It's practical today to do object-oriented modeling in the enterprise, but the tools aren't here to move legacy code automatically into the object-oriented environment. Therefore, the interim answer is to re-engineer legacy code into an IE model.

James Martin, now of James Martin Associates in Chicago, suggests that an organization has seven options in tackling the migration from legacy to modern systems. As an organization moves to a higher-level option, the complexity and expense grow proportionately.

In the first option, the company finds itself with legacy code that works. Here the operative procedure is to do nothing. If it works don't fix it. The second option involves legacy code that requires some minor changes. In this instance, it is more cost-effective to make the changes in the system's present form than to re-engineer it. The third option is to restructure the code, but not to re-engineer it. An example is to take spaghetti Cobol, put it through an engine such as Recoder (from Language Technology in Boston), and turn it into structured code.

Shrink-wrapping the legacy code is the fourth option. It is perhaps the most popular choice today among IT managers. Here the developer freezes the legacy code (unchanged), and makes additions on the outside. This is where object-oriented tools will play a pivotal role, shrink-wrapping legacy code so that it looks rather like an object. Object-oriented requests can then be sent to it.

The fifth option is to re-engineer the code. A developer reverse-engineers the code into a CASE repository so it can ultimately be forward-engineered in CASE fashion. The key for the future will be to link the reverse engineering to the forward engineering.

Re-engineering to an information engineering model is the sixth option. Of course, this implies that the organization possesses data models with the data correctly normalized. The seventh option, which carries the highest cost, is to scrap the code and redevelop it. This option is not as expensive as it may appear, however. Today developers are likely to regenerate it with code generators and CASE tools, so the cost of scrapping it is much lower than it would have been with ordinary Cobol. In ordinary Cobol the rule of thumb is that if more than 12 percent of the lines of code must be changed, it's cheaper to scrap or redevelop it than attempt to maintain it.

An organization would be making a mistake to force legacy code to object orientation today, since for the most part the tools are just not here. The organization would be spending a lot of money and not getting a lot of functionality. Instead, the IT manager should make CEO-like decisions when judging the migration to object orientation. Return on investment (ROI) should be the deciding factor in the decision. Right now this activity would be very expensive, so ROI would almost certainly be negative.

First Union National Bank enlisted the help of Knowledge Systems of Cary, North Carolina, in its move to object orientation. The bank utilized Knowledge Systems' expertise primarily for training in the Smalltalk object-oriented programming language. Knowledge Systems' goal, on assignments such as these, is to fit object technology into the environment that companies now have. Objects are what business needs to do. Most organizations recognize that objects are part of the solution.

Screen scraping, a phrase used to describe building a GUI front end to a legacy system, is good for only a limited set of applications. Tools that provide this sort of functionality are not really object-oriented, but more like scripting languages. These scripting languages simply do not have the expressive power to describe the business and the business rules associated with it.

When Knowledge Systems takes on a client, it first determines whether the application is appropriate for object orientation. Usually the deciding factor is whether the company's present application is running out of gas. For instance, an organization had credit card files sitting in DB2 on the mainframe and image files on an Image Plus system. The company needed to be able to put this all together, so it spent a year writing code which never did work. But after 3 or 4 months of using object technology, the organization had a working system deployed.

One company which thinks that an object-oriented solution for legacy code is already at hand is Neuron Data of Palo Alto, California. The company originally positioned itself in 1986 as a supplier of the expert system development tool Nexpert Object. In response to demands from its customers, Neuron Data began marketing a portable GUI builder tool developed internally. Neuron's Open Interface is now responsible for about 50 percent of the firm's revenues.

Part of Neuron Data's marketing strategy is to target software suppliers whose development resources are strained in an effort to support multiple GUIs. One such client is American Management Systems (AMS) of Arlington, Virginia, which sells professional ser-

vices and proprietary application packages. AMS is using Neuron's
Open Interface to provide Microsoft Windows and IBM OS/2 GUI support to its range of mainframe applications. AMS is building a communications application program interface (API) layer that lets Neuron's
Open Interface appear as a 3270 session to the host. Neuron Data provides the API for the GUI client, essentially gluing the two worlds of
legacy and object-orientation together.

Moving from Legacy to Object-Oriented Development

Object orientation (OO), which views the abstractions manipulated by
computer software as counterparts to real-world objects, promises
developers a brave new world. According to industry savants, object-
oriented development is emerging as the dominant software development methodology of the 1990s. Not surprisingly, vendors are rushing
to provide OO development tools.

On the very high end are complete object-oriented application development environments. In the commercial CASE arena, vendors are
offering, or have announced, varying degrees of OO within their CASE
products. Finally, there is the category of development tool that integrates various technologies, such as expert systems, hypertext, and
OO environments. It is also worth noting that there are varying
degrees of OO in general. That is, OO is less a single paradigm than a
family of paradigms.

CASE vendors have been particularly aggressive in claiming OO
characteristics for their current programs. However, there is a great
deal of confusion about the meaning of object orientation, and those
looking at this solution should take heed. Caveat developer.

No matter. Object orientation is destined for the commercial arena
via CASE. Most large-scale commercial applications will be developed
with OO toolkits within the next 3 to 5 years.

The appeal of CASE is that it is a Trojan horse for bringing the benefits of object orientation into the commercial arena without the considerable sociopathological disadvantages—that is, without posing a
threat to the established way of doing things. In the words of Chairman
Mao: "I don't care if a cat is black or white as long as it catches mice."
The same is true for OO technology. If it's transparent to users, all the
users care about is that it allows them to work rapidly, flexibly, and,
ultimately, productively.

The concept of an *object* is the fundamental building block on which
the object-oriented paradigm rests. There are four pivotal concepts
behind object orientation. These are encapsulation, inheritance, message passing, and dynamic binding (see below). And to the extent that

TABLE 8.2   Terms Used in Object-Oriented Technology

Class—A template comprising a definition of behavior and supporting information; each instance created from the class has its own copy of the information and utilizes a single copy of the methods that implement the class' behavior.

Class Hierarchy—A tree-structured aggregation of class definitions in which vertical link establishes a superclass-subclass relationship between a pair of classes; the subclass is a specialization of the superclass.

Information Hiding—A technique by which the structure and precise usage of information (data) is concealed. The information is private to its owning objects and accessible to all other objects only via message sends to the owner; this is the basis of encapsulation.

Instance—A particular occurrence of an object defined by a class. All instances of a class share the behavior implemented and inherited by the class; each instance has its own private set of the instance variables implemented and inherited by the class.

Instantiation—The act of creating an instance of a class.

Method—A procedure whose code implements the behavior invoked by a message send.

Object—An entity capable of exhibiting a defined set of behaviors and interacting with other objects.

Object-oriented Technology—A collection of languages, tools, environments and methodologies aimed at supporting development of software applications centered around interrelated, interacting objects.

Reuse and Reusability—An approach to software engineering that emphasizes: reusing software assets, including designs and code; and building software assets likely to be reusable in future applications.

a tool or language incorporates these concepts, it becomes qualified as an OO toolkit. Table 8.2 summarizes some of the key terms in OO technology.

Let's look at an example. Suppose a user writes an E-mail letter to a colleague in another department. The letter itself is an object. It has many properties in common with other letters: It contains information and has associated procedures that allow the user to manipulate it (read, write, and send). These properties, when grouped together, constitute the concept of the letter object. This process of combining data and functions all in one object is called *encapsulation*.

Now suppose the E-mail system allows users to write letters in English, but the company has just hired an employee who speaks only Japanese. The company now needs the facility to create and manipu-

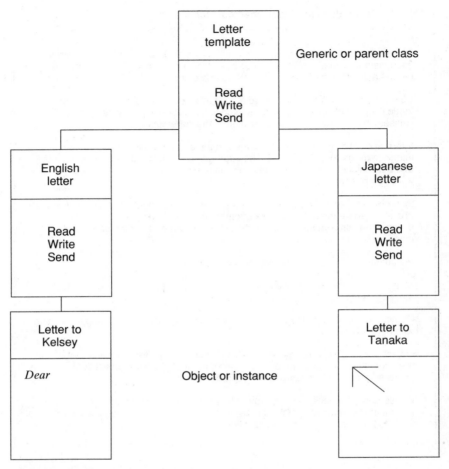

Figure 8.3   Inheriting functionality. (*Source: Hewlett-Packard.*)

late Japanese characters. This is done by putting letter objects in discrete categories, or classes (see Figure 8.3).

A *class* is a collection of objects that share the same functionality
and characteristics (procedures and data). In this example, two classes
are created: an English letter class and a Japanese letter class. Both
the Japanese letter class and the English letter class have many functions and characteristics in common. By identifying those things held
in common we can create a super or parent class. Thus, the English
letter and the Japanese letter become subclasses, with each pinpoint-
ing how it differs from its parent and siblings.

Inheriting functionality

The English and Japanese letter subclasses inherit the "read, write, and send" functionality from the parent object. But the Japanese subclass is different in that it has the extra characteristic of translating text into the Japanese language, and the English subclass is different in that it translates into English. This is the meat behind the OO concept of *inheritance*.

The letter object permits the user to request certain tasks or services, such as "read a letter," "write a letter," "send a letter." This is commonly called "sending a message to an object." In OO parlance, it is *message passing*.

Sending a message is not quite the same as issuing a function call, a process familiar to most developers. Different objects can respond to the same message in different ways. For example, as discussed above, the "read" message is handled one way by the English object and another way by the Japanese object. In fact, the OO term *polymorphism* is used to describe the ability to send general-purpose messages to objects that will then handle them appropriately. The objects themselves handle the specific details.

In sending these messages, the user never has to specify the type of object with which he or she is dealing. OO systems utilize what is known as *dynamic binding* to determine the object type at run time when the code is executed.

Rao Mikkilineni, director of Advanced Technologies at U.S. West, a regional telecommunications company in Englewood, Colorado, is responsible for building productivity into the firm's software development groups. He said he has found an answer in OO. When asked what makes OO more productive, Mikkilineni answers: reusability and a nice modeling technology. U.S. West is using Hewlett-Packard's C++ and SoftBench, an integrated application development environment.

U.S. West continually looks at advances in several areas, including programming languages, databases, and expert systems. From Mikkilineni's perspective, if you look at all these three areas—database technology and advances in database technology; programming languages and advances in programming languages; and expert systems—you find one thing in common: objects.

Overcoming the steep learning curve

One drawback to OO technology is the steep learning curve. Another is that it could lead to a lot of inheritance abuse and a lot of subtyping abuse in creating object hierarchies. As a result, many developers consider object orientation somewhat of a resource hog compared with conventional technologies.

But perhaps the greatest limitation of OO technology is a general confusion about what constitutes an OO-infused toolset, and how it can be related to existing software development methodologies. OO technology has a lot of promise. But one methodology to the exclusion of all others seldom works. Developers want a technology that they can bend around as needed to suit the business problem at hand.

Methodology is the cornerstone of OO

When you talk about an object-oriented CASE tool, there are two different spins on it. First there are those CASE tools designed using OO *programming methodologies*. In this scenario, object orientation is essentially hidden from the user. Under the covers, CASE vendors are using object-oriented techniques to build the most effective CASE tool.

The underpinnings of these CASE tools are important, because object orientation buys developers some advantages as they try to build more features into the tools. Object-oriented tools will be more amenable to change and better able to handle the requirements of what a CASE tool will be in a couple of years.

The other spin on OO CASE tools are those being developed to support current and future OO applications. Developers building today's applications are essentially using the *process methodologies* of people like Ed Yourdon, Tom DeMarco, and Chris Gane and Trish Sarson, as well as the data-modeling methodology pioneered by Peter Chen.

Currently, IE techniques pivot around data and its relationships, as documented in data-flow diagrams and entity-relationship diagrams. But structured analysis is not based on objects.

If systems are to be built in an object-oriented way, there must be new techniques for discovering what the objects are. A new notation as well as a new methodology will be needed to support OO design. But you'll be biting off more than you can chew if you go directly to OO design without passing through structured analysis. Perhaps the best bet is to merge structured and object paradigms. Data models and process models can be drawn at one level. When you try to put the data model and the process model together, the object-oriented approach is the perfect way to do it.

Focusing on OO Benefits

But we just might be missing the point if we focus on the features of object orientation and miss the benefits. Development toolsets will go down the route of enabling OO design in a way that is nonintrusive and noninvasive. People just do it because it's the right thing to do, feels comfortable, and can build fairly good systems—not because it's object-oriented.

Iconographic orientation, or point-and-click graphical interfacing, has little, if anything, to do with a true OO approach. The truth of the matter is that not all users need a completely object-oriented solution for their software problem.

Professor Paul Wegner of Brown University has defined three levels of object orientation for this purpose. The first level is *object-based.* Object-based languages, tools, and methodologies support the concept of the object and the use of messages to communicate between objects. The second level is *class-based,* which supports the concepts of objects, messaging, and classes. The third level is *object-oriented,* which supports the definition that this chapter has already supplied.

So how can a developer choose from the myriad of object-oriented, class-based, and object-based development tools? Perhaps it's best not to worry too much about this point. Instead, users should ask themselves, "What are the benefits that this is going to deliver—and how?"

Brian Moore of Andersen Consulting in New York City did exactly this. Con Edison of New York chose Andersen to work on a very large project in design recovery. Con Edison's 17-year-old customer information system was in need of redesign. But buried within this 2-million-line Cobol system were veritable gems of Con Ed knowledge.

Moore surveyed the CASE tool market and found nothing suitable for his purposes of design recovery. He needed a tool with the ability to look inside a very large integrated system and extract the design of that system. In the Con Ed customer information system, the design was embodied in a decision table structure. The system consisted of some 5000 decision tables.

The team decided to build its own design recovery tool for Con Ed. Moore viewed the problem as twofold: first, as an intellectual problem whose goal was to recover what is reasonable; second, as a hypermedia type of problem. Moore stressed that a hypermedia front end would be critical to the success of the final tool.

Andersen's recommended methodology was that an expert in a given area—say, covering 200 decision tables—would outline an approach and then send some junior analysts off to recover the design and produce a repository of business rules, implications, and side effects of these rules on transactions. A full object-oriented approach would provide the greatest of benefits. Andersen chose the Objectworks development environment, from ParcPlace Systems of Mountain View, California, to develop the in-house CASE tool.

The Andersen team wanted a certain amount of custom development. It wanted to exploit the features of the product in the development of this toolset. These features came in very handy in the development of a *browser*—the navigational and analytical tool that Andersen ultimately built.

A Con Ed analysis function might be: "Show me all the paths to this particular statement" or "Show me all the paths that use this paragraph." Using OO principles of encapsulation and inheritance, Objectworks gave the team the ability to extend existing, basic functions very, very rapidly.

ParcPlace was one of the first vendors of object-oriented toolkits. The firm is best known for its implementation of Smalltalk, which was conceived in the early 1970s by the research labs at the Xerox Palo Alto Research Center: ParcPlace is a spinoff of Xerox Palo Alto.

ParcPlace's object-oriented toolkits are not CASE tools—either upper or lower CASE. They do not assist in analysis or design (upper), or generate code (lower). What they do is offer a robust programming environment that permits the developer to develop applications based on the four pivotal concepts—encapsulation, inheritance, message passing, and dynamic binding.

Today, object orientation is an emerging technology that needs several years to mature. Yet a hierarchy of OO tools is available for today's intrigued user. On the very high end are tools such as Smalltalk/Objectworks and its primary competitor, Actor, which provide extremely robust and true-blue application development environments.

In the commercial CASE arena, vendors are rushing to embrace object orientation—or at least one of Professor Wegner's three forms of it.

Finally, there is a category of development tool that aspires to be "the great integrator." Even though object orientation may be the "new kid on the block" in software engineering, the OO concept has been around for quite a long time. In fact, those involved in developing expert systems have been familiar with OO constructs for more than a decade. The hard edges of the different disciplines of information technology are blurring and beginning to overlap.

Artificial intelligence (AI) has integrated hypertext (see Table 8.3). OO techniques are now infiltrating programming. Software categories are like plastic buckets. Anything that fits in a category you put into a bucket. And there are lots of buckets. You have to decide which bucket to put it in. Is it object-oriented? Is it expert systems? Is it hypertext? And what's happening is that the plastic that these buckets are made of is melting.

Perhaps the ultimate contribution of object orientation is that it will act as the glue that finally binds all the discrete methodologies together. But object orientation will not usurp any of the current methodologies. Rather, it will lead to the creation of tools which permit you to browse very large information spaces. You need to integrate to relational databases that are out there. You need to browse the large information space as if it's one thing.

TABLE 8.3   A Glossary of AI Terms

Artificial Intelligence—A subfield of computer science aimed at pursuing the possibility that a computer can be made to behave in ways that humans recognize as "intelligent" human behavior.

Class—A set of information similar to a file.

Class Member—The elements of information within a class, similar to a record within a file.

Conflict Resolution—The process by which a rule is chosen to fire.

Control—Within the context of a knowledge based system Control refers to the regulation of the ordering in which reasoning occurs.

Encapsulation—Refers to the fact that an object can be considered a mini-program. It is independent from other objects, with its own attributes, values and procedures.

IF. .THEN Rule—A statement of relationship in the form of IF A THEN B.

Inference—The process by which new facts are derived from known facts.

Inference Engine—The working program of the knowledge system that contains inference and control strategies. The term has also become linked with the attributes of user interface, external file interface, explanation features as well as other attributes.

Inheritance—Attributes of the parent object can be inherited by the child. For example, in the object CAR a parent attribute is that it has four wheels. The child object, MERCEDES, inherits this attribute from its parent CAR.

Knowledge base—That portion of a knowledge-based system that consists of the facts and heuristics about an area called a domain. Can be composed of rules, objects and other methodologies for storing knowledge.

Knowledge-based System—A computer system that performs logic, or judgment processing, rather than merely procedural processing.

Knowledge Representation—Methods used to encode and store facts and relationships. Examples are rules and objects.

Object—Building block of the more robust AI-based systems. Contains data and methods, or procedures. Objects communicate with each other by passing messages. Each object is responsible for its own behavior.

Rule-based System—A program that represents knowledge by means of rules only.

Shell—A prewritten knowledge-based system tool. Includes interfaces and interface engine.

The benefits of OO technology can be summed up as follows: quality, productivity, predictability, and control of complexity. In the end, object orientation just may be the key to integrated software engineering.

Surrounding Legacy Data with Intelligent Tools

The folk ballad "Loch Lomond" begins, "I'll take the high road and you take the low road, and I'll be in Scotland before you." This refrain is a timely metaphor to describe the two divergent paths that knowledge-based systems and database systems have taken over the past 10 years.

Some observers consider knowledge-based systems very much the high road (see Figure 8.4). A recent survey revealed that the use of knowledge-based systems increased by 25 percent between 1991 and 1992. However, the number of deployed knowledge-based systems is still low; 45 percent of respondents have at least one deployed application.[2]

Early resistance to knowledge-based systems centered on technological issues. The initial implementations required costly, proprietary hardware and software systems that were incompatible with standard data-processing platforms. To create the robust logic underlying knowledge-based systems that modeled judgment required difficult-to-learn and difficult-to-code programming languages such as Lisp and Prolog.

In the early 1980s, academicians-turned-AI-vendors made headlines with the emergence of software that promised to put the capabilities of building these logic systems into the hands of ordinary programmers. But the software, often called a *shell,* fell short of its promise to users and corporate management. As a result, skeptical IT departments

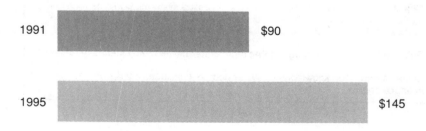

1991 $90

1995 $145

Millions of dollars

Figure 8.4 Expected growth in software revenue from knowledge-based systems. (*Source: International Data Corp.*)

have proceeded cautiously. Perhaps the most serious problem was the inability of the knowledge-based shell to satisfactorily integrate itself to a database environment.

This is, in effect, the very problem that Ted Craven found when he began to develop knowledge-based systems for his customers. Craven, a founder of Toronto-based Knowledge Management Systems, was weary of these same broken promises, so he chose an alternative path. He selected a PC-based integrated toolset called Guru, which is to the knowledge-based world as Lotus is to the spreadsheet world.

Guru, from MDBS, Inc. of Lafayette, Indiana, comes with its own integrated database. Craven chose Guru because in 1985 there were few database/knowledge-based combinations, and Guru was robust. The database manipulation language and the knowledge-based manipulation language exist on a par with each other. They are the same program, so they exist in the same memory space.

Craven used Guru to build a screening-test application for a company's human resources department. The system's goal is to assess applicants' personality traits to determine their ability to perform certain jobs. Guru's knowledge-based component associates the results of the screen-test analysis with text fragments. The knowledge-based system culls together these fragments into perfect English syntax for output to a two- to four-page report. The database component stores the text fragments and also keeps track of people taking the test.

Key players push integration

Even when knowledge-based systems began to gather steam in the commercial sector, database/knowledge-based integration facilities were less than perfect. Even though it was possible, it was real hard to do. The database interface wasn't designed into the product. It was sort of an afterthought, or an exit point that opened the door and "allowed" you to do it. But the system didn't help you at all.

To enable database access translates into defining the concept of the database as an object storage facility. Most high-end knowledge-based systems have added the facility to handle objects as well as the more familiar rules. In an object-oriented system, numbers, arrays, and even files are objects. An object's capabilities are determined by the methods defined for it. Methods are, in turn, equivalent to the function definitions used in procedural languages. Thus, an object can contain procedural code, rules, and even data, as shown in Figure 8.5.

Because all objects are equal to each other within the confines of an OO knowledge-based system, a "database object" is on par with an object created internally by the knowledge-based system—that is, a visualization of database access.

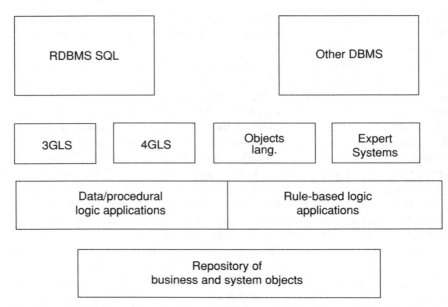

Figure 8.5 Integration of expert systems, CASE, and objects. (*Source: Meta Group*)

Paul Melcher, coordinator for knowledge-based systems at the Peoria, Illinois, headquarters of Caterpillar Inc., believes that knowledge-based systems must seamlessly integrate to existing infostructures. In his view, if companies can't use these current resources with a knowledge-based product, they're not going to buy the product.

Melcher is involved in transferring knowledge-based technologies into mainstream information processing. Early on, Caterpillar saw a great utility in the use of knowledge-based systems. But the company has massive databases and other external data resources that are required as input into these knowledge-based systems.

An example is the Material Coder. The goal of this knowledge-based system is to generate a 10-digit Production Material Commodity Code, which is used by different departments within Caterpillar. For example, the material code 0310209913 is actually an abbreviated specification for a flat steel bar with a particular material specification: a hot-rolled, dry-pickled type of finish and a thickness of .25, width of .88, and length of 192 inches.

Prior to the development of this knowledge-based system, Caterpillar derived the material codes manually using guidelines published in expansive volumes of documentation kept on a text database. Caterpillar, realizing the inherent weakness of the manual system, moved toward a knowledge-based system. However, the Material Coder requires data to be obtained from DB2 and other files stored on the IBM mainframe.

Fortunately, there were a few AI vendors around who understood the necessity of easy linkage to corporate data. In using Trinzic's (Waltham, Massachusetts) ADS knowledge-based tool to develop the Material Coder, Melcher found the process of joining knowledge bases to databases relatively easy. Because ADS is an object-oriented tool, a process object can be defined. From within this defined process object, an external program or data file can be called or accessed on any computer, local or remote. Thus, from within ADS, Melcher can go out and execute a Cobol program and bring back some results. He can also directly access database management systems. It's very simple.

Two schools of thought

Given the robustness of many of the tools mentioned, experienced developers found few integration problems. To them, combining database and knowledge base presented no significant hurdles. But in an era of increasing integration, questions arise about the future direction of knowledge bases and databases. Will they evolve on completely divergent paths? Or will the two technologies converge into what may be called an information base?

There are several distinct approaches to the integration of AI technology and databases, and they will continue to evolve separately into the future. One approach is to embed AI technology directly into the database. There are two major avenues here. One is in object orientation. The second is in providing more intelligence to query processing in database management systems, such that you can ask the database a set of questions that is larger than the specific data items that are stored.

The Glue That Binds

The mantle of object orientation will more than likely become the framework for future systems. Object orientation will not be just a programming technique under the auspices of knowledge-based systems. Rather, it will be the glue that binds the disconnected technologies.

The biggest problem in connecting knowledge bases to databases is that they don't talk clearly. The theory is that by subsuming both knowledge-based systems and database systems under an integrative OO framework, they will indeed talk the same language.

Perhaps the closest existing integrative OO framework is the emerging technology of object-oriented database management systems

(OODBMS). Itasca Systems, Inc. of Minneapolis is one of the leading vendors of this innovative technology. The Itasca OODBMS appears to be the next evolutionary step in database technology.

OODBMS technology takes a modular approach to program development and database structure. It is based on *persistent objects,* or modules of code plus data that form prefabricated building blocks for faster and more streamlined application building.

Over the last decade, hardware speed and power have increased at an annual rate of 30 percent, yet software development productivity has increased by only 4 percent. Current development techniques, coupled with nonintegrative software technologies, have been a large factor in this persistent deficiency.

One of the solutions will be the evolution of AI-intelligent front ends to database inquiries. Although this application of AI utilizes physical knowledge bases only tangentially, it is worth noting, since much movement is being made in this direction.

Topic is the primary product of Verity, based in Mountain View, California. Called an intelligent document retrieval package, Topic provides an intelligent front end to enterprise databases, permitting rapid retrieval of information by searching for concepts. This is very different from keyword searching, in which we know what we are looking for. Topic falls under the category of software that searches for information which might be of assistance to us, but the exact parameters of which we do not know until after we have retrieved it.

Another good example of this type of software is Metamorph, from Cleveland-based Thunderstone Software. Mike Pincus, president of Thunderstone, describes the power of Metamorph as synthetic intelligence. Metamorph was developed by a team of linguists and software engineers for use by government agencies, such as the Department of Energy and the Department of Defense. It was even used to restructure the databases at NASA after the *Challenger* explosion.

Metamorph has one basic goal: It reads information and makes logical conclusions about what piece of information is connected to another piece of information conceptually. No mere matching program, it uses a series of complex, pattern-matching algorithms to quickly and precisely look for conceptual relationships. It does so by performing morphological analysis on the text. (A *morpheme* is the smallest meaningful unit of language, so by breaking down a word into its component morphemes, Metamorph can achieve a high level of accuracy.)

Metamorph can be described as a free-text linear searcher. Using a parser, which is a sophisticated piece of software that deconstructs sentences, the software can locate single words, lists of words, expressions, and even approximations within large databases. Standard database query languages easily retrieve information, but only if the user knows specifically what he or she is looking for. Metamorph can search large databases for nonspecific information.

Another class of information is unknown information. Upon analysis of a large database it is possible to discover patterns, rules, and often unexpected relationships among data items that were previously unrealized. The induction on an extremely large (IXL) database tool from IntelligenceWare (Los Angeles) does just this. IXL uses statistics and machine learning to generate easy-to-read rules that characterize data, providing new insight and understanding.

A More Intelligent Approach

Metamorph, IXL, and Topic are headed in the right direction as they approach a long-term solution to the problem of integrating diverse technologies. The idea of the "intelligent database" just may be key to the troublesome issue of full integration of the database world to the knowledge-based world. And since IXL and other tools like it play an important role, this solution might indeed be the breakthrough for which users have been waiting.

There is a strong case for this emerging technology. The idea for intelligent databases came up about 3 years ago when Kamran Parsaye, president of IntelligenceWare, was looking at the next direction of databases. It was clear at that time, and still is, that the question of data access has to some extent been resolved. IT users can now access data. But they have so much data that (1) they don't know what to access and (2) after they've accessed it, they still get too much data back.

Parsaye also realized that many existing technologies are underutilized and tend to be treated in isolation. Parsaye's concept of an intelligent database involves integrating these separate technical leaps into a unified framework.

The intelligent database model is based on seven information technologies:

- Knowledge discovery
- Data integrity and quality control
- Hypermedia management
- Data preparation and display
- Decision support and scenario analysis
- Data format management
- Intelligent system design tools

One of the major problems in knowledge-based integration involves how the database model should be extended so as to construct intelligent databases. Parsaye's proposed solution is to add extra knowledge representation and inferencing capabilities—now within the domain of knowledge-based systems.

Parsaye views knowledge-based systems as primarily high-level programming environments for information and knowledge-intensive tasks. Within this perspective, a relational database can be closely integrated with a knowledge base using relational predicates and objects. Parsaye contends that the relational predicate model and the object model can be fully interchangeable, forming the basis of a fully integrated intelligent database.

Intelligent databases and object-oriented databases are two routes that vendors are taking to create a bridge between corporate data and knowledge-based systems. Both are logical extensions of the path that many developers are following today. Although they are seemingly robust solutions to the problem, they are also exotic solutions. Thus, the skeptical IT user may not buy into these newer technologies.

Perhaps the most immediate solution, and the one that is the most palatable to IT developers, will come from a more familiar direction. Trinzic Corp. has a persuasive and innovative approach to development environment integration. The company contends that integration must occur across the entire life cycle, including metadata integration, tool and methodology integration, and life-cycle management integration.

In a development phase that the firm calls "knowledge integration," a single methodology supports the entire development process. An integrated CASE/knowledge workstation will support this methodology through a single tool. An associated repository has both knowledge-based and CASE information stored indistinguishably. Thus, knowledge-based systems and database systems will, in effect, be indistinguishable as well.

Computer Associates (CA) of Garden City, New York, would like to see an even simpler approach. As a vendor of both database and knowledge-based systems, CA is in the unique position of being able to put some muscle behind its viewpoint.

CA has developed a "single database strategy," in which the database engine would grow to add the capabilities required by knowledge-based systems. The CA approach is to add capabilities as needed. The developer does so by looking at the engine architecturally, determining the common and noncommon features across the two different semantic methods, and adding only the new ones.

It is foolish to continually throw away what works just to go to a new technology. For example, moving from DL/I to DB2 required people to rewrite many of their applications. But what if DB2 utilized much of the code inherent in DL/I and added only new functionality? In essence, this is Computer Associates's philosophy. It follows then that if CA can provide base navigational capabilities within its database engine, it is possible to augment the engine on a different layer when multiple navigational paths must be provided. This approach may offer the optimum solution to integrating databases to knowledge bases—and, ultimately, legacy systems to object-oriented systems.

Knowledge-based systems call for the merging of AI technology with database technology. The way it has to be done, in my view, is to add OO capabilities to the existing database engine and so be able to integrate the repository information with the knowledge. This might be the real answer to the question of true knowledge base and database integration. After all, if technology is revolutionized every 4 years, will we have to get rid of everything we have every 4 years? Or will we have the luxury of integrating this new technology as an attachment to existing technology?

References

1. Elliot Chikofsky and James Cross, "Reverse Engineering and Design Recovery: A Taxonomy," *IEEE Software,* January 1990.
2. "Knowledge Systems on the Rise," *Computer Market Letter,* September 1993.

9

In Search
of a Methodology

Many years have gone by since Ed Yourdon, Chris Gane, James Martin, and Clive Finkelstein developed their noted software development methodologies. Those were indeed simpler days. Simpler computers and simpler applications. But in the 20-odd years since, the pace of deployment of advanced technologies into mainstream computing has rapidly accelerated.

In a world driven to client/server, object orientation, GUIs, and massively parallel computers, do the methodologies of yore need to be thrown out or tweaked? Or can they be left intact?

Key industry leaders, observer, and users responded to this question with some surprising answers. The results tend to indicate that in spite of two decades of experience in developing software, the question of *the best methodology* is still largely unanswered.

This chapter examines the need for a methodology and provides an introduction to the various and sundry methodologies that are currently in use.

A Question of Methodology

Perhaps the most well-known of structured development methodologies is that created by Ed Yourdon. It is the one, after all, that has been taught at the most academic institutions and for the longest period of time. Yourdon, now publisher of the New York City–based *American Programmer* magazine, admits that the methodology he pioneered back in the 1970s may be a bit dated. It was developed in the days when things like user interfaces were irrelevant. The methodology didn't speak to that need at all. It was card input and tape output.

If we accept the premise that everyone is moving to the brave new technological world of the twenty-first century, then we do need something new. The problem is that everyone is not really on the leading edge. Not everyone is into GUIs or client/server or object orientation. In fact, movement to new technologies follows a bell-shaped curve. The leading 10 percent are doing all these marvelous things, while the trailing 10 percent are still using "relics" like Autocoder and 1401 computer systems.

Most organizations sit squarely in the middle of this curve, shuffling along trying to catch up. And the methodologies, in a sense, mirror that. Migrating to methodologies, however, is like following a fashion trend. Companies may want a new methodology just because they're bored or jaded. But for an awful lot of people, the systems they are building today may turn out to be reasonably well handled by conventional methodologies.

The main concern is that many companies today assume they're on the leading edge and feel that they must abandon whatever they're currently doing and jump over to some brand of new methodology. If you look at the way these firms are using methodology, it turns out that the vast majority of them never did get to the point of adopting the methodologies of the 1970s.

Elliot Chikofsky was one of the principal architects of the Excelerator CASE tool. As a technician, industry observer, and professor at Northeastern University in Boston, Chikofsky echoes Yourdon's view. The first question Chikofsky asks is: "Did we even understand or ever apply the old methods?"

Chikofsky contends that part of the problem is that people adopt the form of a method but not its content. When he gives a speech, he always asks, "How many people use structured design?" Most of the hands in the audience get raised. But when Chikofsky follows with "Keep your hand up if you can tell me what cohesion and coupling are," usually only one hand remains raised.

Cohesion and coupling are the measures of what constitutes a good quality design. The reason Chikofsky's question is so telling and the response so disconcerting is that discussion of these measures constitutes at least two-thirds of any book on structured design.

It would seem, therefore, that organizations as a whole have given only lip service to these methods. People draw data-flow diagrams, but they don't do structured analysis. This is an important distinction.

Janet McCabe, director of methodology at American Management Systems in Arlington, Virginia, agrees that organizations have been paying little more than lip service to these methodologies and that, as a result, the methodologies have not gained widespread acceptance. The reason, she feels, is that these are not methodologies at all, but merely techniques for developing software.

McCabe maintains that today's methodologies and their applications in the real world come up short. They do not cover the complete breadth of activities that need to go on during a software development effort. Not only should a methodology cover the many aspects of software development; it must also cover the issues of testing, conversion, implementation, and even user procedures. Ultimately, a real methodology will go step by step and explain how to do something.

An era of GUIs

One of the technologies that is changing the shape of software development today is the graphical user interface. And one of the most well-known advocates of GUIs is Umang Gupta, president, founder, and CEO of Gupta Technologies. The company has become a leader in the field of SQL-based products.

In Gupta's view, we're moving from an era of character-based systems to graphical-based systems and from an era of structured, top-down programming techniques to object-oriented programming techniques. With all these changes taking place at the same time, we really need a whole new generation of design and development methodologies.

Interestingly, Yourdon and others felt the same way and came up with a whole new type of methodology—object-oriented analysis (OOA) and design (OOD). But since most of us aren't using object-oriented programming techniques (save for same GUI front-end building), adopting OOA and OOD techniques is rather like putting the cart before the horse. In other words, more than just our method of doing analysis and design has to change. The whole way of doing development has to change.

During one internal development project, Gupta used a single programmer to build a key strategic system. Gupta's order management system permits his staff to send orders electronically from around the world to a centralized shipping department. The system resides on departmental SQL servers with bar code input. Instead of using a formal specification process, the programmer did the spec on the computer, essentially building an iterative prototype. From Gupta's perspective, not a single methodology exists today that would significantly improve this prototyping cycle.

Gupta notes that these changes, which have shortened the life cycle, are evolutionary rather than revolutionary. And because they are evolutionary, what we will need is mixture of methodologies, just as we have a mixture of tools.

Savvy developers have used fourth-generation languages for at least 10 years. In shops that emphasize joint or rapid application development, 4GLs have proved to be the tool of choice. What we have begun see in the 1990s is a coupling of CASE with 4GLs. This trend is apparent not only at traditional CASE companies but at companies such as Unisys Corp. of Blue Bell, Pennsylvania, which introduced the Linc CASE/4GL combination.

A Well-Oiled Methodology

In a world largely dependent upon fossil fuels, the one thing that most of us hope for, aside from a clean and safe environment, is lower prices. And although many of the variables that go into fuel oil pricing are uncontrollable, oil companies, like all U.S. companies in the 1990s, are looking for ways to shave the bottom line by increasing efficiencies and reducing costs.

Global Petroleum, Inc. of Waltham, Massachusetts, is a multi-billion-dollar company specializing in petroleum distribution. Since there is no direct pipeline between oil fields in Iran and an apartment building's boiler, the industry has created a web of companies that act as distributors.

Global buys petroleum from any source that will sell it. This can be the stock market or Venezuela. Internally, the company has developed an extensive web of connections that permit Global to service a wide variety of customers. Global sells oil to power plants, the U.S. federal government, paper mills, city transit departments, and so on—down to the elderly couple who live on the corner.

Selling a commodity product like home heating oil forces Global to be keenly aware of price and availability as the product's primary selling points. To monitor these two factors, Global has had to rely heavily on computers. Because the customer base and marketing base are constantly changing, Global performs an enormous amount of computerized gyrations to track where the product is, how much it costs, and how it should be priced.

Global and its computer systems have to be responsive to change to stay competitive. This flexibility was put to test in October 1991, when management made the decision to add natural gas. Even though selling gas is basically the same business as selling oil, to Global's computer systems, natural gas was as different from petroleum as oranges from apples. The computer systems needed to "think about" the two products differently in terms of units of measurement, price, and storage. Oil, for example, is measured in gallons, and gas is measured in BTUs.

In most computer shops, any effort to radically overhaul a working system in a few weeks would be monumental, if not impossible. And what if this change had to be accomplished in a shop whose worth was over $3 billion but whose IT department contained a mere four staffers?

Global's IT department consists of one MIS director, two programmers, and one consultant. Though lean, the shop is highly productive.

Aside from an emphasis on understanding the business, the secret to Global's success resides largely in its choice of tools and surrounding methodologies.

Global has been using Unisys mainframe processors since the company decided to automate in the mid-1970s. Even though some of Global's most important systems are Cobol-based, it is the extensive use of fourth-generation languages that makes Global competitive.

Competition, and the productivity-enhancing tactics taken to foster it, is something that most industries have just begun to be keenly aware of. For the oil industry, this realization came more than a decade earlier than for most other industries. It was during the oil crisis in 1979 that Global realized it needed to have a business that was very flexible, a business that modeled information technology and not the reverse. As a result, the mandate from management was to give the technology people the tools and methods to do the job.

The Linc toolset provided by Unisys includes a robust 4GL with which systems can be quickly developed and modified. Using it has dramatically decreased the number of staff members Global needs as well as the amount of time it takes to complete a job.

For example, not too long ago the IT department was required to make a modification to a product code field. The original length was three digits and it needed to be changed to four. This required making modifications to more than 80 reports and more than 50 screens. Using the Linc data dictionary, Global was able to perform an impact analysis to determine the specific screens and programs that would be affected, saving a great deal of time and effort.

Perhaps the most useful feature of Linc is its ability to paint a system. This graphical capability gave Global a facile way to maintain the definitions of all reports and all screens. With help from the Linc toolset, maintenance took a mere 10 days. The best estimate for a non-4GL approach to the same level of changes is 6 to 8 weeks.

Using a 4GL such as Linc fosters a change in methodologies as well. Because the development team can rapidly prototype and even develop, Global's involvement with end users has become more frequent and more intense. This technique is often called *joint application development* (JAD). But JAD cannot work unless the tools are there to support the process.

Using Linc, Global's IT staff can bring a user in and say, "This is the way the screen is going to look." The user is then free to indicate changes more quickly, enabling the development team to be much more reactive to Global's business requirements.

One of the things Global likes best about Linc is its flexible methodology. The Unisys *Linc Systems Approach* manual details a system development methodology that is consistent with the use of a higher-order, CASE/4GL tool.

In order to gain competitive and productivity-enhancing benefits, information systems must be developed along two concepts: The information system must be an accurate model of the business system, and the system must have the ability to evolve developmentally. Changes to the information system must take place at the same pace as changes to the business.

The Linc systems approach (LSA) methodology adheres to these two constructs. LSA is based on evolutionary prototyping, incremental functional delivery, and object-based design. LSA was specifically created to take advantage of the Linc advanced toolset. Linc is actually more than a 4GL; it is also a set of upper and lower CASE tools.

In using LSA as a system development methodology, organizations need to understand that the entry point to this method is after enterprise analysis and information strategy planning have already taken place. This is a logical conclusion of the business-model-driven approach. As mentioned, Global's IT group was already well versed in Global's business needs, so it was a very short leap toward completing these two preliminary stages.

LSA breaks the system development life cycle into five phases, compared with the eight phases of the "traditional" life cycle (see Figures 9.1 and 9.2). Phase 1 is system investigation. Here the scope and objectives of the system are determined according to analysis of the business unit to be automated. In phase 2, system definition, the actual

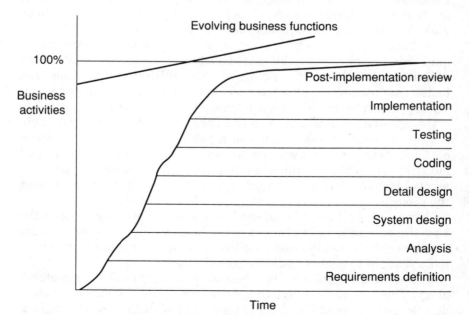

Figure 9.1 Traditional life cycle. (*Source: Unisys*)

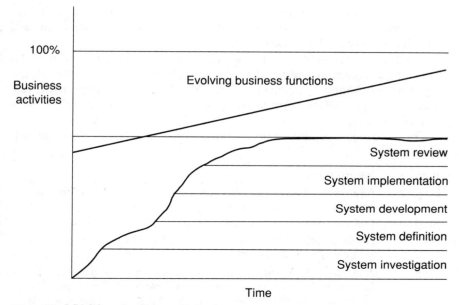

Figure 9.2 LSA life cycle. (*Source: Unisys*)

system is defined. Optimally, an upper CASE tool is used, but it is possible to perform the functions in this phase manually—on a blackboard or with pencil and paper. Once the system is designed, it is defined to the Linc system repository. Phases 3, 4, and 5 are quite similar to conventional methodologies in that they perform development, implementation, and system review.

Although at first glance these system development steps appear familiar, certain nuances of the process actually make LSA quite different from more conventional methodologies. Perhaps the most relevant of these differences is LSA's reliance on an iterative process. The iterative approach fosters a more natural evolution of the system.

For example, let's assume that a particular business functional area is under investigation. During the process, as is the custom, the activities of that functional area continue to change. In a traditional software development life cycle, the goal is to acquire full knowledge of the functional area under investigation prior to the development of a supporting information system.

LSA recognizes that there is a gap between traditional information system development and the business functional area as it changes over time, particularly when significant time is devoted to the development effort.

Aside from, but coupled to, the iterative approach, LSA and the Linc toolset foster the creation of the Linc object model—an important technique in this methodology. LSA is not driven either by data modeling or by process modeling. Rather, both data and process are analyzed simultaneously in the iterative cycle.

The Linc object model is created by describing elements, or objects. These objects are, in essence, Linc building blocks. They can be categorized as components, events, reports, profiles, global logic routines, and external interfaces. Actually, creating the object model is far more complicated.

The Linc object-modeling process contains a number of steps, including:

Step 1   Record the organization's goals.

Step 2   Add recorded activities. The development team should record specifically what the company does.

Step 3   Define implementation boundaries, or functional areas.

Step 4   Group activities into implementation boundaries; note activities that cross organizational boundaries.

Step 5   Analyze each activity. Specifically break down each activity into a Linc object. An object is a component, event, profile, inquiry, global logical routine, or report. Activities are composed of a number of Linc objects and the relationship between these objects. The center of each activity is a business event.

Step 6   Define each event in terms of functions, usage (input, output, or both), transaction volume, data items, edit requirements, screen layout and flows, business rules, and associated objects.

Step 7   Define each component.

Step 8   Build the data dictionary.

Step 9   Define global logic objects. These are routines that are logically encapsulated objects that may be included inside the definition of more than one event, inquiry, component, or report.

Step 10   Define object relationships.

Step 11   Define profiles. Profiles define access paths over data. They can be used to define alternate keys for components, linking several events together.

Step 12   Define reports and inquiries.

Step 13   Review model for functionality.

Step 14   Define external interfaces.

Step 15   Consider security.

Step 16   Consider consolidation and archiving of the detailed data in the event objects.

Step 17   Consider performance.

Step 18   Consider integrity.

Step 19   Review design.

LSA advocates system development using small project teams composed of three to five information analysts together with two to three users of the information system to be implemented. Global end users are an important component of the team, involved from the beginning to the end.

There are few $3 billion companies able to react so quickly to a changing environment. Global believes that what makes it competitive as well as much more productive is a combination of three well-integrated factors. First and foremost is the quality of staff and their closeness to the business units. Second is the decision to forgo traditional tools to concentrate on one high-level but robust toolset that permits the quick, logical, and efficient development of complex applications. Last is the methodology that Global uses to build systems.

A Multimethod Approach

DRT, based in New York City, is the system integration arm of Big Six accounting firm Deloitte and Touche. Ken Hohner, DRT executive vice president, adopts the perspective of someone who's seen hundreds of methodology implementations across dozens of industries. He clearly sees the need for multiple methodologies resident within a single organization.

Hohner supports his multimethodology thesis by using a programming language analogy. How many organizations can get away with picking a language and then adapting applications to it? There are times when this just doesn't work. Cobol isn't good for modeling heuristics. Fortran is a wonderful scientific language but gives you trouble when developing compilers.

Most organizations utilize more than one programming language and allow the development team to pick the language most suited to the task at hand. Hohner advocates extending this freedom to allow the team to pick the best *methodology* for the task at hand.

This decision must be an informed one, though. And as we've already seen so often, most organizations are poorly attuned to methodologies. So how can this be accomplished?

Hohner raises an idea that has, unfortunately, fallen out of favor in many organizations. Originated by IBM, the idea is to have a chief programmer available to assist other programmers in making difficult technical decisions.

Renaming the chief programmer "methodology guru," Hohner envisions having an expert in all facets of methodologies to whom development teams can turn when initiating their projects. The methodology guru would be knowledgeable in the application of all manner of methodologies and methodology-related tools. A required visit to the guru would set the proper path for the development team and eliminate inefficiencies associated with today's utilization of quasi-methodologies.

At least one part of the industry has come down strongly in favor of information engineering as the single, most effective approach to system development (see Figure 9.3). Equally applicable to batch systems as to on-line systems as to object-oriented systems, IE supporters discount any notion of a need for multiple methodologies.

Jim Kerr, an associate director of emerging technologies practice at DMR Group, a Boston consulting company, thinks that the IE approach will really take off in the 1990s. Using IE, you can take advantage of the relational tools that everybody's so hot for today. Also, if you extend IE, you can support object-oriented development.

The IE approach has an interesting history. Although popularized by James Martin, information engineering has its origins in the IBM Palo Alto think tank of the early 1970s. Clive Finkelstein, now chief scientist and founder of Information Engineering Systems Corp. of Alexandria, Virginia, had the idea while at IBM in Palo Alto that the power of relational theory could be combined with the strength of newly emerging strategic-planning concepts to create a new business technique. Later, with James Martin, he co-authored a two-volume report entitled *Information Engineering.*

It was this report that pushed information engineering squarely to the forefront of development methodologies. When Finkelstein first

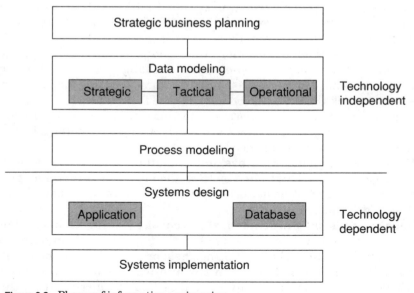

Figure 9.3 Phases of information engineering.

started at IBM in 1972, he looked at different ways to build systems. He felt that there had to be an easier way and was rewarded when he discovered that the relational approach was, indeed, far easier. But relational theory, as a system development technique, had a major flaw. It was rather abstruse for system people, let alone users. But emerging from that focus was the entirely new approach that Finkelstein labeled information engineering. This approach focused more on what you wanted to achieve and how to go about achieving it.

In essence, what Finkelstein discovered was that the secret of developing good, usable systems was based more on business knowledge than on the technology itself. And out of this discovery Finkelstein was able to develop a stable foundation for system development based on data, not on procedures.

Finkelstein contended that moving from process with data which is software engineering, to data-based process which is information engineering, is quite a change. This change filters downward through every component of the software development process, even to the level of development team makeup. Using the business-driven IE approach, team makeup is 80 percent users and 20 percent system analysts, whereas under the software engineering approach the breakdown is typically 80 percent analysts and 20 percent users.

The end results of this change are significant, Finkelstein said, including much higher quality systems and databases, faster development cycles, and prioritization.

There are some subtle benefits as well. Because the system is business-driven, the resultant system is architected in a way that is more flexible to business change. When system design was based on efficiencies of the processor or database model, the inevitable changes to the business model caused a complete revamping of the database structure. Finkelstein's IE approach entirely negated that inflexibility.

Tangible benefits are reaped by the system development staff too. Since the team makeup is changed from 20 percent user to 80 percent user, the team can carry out much of the database and design with only a quarter of the analysts than a traditional approach uses.

Four times the number of projects can be initiated and completed. And while the users are doing much of the analysis and design using the business-driven approach, the analysts can provide much of the project management. The net result is a much lowered maintenance overhead.

As we enter the brave new world of GUIs and object orientation, though, we might ask if Finkelstein's long-standing IE approach is resilient enough to change. He contends that information engineering naturally encapsulates object-oriented techniques. He also notes that object-oriented techniques are not new to the 1990s. Indeed, according to Finkelstein, in its previous incarnation in the 1960s and 1970s, object orientation was called reusable code.

Those who go beyond an elementary understanding of relational theory realize that "third normal form" is not the end of the line when normalizing relational tables. Parsing data down to fifth normal form permits a breakdown of business detail into objects that contain not only data but the associated logic that acts upon that data. Finkelstein's technique is to break down business processes into fourth and fifth business normal form. This permits a natural encapsulation of those processes into objects.

It is the natural object orientation of business-driven databases and systems that reduced maintenance. Business environments changed rapidly in the 1980s, and most automated systems failed to keep up with these structural changes. Systems that were developed along IE principles were able to keep pace with these structural changes. Storing business data and processes within a fifth business normal form, or object, makes it as easy to change a business rule as it is to change a customer's address.

At its data center in Rockville, Maryland, the National Association of Securities Dealers (NASD) has installed Bill Synnott, a Finkelstein follower, as director of information technology. The data center recently embarked on an ambitious data architecture project with far-reaching goals that are unusual for the company. Its emphasis on technology has enabled NASD to increase its prestige and market share dramatically over the last decade, putting it neck and neck with the venerable New York Stock Exchange.

Synnott had long realized that 80 percent of NASD's technology efforts went into unproductive maintenance. His goal was to look for better ways to develop application software. After examining what the company had in place, Synnott realized it would be very difficult to migrate to a new operating environment. He first had to find a way to understand what the current software was doing. They understood that the business logic was, in effect, embedded in that software; so they needed to come up with a suite of methodologies to get them from where they were to the new environment.

NASD's goal was to find something that was a top-down, data-driven approach. Searching through a myriad of methodologies, though, they came up empty. it was then that they came across Martin and Finkelstein's book.

Do We Have the Answer Yet?

Sesha Pratap is president of Centerline Software, Inc. (formerly Saber Software, Inc.) of Cambridge, Massachusetts, which markets C and C++ tools for workstations. His programming tools have indelibly altered the methodology landscape. Pratap is one of a growing number of workstation mavens who, in spite of the Yourdons, Ganes, and Finkelsteins, insist that the software tool itself is the end game and that methodology is simply not part of the equation.

Pratap contends that for a large variety of applications, methodologies are simply not used at all. In the workstation development market, for instance, the adoption of methodology tools is less than 10 percent of the market, Pratap maintains. This, of course, may reflect the fact that many workstations are used primarily for single-user database and intensive applications. Here, what's really needed is a design and an architecture.

But when the system being developed is more than single-user, some sort of "people" communication vehicle must be introduced. This is specifically what a methodology does.

The need for a methodology in this instance is not something that Pratap disputes. In fact, he observes two trends. Software development organizations are trying to adopt tools and technologies that adapt modularity into their software, and these same organizations are trying to automate more and more of the development process. In essence, because of automation and modularization, much of the methodology is wrapped up in programming.

Ultimately, the majority of methodologies in place today are not sufficient to meet the needs of the entire organization. Some methodologies are good at some things, and others are good at other things. The contention that we should take a multimethodology approach just doesn't cut the mustard either. If developers are having trouble with one methodology, they're going to have that much more trouble using two methodologies.

Edward Lanigan, now president of St. Louis–based Lanigan Group, Inc., found this out for himself when he was in charge of a research and development group at McDonnell-Douglas. He was chartered to look at system engineering methodologies and found that few individuals had taken a look at cradle-to-grave development looking at development as both a methodology and a process.

Lanigan's was echoed by many others in the trenches. The software development process is broken. You fix it piece by piece. Consequently, at the one end, you have your up-front methodologies like those put forward by Yourdon and De Marco, which were designed to improve communications for the up-front design—but that's all they were designed to do. And at the other end of the spectrum you have things like optimized compilers. So what you end up with is a very piecemeal approach and when you reach boundaries you come to a screeching halt.

In Lanigan's search for a boundary-free CASE tool that would provide a methodology and toolset for McDonnell Douglas, he began asking CASE tool vendors a telling question: "You are developing CASE tools. The CASE tool itself is a software product but also a tool for helping software developers develop software. Does your development team use your own tool?"

Invariably, the answer was no. What we need, then, is a better answer.

10

And Now for a
Methodology That Works

It's curious that in this age of automation, even those doing the automating often lack the proper tools. Even as these folks work hard and long at developing systems that foster productivity (or at least attempt to) throughout the organization, they themselves are working in less than a productive environment. The question then becomes: Is it even possible to build productivity-enabling systems on a foundation of nonproductivity?

There are more than just a few methodology-driven approaches available to increase productivity. Many of them have been discussed in the last chapter. But some of them are so common that they have become a constant presence in the development environment. One of these is *rapid application development* (RAD) a formal methodology popularized by James Martin.

Without even realizing it most of us practice RAD, even if informally. Pratap's description of rapidly throwing a system together using a screen-painter (discussed in the last chapter) should be familiar to most. We've all done somewhat of the same thing. We give our users PCs and editors and say, "Here, show me what you want." Once they do, we rapidly develop a prototype. And we keep doing this for as long as it takes. I assert, therefore, that today's RAD is something that we've been doing naturally for a long time and although it does improve productivity, it does not do so dramatically unless it is practiced a bit more formally.

My premise is that RAD could make even more of an impact if it were embedded into a methodology whose precepts pushed the twin goals of productivity and reliability to new heights. Essentially, that's what this chapter is about.

The High Cost of Maintenance

Developed systems are very much the mirror image of the process that was used to create them. It's no secret that a full 70 percent or more of the average organization's IT budget is eaten away by the cost of maintenance, as shown in Figure 10.1. Turned around the other way, we can draw the conclusion that only 30 percent of any system actually works the way users expect it to work on its first day in production.

What's interesting to note here is that in spite of a proliferation of tools and techniques, hardware and software (all labeled with the requisite *productivity* buzzword), the 70–30 ratio has pretty much stayed the same over the last dozen years or so. Curious!

There's been much speculation on the reasons for this phenomenon. Obviously, there is no single culprit but rather a combination of factors that has converged to keep productivity in check. Let's look briefly at some of the more esoteric reasons that the system maker's children have a rather low PQ (productivity quotient).

A Case for Productivity

Many managers live by the 10 percent rule. That is, the greatest productivity you can get comes from hiring within the top 10 percentile. Therefore, one of the easiest approaches to developing an efficient IT department is to bring in the better people. Since there is about a 25-to-1 differential between the best people and the worst people, and a 4-

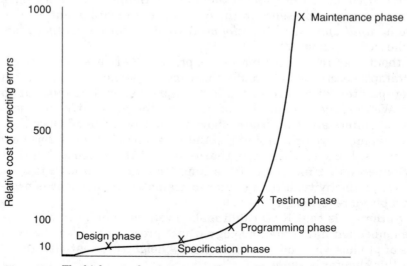

Figure 10.1   The high cost of maintenance. (*Source: Techinsider*)

to-1 differential between the best teams and the worst teams, maybe the best way to improve productivity and quality is just to improve hiring practices.

But just what types of people will improved IT hiring practices find? Perhaps they are the people who are just innately better programmers. If you take a random group of 100 people and put them in a room with a complex programming exercise, one of them will finish 25 times faster than the others. Certain other peopleware techniques could go a much longer way toward increasing productivity. Tom DeMarco, author of a well-received system specification study in 1979, has more recently turned his analytics to productivity. According to his findings, people with adequate office space have substantially higher productivity than people with traditionally allocated amounts of space. DeMarco also stresses the importance of training. In fact, he presents the revolutionary notion of letting people accrue their training days the way they accrue their vacation days.

Productivity can be improved in many other ways as well. One is by training managers to be better at performance reviews. Another is by focusing on the psychological makeup of the development team. Much work has been done, in recent years, on team dynamics. In order for a team to work together successfully, its members must complement one another. Each team needs a distribution of leaders, followers, idea people, testers, debuggers, and so on. Even in an industry whose personality profiles are skewed toward introversion, it is still possible to build an effective working team. All it takes is some good management.

Metrics—the yardstick for measuring

Perhaps the best place to start in raising an organization's PQ is with metrics. If you don't know where you are now and you don't know where your productivity problems are, any solution you seek may turn out to be the wrong one. Perhaps the most popular metric of all, at least as of this writing, is *function points*. Function points is by no means new. It surfaced back in the early 1980s as a metric that would measure functionality rather than mere lines of code. In a nutshell, the function point metric assesses the functionality of the software development process by first counting the number of external inputs (e.g., transaction types), external outputs (e.g., report types), logical internal files (nonphysical), external interface files (files accessed by the application but not updated by it), and external inquiries. After a set of standards is applied to assess complexity, these components are classified as being relatively low, average, or high.

Once the total number of function counts is computed according to a statistical formula, the impact of fourteen general system characteristics is assessed. The fourteen characteristics are:

Data communications

Distributed functions

Performance

Heavily used configuration

Transaction rate

On-line data entry

End-user efficiency

On-line update

Complex processing

Reusability

Installation ease

Operational ease

Multiple sites

Ability to facilitate change

These values are then summed to compute what is known as the *value adjustment factor* (VAF). The VAF is then multiplied with the total function count to create the number of function points.

The popularity of function points as a metric has perhaps been spurred by the formation of the International Function Point User Group (IFPUG) based in Westerfield, Ohio. IFPUG membership has grown dramatically over the years with the coincident rise of interest in measurement. In fact, it is IFPUG that has published the definitive standard on just how to count function points.

But measurement is more than just taking a count. In fact, many astute observers think that the concept of measurement itself is flawed. Most organizations start a measurement program without people understanding the requirements for measuring. Companies should know what the destination target is, and to achieve it they need to develop navigational measures.

Howard Rubin is president of Rubin Associates and a professor of computer science at Hunter College in New York City. He has collected statistics on almost 300 organizations and their attempts to implement measurement programs. The results are presented in Figure 10.2. Rubin stresses that over the last 40 years, measures have evolved through a series of generations, starting with what he calls "the observable generation" and its reliance on lines of code through more analytic periods which rely on measures such as function points. This has now evolved into what he terms "business-directed." In this generation no longer is IT casually linked to business concerns. Now IT measurement is rooted squarely in the lingo of user and

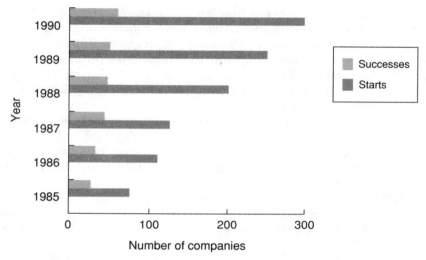

Figure 10.2   Low success rate for metrics. (*Source: Rubin Systems Inc.*)

management concerns, where they are referred to as "measurement stakeholders."

These measurement stakeholders have driven some advanced organizations to adopt a *dashboard* framework for program implementation. Rubin describes these dashboards as consisting of the appropriate gauges to show current performance, baselines, directional trends, and targets in the areas identified by the technique of audience analysis (e.g., user participation). The basic gauges found to be the most useful are the core management concerns of quality, productivity, delivery, demand, overall work distribution, work profile within projects, tool penetration, process maturity, and technology readiness. But in order for this type of measurement program to work, Rubin insists, the IT organization must fully understand how the company itself measures its business success and how IT performance links to company performance.

Productivity Stems from a Good Methodology

Companies that will win the competitive battles of the 1990s are those firms that will leverage their technology investments to create new possibilities. And what is needed so that IT can make a productive contribution are good management, good technical staff (including good estimators and testers), good measurements, good tools, and good methodology.

IT management can choose from many well-known and well-documented methodologies. But are the most popular methodologies actually the most productivity-enabling? To answer this question, think back a bit: You have been using the same methodologies for close to two decades. Has productivity improved during this time? If you've answered in the negative, then perhaps it's time for something slightly different.

A methodology encompasses the processes, or steps, that a technology unit goes through in order to specify, develop, and then implement a computer system. Pursuing technology development without a methodology is akin to making your way through the Yukon without a map. It's surprising, therefore, to find that many companies develop a majority of their systems without a map.

The Pittsburgh-based Software Engineering Institute has produced a well-known chart depicting the software process maturity framework. As shown in Figure 10.3, an IT department goes through five

STAGE 1: INITIAL
—Ad hoc
—Little formalization
—Tools informally applied to the process
KEY ACTIONS TO GET TO NEXT STEP:
—Initiate rigorous project management, management oversight and quality assurance

STAGE 2: REPEATABLE
—Achieved a stable process with a repeatable level of statistical control
KEY ACTIONS TO GET TO NEXT STEP:
—Establish a process group
—Establish a software-development process architecture
—Introduce software engineering methods and technologies

STAGE 3: DEFINED
—Achieved foundation for major and continuing progress
KEY ACTIONS TO GET TO NEXT STEP:
—Establish a basic set of process managements to identify quality and cost parameters
—Establish a process database
—Gather and maintain process data
—Assess relative quality of each product and inform management

STAGE 4: MANAGED
—Substantial quality improvements
—Comprehensive process measurement
KEY ACTIONS TO GET TO NEXT STEP:
—Support automatic gathering of process data
—Use data to analyze and modify the process

STAGE 5: OPTIMIZED
—Major quality and quantity improvements
KEY ACTIONS TO GET TO NEXT STEP:
—Continue improvement and optimization of the process

Figure 10.3 Five steps to maturity. According to the Software Engineering Institute, an IT department goes through five stages of maturity on its way to becoming optimized and productive. (*Source: Software Engineering Institute.*)

levels of maturity on its way to becoming completely optimized and productive. An oft-quoted statistic is that a full 80 percent of us are sitting squarely on top of level 1. This may be because the general computing public has not exactly found what it wants or what it needs from any one of these methodologies. Instead, technologists are all back in their shops trying to put a little bit of what sounded good in one together with what sounded good in another. They're asking, "Is there a way for me to create my own version of these methodologies— and then have some tool that would enforce them for me?"

This, in fact, may be one of the largest factors holding back the penetration of CASE into the IT market. CASE is to more rapidly developing efficient programs what Lotus 1-2-3 is to rapidly developing efficient, and accurate, spreadsheets. Unfortunately, CASE is useless if the technology department doesn't follow a development methodology.

In choosing a methodology, IT would do well to understand the dynamics of the relationships between methodology, CASE, and measurements. The proper sequence of implementation to foster the sought-after improvement in system development, productivity, and quality is to develop a measurement program first, choose a methodology second, and pick a CASE product last of all. Surrounding this trio are the prickly issues of peopleware (see Figure 10.4). Note that the sequence here is iterative, with measurement coming full circle again at the end of the process.

A New Methodology Is Needed

The majority of organizations are simply not using any methodology at all. And while the rest *are* using a methodology, it's apparent that the particular methodology we chose is doing little or nothing to boost our PQ.

The following 26 questions, developed by Sam Holcman, president and founder of Computer & Engineering Consultants, Ltd. of Southfield, Michigan, provide a good basis for selecting a methodology:

1. Does the methodology identify the steps necessary to produce each deliverable of system development or evolution?

2. Does the methodology house and deliver the details necessary for developing or evolving systems?

3. Does the methodology simplify the systems development or evolution process?

4. Does the methodology encourage and provide the means to implement a standard approach to system development?

5. Can any aspect of the methodology be customized to meet specific standards and practices of the using organization?

6. Can changes to the methodology be verified as correct?

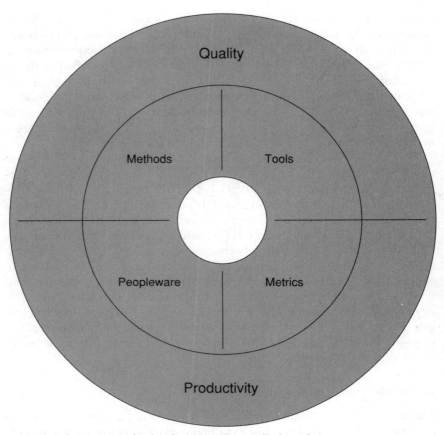

Figure 10.4   Layers to quality/productivity. (*Source: Techinsider*)

7. Does the methodology support current techniques and technology or is it based upon dated practices?

8. Does the methodology cover all aspects of systems activities?

9. Can the methodology be realistically followed by the systems organization or does it present overwhelming details?

10. Can cohesive pieces of the methodology be extracted for use on focused projects?

11. Is the methodology driven by the production of deliverables?

12. Is the methodology organized in terms of discrete methods that are linked by the deliverables they produce?

13. Does the methodology provide techniques that describe how to conduct its methods?

14. Can the methodology embody the standards and practices of the using organization?

15. Does the methodology identify the roles (types of job functions) that are involved in each method?

16. Does the methodology identify the support tools appropriate for the execution of each method?

17. Does the methodology allow for predefined paths that accomplish specific objectives?

18. Is the methodology expressed using formal models whose structural integrity can be automatically verified?

19. Can the methodology be expediently searched to retrieve methodology information?

20. Can select pieces of the methodology be published as project handbooks?

21. Can the methodology be ported to external software (tools)?

22. Is the methodology supported by a complete line of educational services?

23. Are services available to integrate the methodology with the standards, practices, and conventions of the using organization?

24. Is the vendor capable of demonstrating any aspect of the methodology on a real project?

25. Are services available to customize the methodology to incorporate the using organization's experiences?

26. Are services available to guide an effective rollout of the methodology?

For the most part, methodologies in use today reflect the realities of the time period in which they were created. But a lot has changed since the late 1970s. Hardware has become much more powerful and has been downsized to the desktop. A proliferation of programming languages and styles has descended upon the marketplace. But the most important change is that the applications being developed are a hundredfold more sophisticated than the simple payroll and accounting systems of a mere decade ago. Today's systems are real-time, multiuser, and often logic-bound. They launch space shuttles, command missile defense systems, and control billions of dollars through money transfer systems. For systems such as these, the 70–30 ratio is simply not good enough.

Object orientation is looming large as the solution for development ills. There is a problem, though, as alluded to in the last chapter. Most organizations aren't really using OO programming techniques. They may be using OO client/server tools, but for the most part organizations have yet to make the grand leap from Cobol to C++. To adopt OO analysis and design techniques seems, therefore, to be a partial solution. And although object orientation is currently being heralded as the panacea for the industry's productivity problems, this disjointedness is rather disturbing.

For a programming system to work its magic, it must be surrounded by the trappings of methodology. And for a methodology to induce productivity, it must be closely linked to a programming system. Notice, I use the term programming *system* rather than programming *language*. Programming languages connote the hard manual labor of hand-coding the nuances of a sophisticated and complex program—hardly the stuff of increased productivity. Even though CASE tools sporting code generators have been on the market for more than a decade, nearly 95 percent of all code continues to be generated by hand. It's true that most current code generators are simply not robust enough to generate code for real-world problems, but this fact alone is not solely responsible for lack of adoption of these tools. Mindsets have to change as well.

For decades, developers have been responsible for wholesale elimination of certain types of jobs from the global economy—going as far back as factory automation in the first quarter of this century. Yet it's been quite an uphill fight to eliminate any part, archaic or not, of the systems development *process*. Even though elimination of the painful and error-prone task of coding seems a natural way to spur productivity and increase the quality of the code ultimately generated, programming departments routinely inhibit any such improvement.

This may very well be a classic catch-22 situation. On the one hand, programmers and their managers are wary of the plethora of CASE-type tools that (1) appear to diminish the status of the programmer and (2) don't provide the full range of capabilities actually needed. On the other hand, software vendors—very much aware of the seemingly limited market potential (because of hesitant programming staffs) and of the vast complexity (to develop and support) of a full life-cycle tool—seem to be content to offer a patchwork quilt of solutions. While the vocabulary of CASE certainly seems to indicate a software solution for every phase of the life cycle, in reality the pieces are simply not "plug compatible." In spite of their claims, the leading CASE vendors simply have not yet developed a fully integrated life-cycle engineering and development environment that promotes both productivity of staff as well as quality of finished product. Perhaps programmers are rightly wary. Why should they give up their programming medals for only half a solution? Or perhaps we should turn away from the leading vendors and look elsewhere for a solution.

In point of fact, an engineering environment could go a long way toward solving some of the productivity problems that are now deeply entrenched in our current modus operandi. Setting aside some of the human issues such as good management and training, programming environments are much discussed, painstakingly planned, expensively implemented, but often disastrous.

Today's programming environments are little more than adaptations of the old 70–30 rule. They are mere automations of the old way of doing business—even if that business is programmed using the newer object-oriented techniques. If you take an old methodology and surround it with a series of tool fragments (upper CASE tool, lower CASE tool, editor, compiler, debugger, and so on), you wind up with a system of questionable quality and value. What's needed is a radical departure from the same old way of doing things.

Only a short decade ago, developers were building systems for one platform using one programming language. More than likely, these systems were batch and didn't have very heavy-duty requirements. This has changed to a world in which multiprocessing is commonplace, and distributed computing is the order of the day. Any engineering environment worth its name must provide a single uniform series of tools that enable developers to deploy to any number of platforms in any number of locations. In other words, it should be possible to have a set of techniques that work with any number of operating systems, programming languages, graphical user interfaces, and databases. This robust engineering environment should be able to handle C today, ADA tomorrow; or Oracle today, Sybase tomorrow. This engineering environment should be readily adaptable to change.

While tool functionality is most certainly high on the list of environmental attributes, perhaps even more importantly the systems engineering environment should be wrapped around a methodology that promotes quality and reliability.

An Object-Oriented Systems Specification Language

Object-oriented programming languages and environments were developed out of the need to find a way to realistically—and efficiently—model complex systems engineering problems. But while the syntax of the OO languages greatly expedited the code development process of some systems, the foundations of OO are hobbled by its dependence on traditional methodologies. Although some newer object-oriented methodologies are, of late, coming into vogue, the true test of the success of OO will be its ability to model real world problems. What this means is that OO must have the ability to model a business organization as easily as it does a trading system, a factory plant as completely as it does a missile launch system.

The major tenet behind OO is reusability. Therein lies its claim to increased productivity. While it is indisputable that software developers can dramatically reduce the amount of time it takes to develop a system by utilizing prewritten objects, for successful reuse a system has to be worth reusing.

The answer lies in finding a new approach for designing and developing systems which maximizes quality and reliability of the system as well as productivity of the process. There are two ways to accomplish this. One is curative and the other preventive. Curative means to obtain quality by continuing to test the system until the errors are eliminated, while preventive means not letting errors in in the first place.

Systems developed using traditional software engineering techniques, including object-oriented, have limitations which inherently preclude high degrees of reliability and productivity. Simply put, things happen too late. That is, they happen "after the fact" instead of "before the fact."

The following list describes some of the "causes and effects" of an after-the-fact methodology.

Integration. In defining requirements using traditional or even the more modern methodologies, data flow is usually defined using one method, state transitions another, dynamics another, and data structure using still another method. Once defined there is no way to easily integrate these disparate sets of requirements, especially between life-cycle phases. Perhaps even more damaging is the apparent inability to integrate the results of system development efforts when those efforts have been made using widely disparate tool suites. The result? The system is hard to understand, objects cannot be traced, and there is no correspondence to the real world.

Error propagation. A large number of errors are the result of incompatible interfaces that are discovered only after a considerable amount of development effort has already gone into the project. But even more errors are the result of the system development process itself. The result? Errors are propagated throughout the entire system from the very beginning with developers spending inordinate amounts of time taking the errors out "after the fact."

Change flexibility. Requirements are defined to concentrate on the application needs of the user but they do not consider that the user usually changes his or her mind. As a result, changes are not trackable and porting is "new development" for each new architecture, operating system, data base, graphics environment, language, or mode of system distribution (i.e., client/server). The result? Maintenance is the most expensive part of the life cycle.

Reusability. Requirements definitions lack properties to help find, create, and use commonality. All too often, reusability is only considered at the code level. Modelers use informal and manual methods to find ways to divide a system into its functional natural components, or blocks of components. The result? Redundancy instead of reuse.

Run-time performance analysis. A system is usually defined without considering how to separate it from its target environment. Design integrity is usually considered far too late in the process to have any impact. The result? You can't tell if a design is a good one until its implementation has failed or succeeded.

When critical issues are dealt with "after the fact," true reuse is ignored and system integrity is reduced at best. As a result, functionality is compromised.

A whole new way of looking at development

A methodology which solves these problems is the one that comes wrapped up inside Cambridge-based, Hamilton Technologies, Inc., 001™ systems engineering and software development environment.

When Margaret Hamilton was director of the Charles Stark Draper Laboratories at MIT, her projects ranged from the *Apollo* space mission to SkyLab. Developing human-rated projects carries the task of coding to the level of quality that ensures human survival in onerous conditions. But even in this demanding environment there were errors. In the 1970s Hamilton embarked on a stringent empirical analysis of the data collected from these programming efforts, particularly the errors. What she discovered became the basis for a new way of looking at development and ground zero for a new software tool. In effect, what Hamilton, and her company, Higher Order Software, created was the industry's very first CASE tool.

Over the past decade and a half, Hamilton and her new team of engineering gurus have honed and refined her original theory into something distinct and unique in our industry—a paradigm that promotes both quality and dramatically enhanced productivity. And when used in conjunction with the 001 systems engineering and software development environment, it could knock RAD, JAD, and every other current productivity-enabling device right out of the water.

The paradigm, Development Before the Fact, prevents errors from happening by resting on the two strong pillars of reusability and integration. Each portion of a system built under the Development Before the Fact paradigm is reusable, understandable, and seamlessly integratable. Blocks of error-free code can be continually reused and integrated together to create an infinite variety of systems, all of which experience the same extraordinarily high level of error reduction and productivity improvement. And Development Before the Fact goes way beyond these reliable blocks of code. The *mechanisms,* or infrastructure, that connect these reusable, error-free blocks are reliable and error-free as well. Hence, systems are inherently reliable and error-free—from the ground up.

With the Development Before the Fact paradigm a system inherently integrates its parts and the combinations of functionality using these parts. As a result, the system maximizes its own reliability and flexibility to change. A Development Before the Fact system can capitalize on its own parallelism, thereby maximizing the potential for reusing its own definitions. This enables a system built in this manner to support its own automation as well as its own run-time performance analysis. Ultimately, a Development Before the Fact system has the unique ability to understand the integrity of its own design.

Each system is defined with properties which control its own design and development. With this new paradigm, a life cycle inherently produces reusable systems because there is a decided emphasis on defining things right the first time.

The secret of the success of the paradigm lies in the language properties that are used to define Development Before the Fact systems. This language has the capability to define any aspect of any system and integrate it with any other aspect. These aspects are directly related to the real world. The same language can be used to define system requirements, specifications, design, and detailed design for functional, resource, and resource allocation architectures throughout all levels and layers of "seamless" definition, including hardware, software, and peopleware.

The language is used to define and integrate implementation-independent *function*-oriented decompositions with implementation-independent *object*-oriented decompositions. It defines and integrates these decompositions (control hierarchies) with networks of functions and objects. It can be used to define systems with diverse degrees of fidelity and completeness. A systems language with these powerful constructs, by its very nature, can easily support the rigorous demands of real-time, distributed, and client/server systems.

This language also has mechanisms to define mechanisms for defining systems. Although the core language is generic, the user "language," a by-product of a development, can be application-specific, since the language is semantics-dependent but syntax-independent.

Building a Development Before the Fact System

The first step in building a Development Before the Fact system is to define a model with the systems language described above. The model is then automatically analyzed both statically and dynamically (i.e., as an executable, simulated specification) to ensure a proper definition. The next step is to generate, from this same model, a complete and fully production-ready software implementation using a generic generator tailored for one of many possible environments (C, Ada, Motif, Sybase, etc.). What's important to note here is that generated software is tightly integrated. That is, there is total integration of the graphics—client/server as well as algorithmic components of the system. The resulting system can then be executed. If the desired system is software, the system can now be tested for user-intent errors.

Changes to application requirements are made to the requirements definition, not to the code. In fact, the code is never touched at all. Target architecture changes are made to the configuration of the generator environment, not to the code. A complete impact analysis is made available to both the designers and developers. Any changes to the system are then automatically regenerated to integrate with the rest of the already implemented system. If the real system is hardware or peopleware, the software system serves as a simulation upon which the real system can be based.

System definition

With the Development Before the Fact approach, every system is defined as an integrated, hierarchical, functional, and object-oriented network based upon a unique concept of control.[1] This approach is used throughout a life cycle starting with requirements and continuing with functional analysis, simulation, specification, algorithm development, analysis, system architecture, configuration management, software implementation, testing, maintenance, and reverse engineering. It is used by system engineers, software engineers, test engineers, managers, and end users; and it provides a framework of automation (shown in Figure 10.5) to aid the organization in focusing on defining and implementing process improvement (e.g., SEI Levels 1 through 5).[2]

Every model is defined in terms of functional hierarchies (FMaps) and type hierarchies (TMaps) which serve as convenient mechanisms to formalize the definition and/or design although, in effect, there is no real separation of data and function. Associated with each type in the TMap are primitive functions (i.e., methods). An object is a recursive system. FMaps can be used to create primitive functions that can be

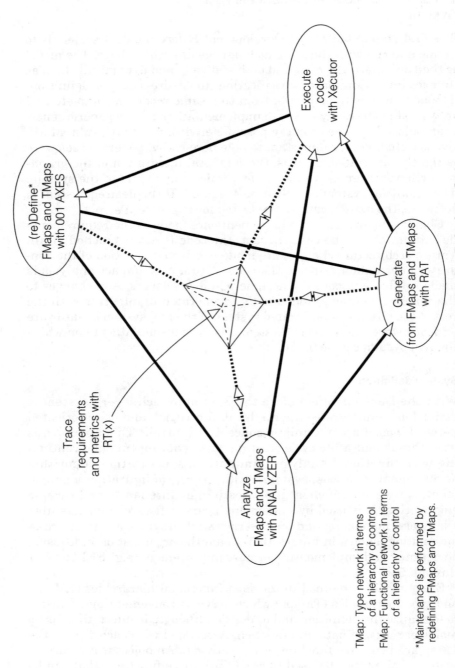

TMap: Type network in terms
of a hierarchy of control
FMap: Functional network in terms
of a hierarchy of control

*Maintenance is performed by
redefining FMaps and TMaps.

Figure 10.5 A framework based on development before the fact. (*Source: Hamilton Technologies, Inc.*)

Trace
requirements
and metrics with
RT(x)

(re)Define*
FMaps and TMaps
with 001 AXES

Execute
code
with Xecutor

Generate
from FMaps and TMaps
with RAT

Analyze
FMaps and TMaps
with ANALYZER

encapsulated to form new types on TMaps. FMaps and TMaps guide designers in thinking through their concepts at all levels of system definition and design. With these hierarchies, everything you need to know (no more, no less) is available. All model viewpoints can be obtained from FMaps and TMaps including data flow, control flow, state transitions, data structure, and dynamics. For example, an E-R (entity relationship) model is a subset of a TMap model, a data flow model is a subset of an FMap model, and a state transition model is a subset of a combination of an FMap and a TMap model. The good news is that all these system aspects are truly integrated in terms of FMaps and TMaps, as shown in Figure 10.6.

Typically, a team of designers will begin to define the problem and/or design a system at any level (this system could be hardware, software, peopleware, or some combination of these) by sketching a TMap of their application. This is where they decide on the types of objects (and the relationships between these objects) that they will have in their system. Often a Road Map (RMap), an index of FMaps and TMaps, will be sketched in parallel with the TMap.

Once an agreement has been reached on the TMap, the FMaps begin almost to fall into place for the designers because of the natural partitioning of functionality (or groups of functionality) provided to the designers by the TMap system. The TMap provides the structural criteria from which to evaluate the functional partitioning of the system (e.g., the shape of the structural partitioning of the FMaps is balanced against the structural organization of the shape of the objects as defined by the TMap). With FMap and TMap hierarchies, all system viewpoints are integrated. They inherently divide a system into an integration of function and OO components which naturally fit and work together.

All FMaps and TMaps are ultimately defined in terms of three primitive control structures: a parent controls its children to have a dependent relationship, independent relationship, or a decision-making relationship. A formal set of rules is associated with each primitive structure. If these rules are followed, interface errors are "removed" before the fact by preventing them in the first place. As a result, all interface errors (75 to 90 percent normally found during testing in a traditional development) are eliminated at the requirements phase. The use of the primitive structures supports a system to be defined from the very beginning to inherently maximize its own reliability.

Any system can be defined completely using only the primitive structures, but less primitive structures can be derived from the primitive ones and used to accelerate the process of defining and understanding a system. For example, user-defined structures including parameterized types can be created for asynchronous, synchronous,

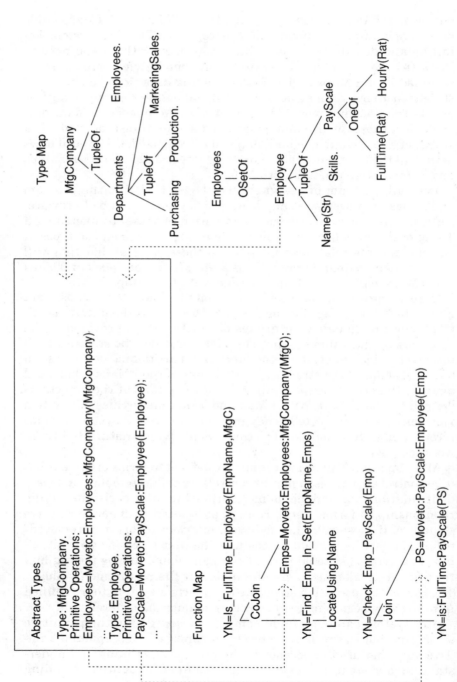

Figure 10.6 FMaps and Tmaps. *(Source: Hamilton Technologies, Inc.)*

and interrupt scenarios used in real-time, distributed systems. Similarly, information retrieval and query structures can be defined for client/server database management systems. Nonprimitive structures can be defined for both FMaps and TMaps. Rules for the nonprimitive structures are inherited from the rules of the primitive structures. Uses (i.e., instances) of each structure inherit the behavior of that structure. This behavior can change depending on the polymorphic properties of the structure itself and the context in which it is used. With the use of mechanisms such as defined structures, a system is defined from the very beginning to inherently maximize the potential for its own reuse.

Run-time performance analysis considerations

When designing a system environment, it is important to understand the performance constraints of the functional architecture. Another important consideration is to have the ability to change configurations rapidly and at will. A system is flexible to changing resource requirements if the functional architecture definition is separated from its resource definitions. The same language is used to define functional architectures, resource architectures, and the allocation of functional architectures to resource architectures. The allocation definition defines how the elements of the resource architecture are applied to the functional architecture.

Using a resource separation method, the functional architecture model can remain the same and therefore be reused for any resource architecture, as shown in Figure 10.7. The resource architecture models can also remain unchanged and become reusable. The only system that would change when going from one resource architecture to another would be the allocation architecture. The use of functional architecture constraints, along with the method of defining a functional architecture to be independent of its resource architectures, provides for a system to inherently support its own run-time performance analysis.

Object-oriented properties

Development Before the Fact systems are by their nature object oriented from the beginning. The definition space, corresponding to real world objects, is defined in terms of FMaps and TMaps. Objects, instantiations of TMaps, are realized in terms of OMaps. Executions of a system (i.e., instantiation of an FMap) are realized in terms of EMaps. From FMaps and TMaps, completely production-ready target system code or documentation is automatically generated and ready to

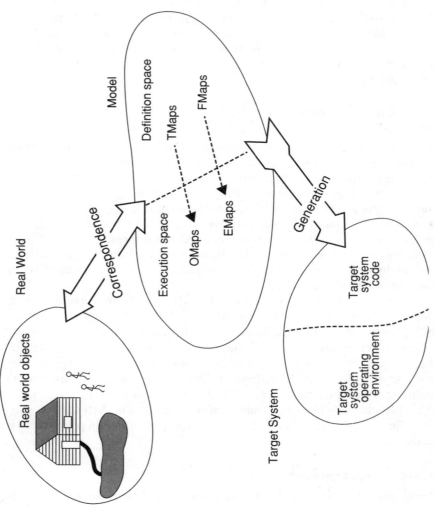

Figure 10.7 Multiplatform. (*Source: Hamilton Technologies, Inc.*)

180

execute. Systems are constructed in a tinker toy–like fashion. Such a technology changes the way software is developed just as word processing changed the way in which offices were managed. The building blocks are definitions, independent of particular object-oriented implementations (e.g., C++, Smalltalk). Properties of classical object-oriented systems such as inheritance, encapsulation, polymorphism, and persistence are supported with the use of generalized functions on OMaps and TMaps.

Results

Many systems have been designed and developed with the Development Before the Fact paradigm, including those which reside within manufacturing, aerospace, software tool development, data base management, domain analysis, transaction processing, process control, and simulation environments. Approximately a third of these efforts were system engineering projects, another third was composed of software development projects, while the remaining third were both systems engineering and software development projects. We have analyzed our results on an ongoing basis in order to understand more fully the impact that properties of a system's definition have on the productivity in its development (Figure 10.8).

An example of a system with a full life cycle is that which was developed for the National Test Bed during a rigorous comparison of three advanced methodologies, Development Before the Fact among them. The task at the center of the experiment was to develop a real-time, distributed, radar tracking system which consisted of a command center element, a number of radar elements, and a central simulation executive. This problem, representative of the type of problem required to be solved by system engineers and software developers on a daily basis within the defense community, is also indicative of the most complex and demanding problems that are required to be solved within the commercial arena (i.e., telecommunications, money transfer, client/server).

The results show that the Development Before the Fact approach clearly outperformed its competitors.[3] Where the Development Before the Fact team[4] was able to complete 90 percent of the specified problem in the narrow competition window, the statistics on its two competitors were a disappointing 75 percent and 50 percent, respectively.

Continuing measurements of the Development Before the Fact paradigm range between 10 to 1 and 50 to 1, depending on factors such as experience level of the systems engineer and/or software developer and the length of time the methodology has been in use.

Experience strongly confirms that quality and productivity increase with the increased use of Development Before the Fact properties and

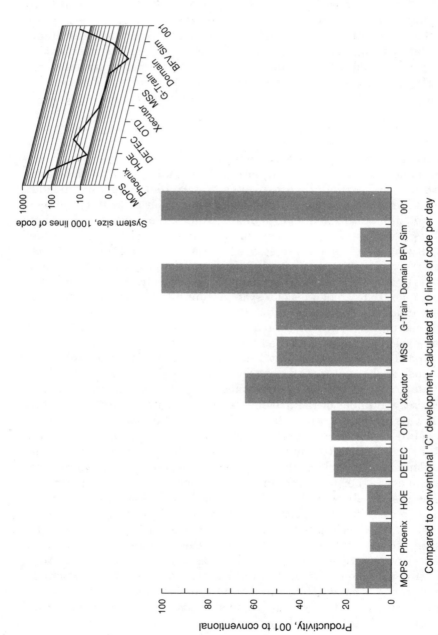

Compared to conventional "C" development, calculated at 10 lines of code per day

Figure 10.8 Productivity gains. (*Source: Hamilton Technologies, Inc.*)

its associated systems language. For the most part, this has to do with the inherent reuse capabilities of Development Before the Fact systems. Taken together, many of these properties can be mapped to a combined integration and abstraction of the best parts of some of the newer, yet more traditional, methods; each of these methods presented a partial solution and it was not possible to find a perfect mate to integrate it with to form a total system solution.

Yet systems developed with Before the Fact properties do not exhibit many of the known shortfalls of these methods. Further, implementation inefficiencies often resulted from taking an indirect path to a solution forced by attempting to integrate methods that are not a natural fit. These approaches still suffered from "after the fact" development. "After the fact" development is often redundant where reuse is abandoned for most of the life cycle. Productivity gains over traditional approaches can be significant with a before the fact paradigm since reuse is inherent.

The paradigm shift occurs once a designer realizes that many of the things that he or she used before are no longer needed to design and develop a system. For example, with one formal semantic language to define and integrate all aspects of a system, diverse modeling languages (and methodologies for using them), each of which defines only part of a system, are no longer a necessary part of the process. There is no longer a need to go to great lengths to reconcile multiple techniques with semantics that interfere with each other and then not be able to automatically produce complete production-ready systems.

Techniques for bridging the gap from one phase of the life cycle to another are no longer needed, since this approach is seamless. Techniques for maintaining source code as a separate process are no longer needed since the source is automatically generated from the requirements specification. Verification (i.e., the process of verifying that the implementation matches the requirements) becomes an obsolete process as well. Techniques for managing paper documents can be replaced by entering requirements and their changes directly into the requirements specification data base that supports the requirements, such as generating documentation from them. Testing procedures and tools for finding the majority of errors are no longer needed because those errors no longer exist. Programming can become an art relegated once more to a select few.

With Development Before the Fact, all aspects of system design and development are integrated with one systems language and its associated automation. Reuse naturally takes place throughout the life cycle. Because of these properties, a system can be automatically developed with high quality, high reliability and rapidly without a compromise in efficiency, completeness, or production readiness. It can be safely reused to increase even further the productivity of the systems developed with it.

The Development Before the Fact approach was derived from the combination of steps taken to solve the problems of the traditional after the fact approach. The solution is in the results.

References and Notes

1. M. Hamilton and R. Hackler, "001: A Rapid Development Approach for Rapid Prototyping Based on a System that Supports Its Own Life Cycle," IEEE Proceedings, *First International Workshop on Rapid System Prototyping*, Research Triangle Park, N.C., June 4, 1990.
2. W. S. Humphrey and W. L. Sweet, "A Method for Assessing the Software Engineering Capability of Contractors," CMU/SEI-87-TR-23, ESD/TR-87-185, SEI, Carnegie Mellon, Pittsburgh, Pa., September 1987.
3. Software Engineering Tools Experiment—Final report. Vol. 1, *Experiment Summary*. Department of Defense, Strategic Defense Initiative. Washington, D.C. 20301-7100.
4. The NTB experiment was designed to emulate the NTB environment, which consists of a series of distributed agency nodes. The node teams, which consisted of vendor representatives as well as representatives from member agencies, had a mix of expertise with tools, varying from novice to moderate amounts of experience. This combination of participants also met the requirement for a geographically separate development, to be followed by integration and centralized running of the experiment. Monitors were chosen to watch and observe both the node and the vendor teams' work during training and the experiment.

11

From Information to Knowledge

One of the reasons the computer hasn't produced the spurt of productivity that we all expected is that we are still dealing with bits and bytes of information. We still haven't learned how to turn it into certifiable knowledge. That's because most of us are still building traditional systems—that is, systems that provide merely tactical information—rather than smart systems that provide competitive advantage: systems that provide knowledge.

This chapter presents a series of case studies in the application of smart systems. You'll notice that they are all knowledge-based systems. I admit I'm biased toward artificial intelligence (AI). However, you don't always need AI to build smart systems. With today's crop of object-oriented tools, it's more than possible to build the smartest of smart systems.

For this chapter, forget the tools used to create the system, and instead concentrate on the substance of each system. They're not your traditional systems.

Transforming Information into Knowledge

Perhaps the industry with the largest share of traditional systems is the banking industry. No one personifies banking more, or has done more for the industry, than Citicorp's chairman emeritus Walter Wriston. In his 17 years as chief executive officer, he revolutionized the international banking environment. And one of the tools in his toolbox of change was the computer. With over a trillion dollars a day changing hands in the New York market alone, the banking industry is gearing up for an alliance between technology and strategy. Wriston envisions a banking environment in which the interface between user and machine permits easy access to complex information. Artificial intelligence, predicts Wriston, will become the norm and not the exception. He looks forward to a day when he can walk up to a smart system in a bank lobby that will be able to answer complex questions about his account. "Can I invest in a tax-free fund? Can I do brokerage transactions?"

Quaker Oats in Chicago was one of the first consumer goods marketers to realize the potential of strategic technology. More than 15 years ago it set up its own computer program to analyze some 2 billion facts about different products and competitors. Use of the system permitted the Quaker Oats people to understand this data and to draw insights from it. As a result, they moved to the number-one spot in such product categories as Rice-A-Roni and the ever-popular Aunt Jemima Pancakes. More recently they began to realize that new technology was making the system obsolete. So without hesitation out it went and in came Express MDB. With it the folks at Quaker Oats can perform the intricate "what if" analyses that will keep them number one.

This brand of filtering methodology is a technology very much in vogue as more and more entrepreneurial start-ups compete to slay the information dragon. MIT stepped in to become a knight in shining armor when it devised a novel way to separate the E-mail wheat from the chaff. For many of us, electronic mail messages rate right up there with junk mail. The MIT system found a novel way to categorize messages as top priority if they came from certain people or if they implied the need for a response within a few days. Joining this Knights of the Round Table is a former Lotus development executive. He started a company called Beyond Inc. based on just this technology. Lotus itself has its own mail sifter. NOTES uses graphical displays to permit senders to imprint distinctive logos on their electronic missives. You can direct your mailbox to turn up its nose at certain logos and permit others access. I suppose some enterprising start-up company will find a comfortable niche in producing counterfeit logos for gate-crashing. Or will we call it logo-crashing?

Filters work for more than just turning up your nose at an uninvited electronic guest. They are also mainstays in the marketing arena. For years marketers used technology to filter relevancies out of information glut. It started with the first totally computerized census back in 1970. The U.S. Census Bureau created demographic data on computer tapes, providing a plethora of information on neighborhoods right down to your very own city block. By the time the 1980 census rolled around these stats had ballooned into 300,000 pages of statistics. And a whopping ten times that amount sat patiently on computer tapes. Today the personal computer has put this same information on a desktop.

Some in the financial industry quickly followed suit. Investors Services, out of Bridgeport, Connecticut, has been collecting data for some 30 years. Today it manages Worldscope, an international database containing a wealth of information on some 5000 companies. The key here is smart filtering.

A company in Brookline, Massachusetts, seems to have found the key as well. Individual Inc. sifts through full text articles and pinpoints items of interest to its subscribers. "We are operating an information refinery that takes a broad stream of raw data and turns it into actionable knowledge," says company founder, Yosi Amram.

Dean LeBaron agrees to this approach. He was very much in the avant-garde in the middle 1970s. That's when he preached the use of computers to improve the quality of investing. Today Batterymarch Financial Management is one of Boston's leading money management firms, with a portfolio of over $11 billion. LeBaron runs Batterymarch as one large expert system. It's designed to operate the way an intelligent institutional investor would operate if put on a silicon substrate.

Wriston, LeBaron, and the rest of these folks recognized early on the advantages of using smarter technology. And all revel in number-one spots in their respective marketplaces. These companies have learned to distinguish between information and knowledge. The rest of this chapter will profile the development of several "smart systems" in the hope that you will begin to discern a pattern that can be applied to your own organization.

AI on Wall Street

What better place to start than in the den of the money lions. Wall Street grabbed onto the idea of intelligent systems in a big way back in the early 1990s. The goal? To make more money, of course. The financial markets are the most complex of systems, characterized by literally thousands of variables. While there are some shrewd wheeler-dealers around who trust their own intuition, for the most part Wall Street relies on superintelligent systems to make sense of all that chaos.

Oh, the joy of it all. To be on the floor of the New York Stock Exchange is to be at the center of the universe. The roar of the crowd, the scent of a fresh kill quickens the pulse and flushes the cheeks. But let's exit through the side door and walk down any street. Look, over there, in that tall gray limestone building. That's where all the real action is.

Behind locked doors a blinking, whirring gray box chugs away uninterrupted. A few feet away a shirtsleeved denizen of the Wall Street canyon stands watching this magic box perform its magnum opus. Suddenly the printer begins its dance and the Wall Street trading fiend scrambles to rip the report, ink still wet, from the printer. Running to the phone, our intrepid, but frazzled ivy league investment banker screams into the receiver, "Buy Disney!"

Oh, the joy of it all. To have a computer that is expert. Balderdash, you say? An expert computer can't beat the system! Well, in rebuttal to this rebuff, let's hop a plane to sunny Orinda, California, and visit some with Barr Rosenberg of Institutional Equity Management. In 2 out of the last 3 years Rosenberg's not-so-little expert system, which picks stock portfolios all by its very self, has beaten the market at its own game. That is, Rosenberg's total return in 1988 was 23.1 percent, versus a paltry 16.6 percent for the Standard & Poor (S&P) 500 stock index. Around the same time that he opened his company, Barr Rosenberg started working away on his expert computer system. It now works with over 200 factors, such as book values and price-to-earnings ratios, to spot undervalued companies. Rosenberg's system has figured in every conceivable factor.that makes the market tick— including economics, psychological factors, short-term technical market patterns, and maybe even the kitchen sink.

In October 1987, even the kitchen sink was in jeopardy as the market dropped over 500 points in the largest one-day decline in Wall Street's history. And now that the shock wave has passed, Wall Street has revved up, spending on the big iron and the stuff that goes with it—all in an often frustrating attempt to deal with market volatility, increasing globalization, and the proliferation of products on the market. So it's no wonder that some formerly heretic disbelievers are increasingly turning to artificial intelligence to get the upper hand. Expert system applications not only will be used but will be necessary to respond to the enormous amount of data generated by changes in the European financial markets. So predicts Joel Kaplan, a principal in the proprietary trading group at Morgan Stanley & Company, who's a big believer. In an otherwise normally secretive Wall Street atmosphere, Kaplan is unusually candid about the system he uses. Perhaps because Expert Tick is an unqualified success.

Expert Tick is used on Morgan's profit-and-loss desk. And it solves what had been a costly dilemma. When a trader is busy, often there's no time to review the real-time ticker and make sure that the trade just made is quoted. One of the best-known expert systems on the street, Expert Tick's goal in life is to look at all the information and figure out the likelihood that the trade hit the ticker.

Perhaps the best applications for smart systems are on the other side of the ticker. Almost every Wall Street firm has one or more projects under way to give the trader a toolset that will provide real-time insights and a Wall Street type of expertise. Larry Geisel, president of Intelligent Technology Group in Pittsburgh, talks of the chaotic world we live in and insists that computers and automation of investing, hedging, and tracking will yield strategic leverage.

To do this, firms large and small are investing in a combination of smart systems and advanced workstation technology. Prudential Bache's head of computer systems, William H. Anderson, calculates that most analytics folks are looking for 50 to 100 MIPS (millions of instructions per second). Combining artificial intelligence and the speed of workstation technology gives the trading room a heady combination. Workstations account for one out of every seven workstations sold. Citicorp Investment Bank, in New York, ordered 3000 DEC workstations. The purpose of this grand scheme is to tie its traders into a global network. This network provides each Citicorp trader with the ability to see prices on several markets. It also performs instantaneous portfolio analysis and even automatically executes orders. Yes, the integrated AI workstation approach is a potent weapon, with everyone up and down the Street clamoring to get a piece of the pie. Paine Webber's Hedging Assistant prototype made use of this strategy, as does the Chicago Board of Trade's Aurora system.

Perhaps the best use of AI would be as an embedded component in a quantitative investment algorithm. This could, in fact, change the face of the Street. And such a change is starting to take place now. Larry Geisel's Intelligent Technology Group has developed a model that does just this, and it appears to be extraordinarily powerful.

In the early 1980s, Charles Dym pioneered a quantitative investment theory that butted heads with the three theories most widely held: the modern portfolio theory, the efficient market theory, and the random walk theory. Dym's approach combined pattern recognition and probability theory. A test pilot of this theory did so well that it ranked in the second percentile of the annual Becker rankings. Later Dym joined Larry Geisel with the goal of taking his 14-year-old theory and adding two additional components: the experience of the last decade and the ITG expert system.

Not every Wall Street smart system needs to run on a workstation or needs the power of Charles Dym's theories. The most widely used smart systems are those that come off the shelf, and many of them run on PCs. Steward Pahn, a Thomson McKinnon broker who has over $350 million in assets under management, uses a product aptly called the Intelligent Trading System (ITS). Marketed by Providence Research in San Mateo, California, this product works within the level of risk agreed to by each investor and defines good investment opportunities. ITS comes in two parts. The first is based on 42 expert rules to arrive at a buy/sell decision by examining the stock price information fed to it each day. The second part of this expert system scrutinizes how much of the investor's money will be spent in executing the trade.

Brooks Martin, a stockbroker with Rodman and Renshaw in New York, says that he too "can't live without" his expert system. He uses a trio of products from AIQ systems, based in Incline, Nevada. While we'll look at length at StockExpert, the company markets two other expert products, IndexExpert and MarketExpert, that Martin raves about.

The list goes on. As early as 1987, Coopers and Lybrand worked with Drexel Burnham to develop an expert system that would have the capability of recognizing patterns in auditing trading data. Another innovator, Manning and Napier Advisors, out of Rochester, New York, found a novel way to handle its ever-increasing trading volumes. This novel approach includes using the Wang VS computer to build a rule-based system that guides the trader through the process of determining how many shares to buy and for what accounts. The system tracks many variables, including market value, position size, and objectives of the account. Not only does the system permit Manning to take advantage of smaller commissions and reduced commission rates, but it's much faster than the old way of doing business. The company likes to quote the statistic of the new 1.5 hour program versus the old 7.5 hours to complete a trading program. Even venerable old Merrill Lynch uses TradeCenter, an off-the-shelf expert trading package, to assist in making buy/sell recommendations.

There's great potential here. From front office to back office, the expert system is being used to stem the information crunch in the same way the computer itself was used to stem the great paper crush of the early 1970s. Perhaps the most exotic use of all is on the floor of a stock exchange.

Trading Theories Take on a New Ally: AI

> "Computers Challenge the Stock Market Gurus."
> "Bold New Theory Could Make Investors' Day."

These are headlines in the trades. Everybody, from the CEO on down to the mail clerk who dabbles in securities on the side, is waiting for smart trading systems to take their bow.

Charles Dym was a pioneer 14 years ago and he's a pioneer today at the Pittsburgh-based Intelligent Technology Group. With his AI-analytic approach to trading that seems to outperform the S&P 500, AI is getting a really good name on the Street.

Dym is your atypical Wall Street quant. He talks theory. About the modern portfolio theory, which is the darling of the Street. Here, it is stated, there is reason for everything. Even though there's reason and rationale to all things, these reasons may not be easily seen or understood. On the other extreme is the random walk theory, which insists that everything that happens is at random. Dym's novel theory falls somewhere in between. His approach is to first establish the odds and then utilize a consistent investment strategy.

"Human judgment is a wild card in my theory," Dym explains. His method works like a casino. It plays the odds and plays a consistent game, and the odds work progressively in the house's favor.

Dym's model works with the information that's readily available—no secret stuff here. The model decides rather than advises, which is somewhat of an anomaly in an era of "adviser" systems. The model buys groups of stocks and follows them consistently. It uses a buy-and-hold strategy, making recommendations quarterly. Dym's model also works with readily available hardware and software. Running on a DEC PDP-10 minicomputer, it is written in Fortran IV with the Oliver Database Management system as the expert system front end. Sporting a rule base of 30 rules, it works with downloaded information each night to bring up the answers bright and early in the morning.

Dym's theory defines risk as a function of the decision-making methodology used by the model. Choices are based on the probability that the model's portfolios will exceed the S&P 500 a certain percentage of the time. In certain of the model's portfolios it is expected that its performance will exceed the S&P 500 97 percent of the time. Dym believes that risk and reward are inversely proportional to each other and not symmetrical as other theories tend to be. Risk is based on a probabilistic analog in which a continuous, consistent strategy is played and to which the advantage steadily accrues. Although the behavior of one individual stock may be random, the behavior of groups of stocks is considered to be probabilistic rather than random. This will produce stable behavior, and this model's logic understands this behavior. Dym's model also understands the three major groups of players in the market. The fundamentalists, the technical analysts, and the modern portfolio theorists collectively represent stable behaviors probabilistically.

Since Dym's expert-system-infused trading strategy works like a charm, and since it is so radically different from the way traditional fundamental research and technical analysis are done, this is one expert system that could forever change the face of the Street.

To Hedge or Not to Hedge

There they sit. The gamblers. Eyes glued to the gaming table. Millions are lost and won in the flicker of an eyelash. Beads of perspiration quickly wiped aside with damp handkerchiefs. Knots in the stomach. Eyes red with fatigue. Minds calculating the odds. Making quick decisions to hedge their bets. This game is not played out in Atlantic City; it's played out 20 stories above Wall Street. And the gaming table is the block trading desk.

Traders have to have strong stomachs and nerves of steel. After all, they're putting their firm's capital on the line in the name of institutional trading. The smart ones hedge. Think of a seesaw. Little Joe jumps on but unless his little friend hops onto to the other end, Little Joe will stay firmly planted to the ground. Once Little Nell is enthroned, they both giggle happily, balanced perfectly. A shrewd trader will try to counterbalance a large block trade with a combination of products such as options and index futures. This lessens risk and protects the block desks from the erratic movement of the markets.

The trader is only human. Just making it through the tumult of a typical trading day is cause for celebration. To ask a trader to perform complex statistical calculations in rapid-fire time amid all this furor is to seek the impossible.

The smarter brokerage firms recognize the value of hedging but also see the impracticability of asking their already harried traders to perform the necessary calculations to arrive at a hedging decision. The more innovative firms are at least trying. And at least one of them made the grand attempt to install something a bit elegant.

In late September 1987 the capital market systems group at Paine Webber in New York decided to expert systematize the art of choosing a hedging strategy. There is no single strategy but an array to choose from. Selecting among these alternatives is a process involving complex quantitative analytical methodologies.

W. Leo Hoarty, then head of the capital market systems group, was presented with a twofold problem. Problem one involved the necessity of "cleaning up" the typical crammed desks of the traders. Traders need instant access to data that typically is displayed on various and diverse terminals. So good idea number one was to integrate all these services under one roof. For the prototype the group voted for the UNIX-based Sun workstation. This decided, a more difficult decision needed to be made: How to turn the often judgmental knowledge of the art of the hedge into a coherent and working system? A development tool was needed that would be easy to work with as well as easy to change, and that would accommodate this sort of specialized knowledge. Paine Webber decided against conventional coding languages, forecasting a nightmare in maintenance and long lead times for development.

Instead the company opted for an expert system. Since Paine Webber had little or no expertise in the building of rule-based systems, it opted to speed up to the top of the learning curve by hiring an outside consulting firm. Integrated Analytics of Los Angeles was chosen to do the hard part—the knowledge engineering.

Within 2 months a working prototype was built, and within 8 months the system was fielded out for beta testing. Paine Webber chose a narrow domain: only one trader handling up to eight stocks. And this most certainly had a lot to do with the speed of prototype development. However, the ease of use of the expert system tool, which permits rapid insertion, deletion, or change of rules, certainly account-ed for something.

Paine Webber shrouded this project in mystery. The company believed that the expert system methodology would most certainly add an extra edge to the competitive sword it carried. So officials were nec-essarily vague about the details of the Hedging Assistant. However, Integrated Analytics published a paper called "Intelligent Trading Systems," which discusses an anonymous firm that clearly suggests Paine Webber ownership.

This paper describes a network of workstations on which traders state the symbol and size of the block they wish to hedge. The system processes through a series of alternative evaluative algorithms and selects up to four alternatives that reflect the current market as well as adhere to the trader's stated preferences. This is all done in under 4 seconds, which is the absolute maximum response time for a system in a high-pressure trading environment.

And high pressure it is, especially after the crash of 1987 and the corrections of 1989. We're talking $25 million in losses for the year for the typical big-league firm. So it's no wonder that wise brokerage man-agements began looking for a better way to handle something as imprecise and inconsistent as individual hedging strategies.

After the initial flurry of activity and publicity surrounding the Hedging Assistant, the system appears to have been put out to the AI-pasture, waiting to be resurrected during the next market boom.

The Watchdog

Washington Square Advisors (WSA) manages over $6 billion. With a client asset base of such magnitude, this subsidiary of Northwestern National Life Insurance Company decided to use an AI solution to the problem of analyzing the bond market to minimize losses and maxi-mize revenues.

Before the decision was made in 1987 to proceed with development of the system, which was dubbed the Watchdog, two senior financial analysts were given a seemingly impossible task: to screen voluminous and quite complex financial data on individual companies of interest. The process required some 15 ratios to be applied. The two analysts searched out increases and decreases of these ratios in an attempt to predict future performance. They attempted to discover causes for ratio fluctuations. They then used this information in their evalua-tions for each company, which in turn led to buy/sell recommenda-tions. The financial analysts really needed some tool to help them do this process faster and better. As one WSA analyst put it, "We just can-not process all of this information in our heads!"

Since this was the first endeavor into AI, project manager Chris Evers wanted to build a system that not only was cost-effective but would also serve as a base for future AI development efforts. Toward this end, an outside AI company was chosen both for its experience at knowledge engineering and for its AI toolset.

In October of 1987, a notable date for the world's securities and bond markets, a PC-based investment watchdog system that would keep an eye on current and potential holdings was given the go-ahead. The only caveat was that it had to be complete and show demonstrable value by the end of the year. And that was only 3 months away.

Apparently PEAKSolutions, based in Minneapolis, Minnesota, was up to the challenge. Using the KEYSTONE Expert System Development Environment from Technology Applications, the team managed to pull together an elegant solution that belies its short time frame. The system was developed to act as an assistant to financial analysts who were not very computer literate. It had to be able to access external files such as a commercially available database containing current information on over 7000 companies. It needed to have a robust form of knowledge representation and inferencing mechanisms to perform the type of financial ratio analysis that was now being done by the expert analysts.

The PC-based KEYSTONE product appeared to possess all the above and more. KEYSTONE provides many of the capabilities of the toolsets that traditionally have run on workstations or minis. These include object orientation, use of production rules, mouse-driven graphic displays, and an underlying LISP environment which the programmer has access to.

It was envisioned that the Watchdog would have the capability of real-time access to the corporate financial data of over 7000 companies. For each company, the user would have the option of selecting different time periods to narrow the financial analysis. At this point, the Watchdog would analyze the performance of each company, using the same methodology that the human analysts had been performing for years. This in-depth financial analysis would be coupled with the subjective judgment of the human analysts.

This objective was obtained during the knowledge engineering sessions performed by PEAKSolutions. In addition, the knowledge base was made even smarter by loading in the determined causes of previous ratio fluctuations. The system's output is a screening report which shows changes in performance of each company in various sort categories as well as more detailed reporting on each specific company.

PEAKSolutions configured the system into five integrated knowledge bases. Three of the five knowledge bases contain explicit information on how the financial analysis is performed. The fourth and fifth,

WDUSER and Watchdog, control the user interface and the current state of the entire system respectively.

The WDCREDIT knowledge base contains information about the companies which are to be analyzed. Since KEYSTONE is an object-oriented system, objects are used to great advantage here by defining each company as an instance object. Each company object contains both financial and human judgment about the company.

The WDDATA knowledge base contains the specifics of the methodology of financial analysis. Showing its well-integrated nature, WDDATA is able to access WDCREDIT to access financial data about a particular company. Once the data is obtained, the financial analysis of the company can be performed. Here, demons are employed to activate the actual calculation of the financial ratios.

Upon completion of financial analysis, the results need to be analyzed to determine a company's financial performance over time and to project financial performance into the future. This normally human subjective analysis is performed by employing another knowledge base. WDRULES use production IF...THEN rules to approximate the formerly manual judgment applied by the human experts.

The WSA team spent under $100,000 and fewer than 3 months creating a system that had immediate and enormous payback. A human analyst takes over 100 hours to perform this set of procedures for 80 companies. Watchdog takes under 1 hour, proving the point that a little money and a lot of expertise and creativity can go a long way.

The Banking Connection

From Citibank's natural language money transfer system to Chase Lincoln's financial planning system to credit analysis to real estate appraisal to mortgage loan analysis, the depth and breadth of these applications is staggering. That's probably because the type of work that banks do and the numbers of transactions that flitter through their systems are staggering too.

A survey from the National Council of Savings Institutions displayed some pretty interesting statistics. This survey looked into the back offices of 409 member institutions with assets between $50 million and $5 billion. It showed that the banking industry is, and has always been, very reliant on computer technology to service its vast information needs. More than 65 percent of these member banks use automated teller machines. And a whopping 79 percent have automated their platform areas, showing a banking emphasis of placing smart technology within a customer's reach. Fred White, a vice president of Furash and Company, Washington, D.C., which performs consulting to banks and thrifts on technology topics, says that even the most technophobic CEO knows that the computer is the lifeblood of the operation.

The new banking buzzwords call for competitive advantage and the necessity for banking institutions to reach for higher and higher levels of technology.

In today's hostile banking environment banks are no longer assured of the profits of the past and are faced with regulatory changes, competition, and unending mergers and acquisitions. Technology is needed for more than just competitive advantage—it's needed for survival.

Banks need to push away from the tactical data processing of the past. Here the emphasis is in pushing reams of paper through the bank. They need to look to strategic computing. Clark and Wolfarth[1] make recommendations to apply technology in the areas of managing customer information, developing asset-quality tracking, and providing expense control. Perhaps tracking asset quality will provide the biggest bang for the buck in application of technology. Here the overriding concern is to control risks and evaluate asset alternatives. Using technology for competitive advantage can also be applied in evaluating asset alternatives, monitoring nonperformance, and performing impact analyses on customer activities.

An Expert Foreign Exchange System

Money. A delightful topic. Walking about a foreign exchange trading room and hearing the babble of the trading—"50 million deutsche marks," "100 million yen"—makes a visitor tingle with anticipation. The amounts are so astronomical and the pace so rapid-fire, the uninitiated get the distinct impression that this is just so much monopoly money.

The foreign exchange environment

For the foreign exchange trader, this is serious business. The world of the trader is small. Often a lot of people are crammed into very small dealing rooms. Shoulder to shoulder they sit, stand, and sometimes jump up and down acting and reacting to people and blinking equipment. A stressful environment, this. Sometimes six screens are simultaneously flashing information on currency rates and other market data. Pages upon pages of information stream by. Under the glow of these displays are the trader's connection to the outside world. Often, 120-line telephone boards are not even enough, so the intrepid trader installs yet new outside lines to reach clients quickly.

And it is quickly that these traders must react, for they cannot afford the luxury of deep analysis. In the bat of an eyelash they must scan and understand volumes of data, assess the historical trend of this data, discard unnecessary information, and finally reach a simple yes or no answer. To sell, to buy.

No equanimity here. Traders have been known to skip lunch, glued to their displays, eyes red and bulging, waiting for an opportunity. And when it comes, they seize it and are pleased with being right somewhere around 60 percent of the time. It's the other 40 percent that's the killer, however. Traders have been known to go out for an innocent lunch to find, upon their return, that the market did a turn-around and a large amount of money was lost. So many telephones have been ripped out of trading rooms by furious traders that *Ma Bell* has a franchise on the trading floor.

It was to this environment that Manufacturer's Hanover Trust (now Chemical Bank) decided to look for technical innovation. The develop-ment of the Technical Analysis and Reasoning Assistant (TARA) is a case study in how to do everything right in building an AI-based system.

Foreign Exchange trading is a prime banking profit center. It's a legal form of gambling in which you try to forecast which way the price of a particular currency is going. Forecasting is a tricky process. Traders have two techniques that they use to peer into the crystal ball. Fundamental analysis studies such esoteric factors as the world economy, political events, and even market psychology to predict the supply and demand for a particular currency. On the flip side, technical analysis uses the tech-niques of charting and statistical methodologies to forecast on the basis of historical trend analysis. Neither method is practiced to the exclusion of the other, and neither approach has any set formula. Both often rely on the experience and gut instinct of the trader.

It's these gut instincts that Manny Hanny wanted desperately to capture. So a team of heavy hitters was established that could bring the dream of TARA to life.

How "smart" infiltrated the trading room

Back in the late 1980s, the trading room management team took Tom Campfield off the line. Tom, a vice president in the investment bank-ing sector, was one of the more senior traders at the bank. His goal was to seek out innovative technological solutions to the problem of enhancing the trading process. This one act—taking Tom off the line—set Manny Hanny up for the success it ultimately achieved. Tom rep-resented the highest level of knowledge in the trading area. He was a most valuable resource, with his hands-on experience plus his acade-mic credentials in international finance and electrical engineering.

A few miles away, the technology department at Manny Hanny offered a position to Elizabeth Byrnes. With her doctorate in clinical psychology, the bank bought themselves an expert in eliciting knowl-edge from human confusion. The successful development of TARA began with the joining of forces of the trading and technology departments.

Members of the newly formed TARA team decided to do an experiment. They knew that expert systems had been developed successfully before. They had some, but not all, of the ingredients of success. They did have a recognized and willing expert in Tom. The area of knowledge they wished to capture was limited to foreign exchange trading, which was a nice, narrow domain. And they possessed substantial documentation on the process of trading. What they didn't have was a manageably sized database. With live feeds of thousands of pages of data a day, the problem of data access within a reasonable window of time became a cause célèbre to the team. And what the team had too much of was fuzziness. In the world of trading, no two experts agree, each relying on his or her intuition. In fact, many traders are so superstitious that the dealing room is filled with fuzzy bears, Gumbys, and the like, all rubbed, patted, and tossed into the air for luck.

TRADER 1: Why did you sell deutsche marks?

TRADER 2: Because I had the feeling the DM was going to depreciate.

TRADER 1: Why did you feel it was going to depreciate?

TRADER 2: Well, I just spoke to my friend Joe at Salomon Brothers and he said…and then I spoke to my friend Maria at Chemical who does a lot of dealings with deutsche marks, and we just got this feeling that the DM was going to go down.

Sifting through this haze of superstition, gut instincts, and inarticulate traders was stupendously hard.

The prototype

The fearless TARA team spent 3 months in interviewing the traders— 3 months of pulling methods out of the words of the traders. By June of 1987 a working prototype was presented to management. In 1987 the foreign exchange trading department had a comfortable income of $161 million. Management decided that if the system could produce as little as a 1 percent increase to this income, TARA could survive. Manny Hanny also knew that virtually every foreign exchange dealing room on the Street was looking into AI. So it decided to pursue TARA for two simple reasons: honest GREED and competitive advantage.

The TARA team set about looking to enhance the prototype to boost the deal success rate of the trader from the level of 60 percent it now hovered at. The team's motto was "Maximize good trades and minimize bad trades." But the team had a problem. Impatient management. A working system had to be installed by December of 1988. A very short time frame indeed. To accomplish a very complex undertaking in a very short amount of time, the team members needed to make quick decisions and sometimes compromise on solutions that were less than perfect.

Luck was on their side, however, during the initial prototype period. They did make the correct decisions. They had selected a high-power and expensive Symbolics workstation. With its 19-inch monitor, TARA is able to process all that streaming trading data in as many as 50 windows at a time. That's a lot of machine power. The psychological and technical considerations were overwhelming. Data is coming into the system in video form. Previously this data was display only. Now it had to be captured and stored in the appropriate window so the trader could activate the screen on whim. The data also had to be made accessible to the expert programs that used these feeds as input to the "smart forecaster" that was the core of the TARA system. And all this had to be done in a window of less than 3 seconds.

To accomplish this end, the team used heavy-duty software. While most of TARA was written in LISP, Intellicorp's KEE was used for inferencing and knowledge representation. The knowledge representation scheme used was the rule. At the outset of the project, this knowledge base consisted of some 350 rules, of which about 175 were related specifically to currency trading. The rules analyze both technical and economic factors. The technical factors can be considered the dos and don'ts of trading, while economic factors use modeling algorithms. It is only after both analyses, technical and economic, are completed that a trading recommendation is made. KEE's ability to both backward- and forward-chain through the rule base is used to great advantage when the trader wants to review the rationale behind the expert system recommendation.

And sandwiched between the knock-your-socks-off workstation display and the state-of-the-art software was the trader. All dealers have their own styles. Some use the Gumby approach to trading; some use analytical methods. So TARA had to be flexible enough to open all sorts of doors and windows so the dealer could use the system in many different ways.

A working system

Using a rich graphical interface to simulate the foreign exchange trading environment, TARA currently is a deployed real-time system. It can be used in two modes: as a skilled assistant and as an experienced colleague. With its knowledge base of both technical and fundamental trading strategies, TARA can assist in evaluating any of the 30-odd technical trading models stored in its innards. It tracks multiple currency, monitors bond and interest rates, runs algorithms, and fires rules to interpret these models. Net, TARA makes recommendations on whether to buy, sell, or hold a particular market position. As the price of a currency changes, TARA is instantly made aware of it through the diligent monitoring of the live data feed. Appropriate rules and algorithms are triggered, and recommendations and alerts are flashed across the workstation display.

Like a game of tic-tac-toe, a technical model of any particular currency is composed of Xs and Os. The Xs represent increases in price and the Os, decreases. The model filters out insignificant price movements to permit the trader to zero in on the beginning and end of the trend. Each X or O represents a unit of price.

Manny Hanny didn't want to spend huge sums of money on just mimicking currently existing technical charting programs. It wanted to lay a foundation of knowledgeable analysis of this data by encoding technical trading rules which know how to use these charts to trigger a buy-sell-hold recommendation.

TARA does not capture all the instinct of fundamental analysis. It does not yet contain all the rules necessary to handle the unforeseen economic, business, and political problems which make the market so volatile and mesmerizing. But it has been successful. When TARA was unveiled in May of 1988, at first the traders were wary of this large, blinking, and talkative box. When recommendations made by TARA proved to be accurate, the traders passed them off as so much beginner's luck. Gradually, one and then another trader began to sidle over to the workstation and sneak a peek. These peeks turned into glances and the glances into steady use of the system.

TARA is at Manny Hanny to stay. It successfully achieved its goal of increasing the bottom line by 1 percent. In fact, the real increase, although secret, was intimated to be considerably more. With its success came a clamoring for more. TARA is an example of expert systematizing the front line of foreign exchange processing. Let's now take a walk over to Chemical Bank in New York to see an expert system with a slightly different slant on foreign exchange trading.

The Citibank Money Transfer Parser

Yen. Dollars. Pesos. What a nice ring to these words. And sometimes words have a way of getting all jumbled up on messages. Think back some years ago. In the classic sci-fi movie *Close Encounters of the Third Kind* the skies were darkened by the enormity of an alien spacecraft. It was kind of common as spacecraft go. You know, oval with blinking lights. What was different was its attempt to communicate with us lowly earthlings. The aliens, which turned out to be skinny little bald creatures, attempted to speak to us via blinking lights and music. This message was a sort of intergalactic Morse code. Well, the humans on the ground looked up at this monster spaceship in awe and scratched their heads trying to figure out just what the aliens were getting at.

Getting at the Gist

Getting at the gist of the message was terribly important to our visiting sci-fi crowd, for it meant world peace and galactic harmony. Back on earth getting to the gist of the message means money to hundreds of banks that wire billions of dollars in the thousands of funds-transfer messages that are Telexed criss-cross the globe each day.

At Citibank the crew in the institutional bank international service management department would have done marvelously well in interpreting the musical message of our little alien visitors. Each person in this unusual entourage seems to have a musical alter ego. The lead ego plays keyboards and acts while the rest of the group either act or sing, or play the harp. This isn't as unusual as it sounds.

Expertise in the artificial intelligence branch of natural languages requires a unique perspective. After all, what kind of person likes to sit and look at a word and mutter, "I know that this word means two different things in these two contexts. What are all the other contexts?"

The precision of musicianship coupled with the love of the fluidity of the human language makes for fireworks in the application of natural language. Why is natural language needed for funds transfer? In a word, the answer is marketing. A second answer here is customers. Bank customers like to take the easy way out. They're paying big bucks to the banks to move money from one account to another. They want to do this transfer as easily and quickly as possible. They do not want to be encumbered with rigid formats and procedures. They just want to type an English message on a Telex and press GO:

"Pay through Chase for the account of San Juan Bank to the account of John Doe."

"Pay to John Doe of San Juan Bank through Chase."

There are as many ways for a message to be written as there are tentacles on aliens from Mars. Conventional programming systems, those that do accounts payable and human resources, can't cope with the vagaries of the English language. When the study of AI opened the door for use of natural languages in business, the big banks did a jump-start and forged ahead into the heady world of international funds transfer.

Citibank jumped into the deep end of the pool in the institutional banking area about 5 years ago. The forward-thinking Citibank executives decided that natural languages could be the answer to the question of how to process the thousands of garbled funds-transfer messages received by the group each day. They wanted to develop a smart system that could determine whom to debit, whom to credit, what reference numbers to use, and what account numbers to use—all within a short period of time.

So an AI project was funded. As was the way in the mid-1980s, Citibank did a search of outside consulting firms that could do the project. At the time, AI was surrounded by a cloud of mysticism. AI was unique and sexy, and couldn't possibly be done by your everyday programming Joe. Citibank fell into the trap that so many commercial houses had already fallen prey to: the "Can't possibly do it unless you have a Ph.D. from MIT" trap.

When Dr. Expert was finally hired, he was held in such high esteem that the everyday ordinary practicalities of system management were discarded, or at least overlooked. No system planning. No documentation. The team flailed and Citibank failed.

Like the mythological phoenix, Citibank resurrected itself. Resurrection came in the form of a young natural language expert transplanted to New York from California. Greg Parkinson is a guru. An expert in LISP and one mean keyboard player. He also likes to talk in his own disarming way about the events leading up to the successful implementation of his series of natural language systems. Greg was hired to pull Citibank out of a hole. Citibank had spent a goodly sum and had little to show for it.

When our hero arrived he was told, "There are a lot of people who don't believe that anyone can do AI without a Ph.D. And no one with a Ph.D who's smart enough would want to work for the bank. So that's why we have to go to these consulting companies. We don't believe that. We believe that, properly managed, these systems can be successful and that someone who knows what he's doing and has a fair amount of experience can achieve as much or more than a person who has a Ph.D. from MIT. But the way we're going to prove this is by getting the system done in 3 months." Quite a mouthful.

Well Greg walked right into it, didn't he? Evidently he's made of the right stuff because he achieved success, but not without a few sleepless nights. The first problem was the AI tool that was at Citibank at the time. A good natural language tool is many things. At a minimum you would want to have the ability to put in word definitions and patterns. The tool that Citibank had was your very basic pattern matcher. Greg and friends worked long and hard at giving the tool more intelligence. They gave it the ability to do contextual understanding. They gave it the ability to do generalization.

Alpha searching

Greg found that a lot of mythology had been built up around the tools that had been provided by the consulting companies. Part of this excess baggage was Citibank's Alphasearch interface. This slightly smart program was written to compensate for the often nebulous manner in which bank customers write the name of the sending or receiving bank in the message. For example, a bank in Tokyo would send a money transfer to Joe at Citibank New York. Which Citibank? Operators at the receiving end spent much time in looking up the left-out information. The original Alphasearch was left untouched for 2 years. The users, however, compiled a list of over 200 items that were wrong with it.

Now rewritten, this smarter version of Alphasearch hits the right button between 80 to 95 percent of the time. Not your ordinary name lookup function, it uses natural language methodologies to do spelling corrections, expand abbreviations, understand synonyms. It knows that the Commercial Bank of Ghana is the same as Banque Commerciale de Ghana. It knows that Chem Bank is short for Chemical Bank. It also knows that Security Pacific is not enough information. Is it Security Pacific National Bank or Security Pacific Asian Bank?

Picking out the right city in a message is even more difficult than figuring out the right bank name. The secret of a successful money transfer is the interpretation of both bank name and city. You get a message, "Swiss Bank Zurich pay through Chase New York." A person viewing this message would immediately interpret the message as pay through the Chase New York Bank, which is a bank name.

For the computer, it's not so easy. Remember, it's looking for two banks and two cities. In this case it could interpret New York as a designation rather than as part of the bank name. And then there's the problem of messages that contain complete addresses and the street names within these addresses that contain cities. How about "New York Avenue, Chicago, Illinois"? As in all things automated, there is a danger that this smart system is too smart and will spell-correct these addresses into something totally different from what they're supposed to be. To compensate for this, Citibank provides staff members to verify each one.

Structured versus unstructured messages

An average money transfer message is one page long. All messages that are routed over the Telex are unstructured, free-form English of approximately one page in length. SWIFT is another method of sending instructions across the wire. The SWIFT service forces a structure on messages sent across the wire. Given the structured SWIFT format and the unstructured Telex format, bank customers sometimes garble the two. So what you get is pseudo-structure typed into the Telex. Since the SWIFT format is a bit like English Morse code, there is a great potential for system confusion. So the team wrote what it calls a shunt program to determine which format the message is in and to pass it to the appropriate processing program.

With all this expertise in funds-transfer message deciphering, it's no wonder that the bank decided to expand its horizons and use natural language technology to aid in understanding reimbursement claims messages. Here the system analyzes a rather free-form message of the ilk "I didn't get my money." The system determines whether or not this claim is a new one or an old one and then routes the message to the appropriate human staff member at Citibank.

The user's reaction

And what do these humans at Citibank think of their smart computer systems? As Parkinson so delicately puts it, "Some users understand, some users don't." Some users did understand that this was a fuzzy process. No such thing as 100 percent accuracy. You're always dealing in percentages. Many users are quite uncomfortable with this notion. They were born and bred in an era of "The computer is always right." It takes time to make them understand that if you have less than 100 percent accuracy it doesn't mean that it's broken. Still, many distrusted the system to the point of backing out of a release of the system when a very large error was made. The problem was: Whose mistake was it—people, machine, or both?

At the same time that this particular release of the AI system went in, the bank began receiving messages from a new bank customer. This customer had a whole new way of sending in messages, complete with uniquely formatted dates. A whole slew of payments were incorrectly sent out by Citibank on the wrong date because of the way these messages were interpreted by the system. Well, the head of the department blew a gasket and the system was sent to the corner with a dunce cap. After careful investigation it was found that the system was making the same mistakes as the human operators. So our little dunce was called back from the corner and forgiven.

What Citibank learned

What did Citibank learn from its foray into the wild and woolly world of natural language systems? Right off the bat it learned that the best idea was to manage consultants yourself. Don't let them run wild and bypass normal system controls just because the comfort level with the technology is low or because everyone's in awe of the sheepskin diplomas owned by the guru who was hired. Manage. Manage. Manage.

Brace the staff to handle less-than-perfect results. In natural language systems you're always dealing in percentages. Greg Parkinson recommends determining up front just what the minimally acceptable percentage is so that you have an adequate return on investment. This percentage is different for every system. In funds transfer, a minimally acceptable percentage would be somewhere around 99 percent. However, in a tourist information system, for example, an acceptable rate could be far lower—perhaps 85 percent. The more important the system, then, the higher the rate.

Using natural language techniques in deciphering funds-transfer messages will become a standard in the financial services industry. At the same time, of course, any AI-laden trading system is also bound to become the norm. However, it is in the area of credit analysis that the banking community will find AI techniques to offer the power punch.

And Now for Credit Analysis

A man strode into a bank and asked to borrow $100,000.

The loan officer handing him an application said, "Certainly, sir. Can you give me a statement?"

"Yes," said the man. "And you can quote me. I'm very optimistic!"[2]

Ah, the smell of money! Or nowadays, plastic. Open any wallet and out will fall two American Express cards, one personal and one corporate, two Visa cards, two Mastercards, and a slew of various department store charges. Americans have taken to buying things on credit like an oinker takes to a mudbath. We revel in it.

Read $613 billion. That's how many dollars we owed to banks, finance companies, and assorted other credit grantors in 1987. And quite a large portion of this debt can be considered, er, deadbeat. So what's a poor financial company to do?

Banks, finance companies, and the like are in a tight bottleneck in their race to compete for mortgage, charge card, business—ad infinitum—credit dollars. The bottleneck occurs when the loan goes out for credit review. While these credit institutions really do want to grant you the loan, they need to be extra cautious just whom they grant credit to.

The art and science of projecting the creditworthiness of individuals and investors is called *credit analysis*. Here the underwriter attempts to piece together a financial puzzle consisting of many, many pieces. If it's a mortgage you're after, the underwriter looks at such things as your income and debts as well as the type of neighborhood the house or apartment is in. If you're a business, the underwriter looks at revenue, assets, liabilities, cash flow, and a host of other minutiae. The object here is to grant the maximum number of loans with the minimum percentage of bad debt.

This takes time and experience to accomplish. There have always been automated credit analysis systems. But now there are expert credit analysis systems.

Several vendors have jumped on the expert system bandwagon, knowing a good opportunity when they see one. First Security Bank of Idaho in beautiful downtown Boise has been innovatively using Financial Proformas' FAST credit analysis software for years. Financial Proformas, based in Walnut Creek, California, built a system revolving around 550 proprietary rules in its goal to create a system that produces historical analyses and forecast assumptions. Another California company assists loan officers and credit analysts in assessing risk. Syntelligence's Lending Advisor was written to combat the experience void. David LaFluer, vice president of marketing, explains that 50 percent of the people making loans today have under 5 years of experience. Using expert products gives these 5-year-and-under babes in the woods the experience level of 30-year veterans and speeds up the process by 30 to 50 percent to boot.

How do these systems work? The secret inner workings of an expert corporate credit management system were unveiled by two professors who developed a prototype credit-granting system for a nameless Fortune 500 company.

Venkat Srinivasan is the Joseph G. Reisman Research Professor at Northeastern University. Yong H. Kim is a Professor of Finance at the University of Cincinnati. Srinivasan and Kim[3] set out in the middle 1980s to develop a robust, working expert credit grantor. Prototypes of this nature are often more interesting than ones in the industrial segment, since academic models tend to involve leading-edge ideas. In addition, the mix of individuals involved and the numbers of reviews that this project was subjected to ensure the viability and completeness of the finished system.

Development of the system was divided into two segments. As in most expert system development projects, the first step is to elicit the knowledge from a base of one or more experts. In this case our two academics had the cooperation of a participating financial entity. A multitude of in-depth interviews of credit management staff were performed over a period of time. To obtain all viewpoints of the credit-granting process, the team made sure to interview diverse staff members across the management hierarchy. It also performed a detailed analysis of the actual decisions that were made.

Credit granting defined

The team's analysis, which was necessarily iterative, found that the credit-granting process is composed of two different phases. The granting institution must first determine a line of credit, which is reviewed on an annual basis. There are always exceptions to the rule and these must be handled to the satisfaction of both the customer and the credit institution. In the Fortune 500 company that participated in the prototype, the rule was that all major credit lines, which are defined as greater than $20,000, are reviewed once a year. Upon review, credit limits can be increased pending analysis of updated information on the customer. The exceptions to this rule are for new customers and customers who have exceeded their credit limits (join the club!).

Procedural rules for the granting of credit are heavily dependent upon the amount requested. At our nameless Fortune 500 company, requests for less than $5000 are quickly approved after a cursory review of the application form, while requests for credit up to $20,000 include review of bank references. And when more than $20,000 is requested, watch out for that Dun & Bradstreet report.

There are so many subjective decisions to be made that it's a wonder any credit is granted at all. Let's say you stop by the friendly Moolah National Bank for a $30,000 line of credit for your new business. You sit down opposite someone in horn-rimmed glasses who grills you for over an hour, interrogating you as follows:

"What's the growth potential of your business?"

"How are others doing in your location?"

"How good is your management prowess?"

"What are your bank references?"

"What's your market position?"

"What is your order schedule like?"

"What about the other products that you market?"

"What's your payment record like?"

"How long have you been in business and have you ever filed for bankruptcy?"

On and on the interview goes until your shirt is as wet as a sponge and your nerves turn to jelly.

The prototype

The Srinivasan-Kim system was designed around two phases. The first was a customer evaluation phase in which all the information collected in our little scenario above would be evaluated. This entailed the design of both a database and a knowledge base to support the grand plan. After the evaluation phase, a credit limit determination model would be deployed.

While the overall design of the system is interesting and quite insightful—it is rare to find such a complete specification of an expert-type system—it is the rule bases that we are most interested in.

The rule base for both the customer evaluation component and the credit limit determination component is really a series of interconnected rule bases. Using 11 different classifications—such as financial trend rules, business potential rules, and liquidity rules—the large rule base was able to be logically segmented, which was quite innovative for an expert system built in the middle 1980s. Each segment contained rules specifically for that category. The academics shared several of their rules, as presented in Figure 11.1.

The judgmental conclusion of rule evaluation is ultimately passed

Profitability
If sales trend is improving
And customer's net profit margin is greater than 5%
And customer's net profit margin trend is improving
And customer's gross margin is greater than 12%
And customer's gross profit margin trend is improving
Then customer's profitability is excellent

Liquidity
If sales trend is improving
And customer's current ratio is greater than 1.50
And customer's current ratio trend is increasing
And customer's quick ratio is greater than .80
And customer's quick ratio trend is increasing
Then customer's liquidity is excellent

Debt Management
If sales trend is improving
And customer's debt to net worth ratio is less than .30
And customer's debt to net worth ratio trend is decreasing
And customer's short-term debt to total debt is less than .40
And customer's short-term debt to total debt trend is decreasing
And customer's interest coverage is greater than 4.0
Then customer's debt exposure is excellent

Overall Financial Health
If customer's profitability is excellent
And customer's liquidity is excellent
And customer's debt exposure is excellent
Then customer's financial health is excellent

Figure 11.1 Credit-Granting Customer Evaluation Rules. (*Source: Srinivasan and Kim.*)

into the credit limit model . Toward this end, the *AHP-based model* was chosen to assist in making this all-important financial decision. The AHP model had been used in the past in areas such as predicting oil prices, planning, and marketing. Based on the concept of trade-off, AHP works in the following way. First, the problem is broken down into a hierarchy composed of a set of elements and subelements. The very bottom level of this hierarchy is composed of the specific courses of action or conclusions that are under consideration. Each element is assigned a relative weight using a 9-point measurement scale, with 9 being of absolute importance and 1 being of equal importance. You will note that the rules in Figure 11-1 make frequent mention of the word *excellent*. For the purposes of this prototype, an excellent rating was assigned a value of 9 on the 9-point measurement scale. A weight of 3 indicates weak importance of one over another, 5 indicates essential importance, and 7 indicates demonstrated importance. The in-between numbers of 2, 4, 6, and 8 are just that—intermediate values between two adjacent judgments. These pairwise comparisons are then evaluated such that global priority levels or weights are determined. In other words, the decision-making system is required to respond to a question such as "What is the relative importance of customer background over pay habits?" What this all boils down to is a decision to either grant or deny credit.

In comparison with the nonexpert system mode of credit approval, the prototype developed in this academic exercise was deemed to be correct 97 percent of the time, which is quite impressive. Although the prototype omitted many other credit-granting components, such as keeping track of collateral maturities, it provides an interesting insight into the way an expert system is developed in an area of great complexity. Here, a detailed rule base was gleaned from expert users and associated with a statistical model to achieve the desired goal of accurately and consistently granting maximum credit with minimum losses.

American Express—A Great Example of Credit Analysis

Another company that lives by the maxim "Max credit, min losses" is American Express. It's hard to categorize American Express into any of the three slots that describe the financial services industry, i.e., banks, securities, and insurance. What is American Express anyway? For me, American Express is my ticket to exotic places. Tahiti. Paris. China. The company is better known for its unique type of credit card, which is low on the credit (since you can't really carry over a balance unless you have a line of credit with an associated bank) and high on the bells and whistles. Bells and whistles such as no preset credit limit on the gold card, which can get a body into scads of trouble in a duty-free port like St. Thomas in the Virgin Islands, where the streets are virtually littered with jewelry stores.

Why expert systems?

Since American Express provides the most popular and prestigious of the credit cards, the gang at the home office is always on the prowl searching out the new and better.

One of the new and better tools that American Express discovered was a technology tool. The company knew that it had a problem. This problem was not unique to the industry. Banks have dealt with it for centuries. It's called bad debt and fraud. In American Express's case, with such a huge number of cardholders, it's easy to understand why losses from bad credit authorizations and fraud would be substantial. Since conventional computer systems didn't make much of a dent in reducing the problem, the idea of an expert system became more and more appealing.

American Express began development of its expert system, to be called Authorizer's Assistant, in the early days of commercial expert system acceptance. Since few companies tread where American Express dared to go, it developed new techniques which, years later, many other financial companies have endorsed in their own forays into expert systems.

One of these strategies was to create a corporate group that would coordinate the new technology among its several subsidiaries. These subsidiaries were already tackling other expert system projects in such diverse areas as trading, customer service, back-office support, and insurance underwriting. This reflects the wide variety of American Express business interests.

The Authorizer's Assistant was destined to become the pièce de résistance of the American Express Company and perhaps the single most visible expert system anywhere in the annals of financial services.

In a nutshell, the system assists operators in granting credit to a cardholder on the basis of a review of the customer's records. Since there is no preset credit limit, the process can be a bit tricky. The authorizer usually is called into the picture if the customer is making a purchase outside the limits of the normal computerized system. This means that small purchases can be approved by using the ubiquitous telephone automatic approval device. Here the store clerk slides your card through a slot, which picks up your card number, enters the amount, and waits for an approval code. It's when the amount is over a certain limit, which is different for each store, that Authorizer's Assistant goes into play.

The prototype

In developing the system, American Express chose the path of utilizing an outside consulting firm. In this case, the firm was the vendor of the product of the company that they chose to use during prototype mode. Inference Corporation, El Segundo, Calif., sells a heavy-duty expert system shell called the Automated Reasoning Tool (ART). It also sells its services in knowledge engineering. American Express took the package deal.

The goal was to build a system that would assist, but not replace, the human credit authorizer. Using the five best senior American Express credit authorizers, Inference Corp's knowledge engineers went to work at eliciting their knowledge. Their knowledge allowed them to determine whether a current transaction should be approved.

In making this determination, the senior credit authorizers reviewed many items, such as customers' outstanding charges, payment history, and (my favorite) buying habits. You see, the American Express philosophy is that you can charge anything as long as you pay your bills on time. Gradually, over the years that you have your credit card, you can build up the amount that you spend on your card until one day you'll even be permitted to charge a Mercedes on it. Some people have.

The system required about 4.5 months to prototype and consisted of about 520 decision rules. It ran on a stand-alone Symbolic workstation. Using a forward-chaining inferencing strategy, the system permitted the authorizers to speed up their review of the customer's files to grant that request faster. This assistant has the capability of guiding the authorizer through phone dialogues with merchants and cardholders. If the situation warrants, it prompts the authorizer to make an appropriate inquiry of the customer. In addition, as is the forte of expert systems, the system can display its line of reasoning, which is a marvelous asset in the training of new authorizers.

Whereas the prototype contained 520 rules, the pilot contained over 800 rules. When it came time for American Express executives to review this pilot and provide a yay or a nay for wholesale deployment, they came across astonishing statistics. They found a 76 percent reduction in bad credit authorizations. They also found the system to be accurate 96.5 percent of the time, as compared with the human rate of 85 percent. Management gave the nod and the team started to plan for deployment of this system to the 300-odd authorizers.

In order to make Authorizer's Assistant work, the expert system had to be connected to the mainframe as a coprocessor. The system also had the constraint that the hardware currently used could not be changed. The authorizer workbench consisted of a 327X IBM terminal connected to an IBM mainframe. Since American Express had already made a huge investment in this hardware, it was decided to keep it and "embed" the expert system. In embeddable expert systems, the expert system component is called by the conventional mainline processor. It's not obvious to users that this is an expert system; they just notice that extra ingredient of intelligence.

The Citibank Pension Expert

It's not the Ides of March that scare Americans but the Ides of April. The specter of taxes causes weak knees and fits of despair in the strongest of us. We spend the days before April 15 mired in a cocoon of pencils, calculators, and self-help tax books. Fortunately for the mere mortal, April 15 comes but once a year; but the processors of those giant pension funds are not so lucky. For these banking institutions, withholding taxes need to be calculated on a daily basis for hundreds of thousands of pensioners. For them, this is taxes with a twist.

Citibank is one of the largest banks in the world. Its parent Citicorp boggles the mind with 90,000 employees, over 3000 offices, and $200 billion in assets. Its data-processing functions were decentralized long ago. In fact, it has more data centers and more dollars invested in technology than a fair-to middling-size foreign country. Citibank is segmented into three major business lines: individual banking, investment banking, and institutional banking. A common thread among these three diverse areas is the corporate technology group. It is these gurus who set the standards and make recommendations; but it was the hot shots in the line area who really got expert systems heated up.

Citibank–IBM joint effort

Abhik Dasgupta is a quiet man with a burning passion for expert system technology. When a joint IBM–Citibank study was initiated in November 1987 to determine a flagship project for expert systems, Abhik jumped at the chance to get involved. IBM and Citibank looked at three very diverse possibilities in the many far-flung areas of the bank. The first possibility was a statement system. The goal of an expert system here would be to process prior-period corrections of security transactions—a sort of retrofitting of transactions. Another possible system would be in the stock and bond area, where the system would identify dividends in a complex world of stock splits and interest declarations. Last but not least was the system finally chosen.

Pensions are big business to any bank. Hundreds of thousands of checks are processed and mailed to retirees every working day. What sounds like a simple process is complicated by the complex structure of the differing tax laws in our country. The IRS is one thing, but the web of state and local governments is another. Any pension system must be able to process a check with the correct deductions depending on where Joe actually lives and how many exemptions he takes. If Joe lives in New York with a wife and three kids, his pension check will look different than if he had moved to Kalamazoo, Michigan.

Peter J. Coughlin had a problem. Peter, who's a vice president at Citibank, was handed the news that California had passed a new tax law that was to have a profound effect on his pension-processing system, which was then based on Cobol. The Cobol system had the capability of processing only federal taxes. The specter of adding the differing, and quite complex state tax laws was quite unnerving. The Cobol system was dutifully modified. It was a 120 worker-day effort for the state of California alone. The estimation for adding the remainder of the states to the system made Peter think there had to be a better way.

When IBM and Citibank began looking at the pension-processing system as a possibility, Peter and Abhik pushed hard. Their efforts paid off, as the *disbursement online system (DOLS)* took flight. And none too soon, since the user demanded that the final system be implemented within 6 months.

The prototype

Lesser men (and women) would be mortified at having to learn a new tool and new techniques as well as implement a real, not a prototype, system in a 6-month effort. The Citibank–IBM team was apparently up to the job. Citibank had one constraint: The system had to be developed on its IBM 3084 MVS/XA mainframe, forcing the developers into the untried domain of mainframe expert system shells. Around this time, the majority of expert systems were being deployed on AI workstations or personal computers. Given the hundreds of thousands of transactions and the very large databases filled with tax and pensioner information, the mainframe platform was the only game in town. The IBM mainframe expert system shell, Knowledgetool, was selected, since it exhibited the richness of toolset that was necessary for the system. Using a consulting paradigm, Knowledgetool employed forward and backward chaining as it processed each DOLS transaction by residence of the pensioner.

The Knowledgetool inference engine, written in PL/I, is touted to be a high-performance expert system shell. It uses a very efficient, but proprietary, algorithm for pattern matching. Astute users of the tool do well to employ the OS PL/I optimizing compiler on their applications, since this serves to increase throughput. Citibank found that this tool actually enhanced the performance of the system over the more conventional Cobol approach. Remember, the company already had a good benchmark completed with the Cobol system only recently redesigned for the state of California. In fact, Citibank determined that it had a decrease of 14.3 percent in clock time in the running of the expert system version of California.

How do the guts of Knowledgetool work? It processes a knowledge application in a *recognize-act* cycle (or for you conventional programmers, loop). The inference engine matches rule conditions to existing class members and updates the conflict set with the instantiations recognized. We now have a set of rules ready to fire. This is the heart of the process and Knowledgetool uses an IBM version of the OPS5 algorithm, one of the fastest available. During the second step of this process, the inference engine attempts to resolve the conflict set. Here it chooses which rule, among many, to fire next. Citibank took the option of controlling or predetermining the order of rules, which is a Knowledgetool feature. In the last step of the cycle, the rule selected is executed, or to use expert system parlance, *fired*. The rule fired is procedural and might add, change, or delete class members or might even fire a nested recognize-act cycle for a nested block of rules.

Like most large MIS shops, Citibank had adopted Cobol as its programming language of choice. In fact, only one staffer had ever used PL/I. Knowledgetool, written in PL/I, had structured its development environment using a syntax similar to PL/I. So when the project was begun, Citibank was far behind the eight ball. It was unfamiliar with AI, unfamiliar with Knowledgetool, and unfamiliar with PL/I. Here's where IBM stepped up to the gate. Since this was a flagship project, the IBMers supplied large doses of technical help. They were right there to assist with everything from installation to knowledge engineering to training.

The project team consisted of three full-time staff members, one consultant, and one intrepid IBMer. Since PL/I was virtually unknown at Citibank, the group spent 1 week learning the fundamentals. Another 3 days were spent in Knowledgetool training. Armed with the desire to succeed and all this technical know-how, the team spent 2 intensive weeks on the design. At the end it took 3 months to develop the entire system, soup to nuts. The team averaged five to six complex rules per day, to achieve a total labor-hour usage rate in the range of 12 to 13 percent lower than that of the Cobol version. Since the original senior-level management goal was to find tools to increase productivity, Citibank appeared to have found a winner in Knowledgetool.

At the heart of the project was the expert and his or her knowledge. The system goal of this expert system was to apply the tax law at the federal, state, and local levels uniformly and accurately during the processing of pension checks. The stated user goal was to automate and integrate all tax processing. The unstated goal was to eliminate the system department's interference and let the business unit run with the ball. Walter Feldman, vice president for pension disbursement at Citibank, acted as disseminator of tax information. It was Walter who created the rules, based on information from the tax department. And it was Walter who was heavily involved in testing the accuracy of a system that would need to pass muster with the auditors.

Since this system would deal with disbursements of millions of dollars each evening, the team tested and tested and tested some more. A case history approach to validation of the system was used. This is a tried-and-true method of testing for expert systems, since it permits a parallel test of the expert system versus the current system or the manual method, whichever is applicable. In this case, the team jointly worked on a representative sampling of test cases. Each test case was run through the expert system and then compared with the results arrived at manually. The user department painstakingly compared all test results. After all, one misguided rule could result in Grandpa John in St. Petersburg receiving a surprising windfall. Testing completed, the user department gladly signed off with a flourish.

DOLS

The DOLS knowledge or rule base contains over 100 rules. Since some of these rules are generic—that is, they apply to all states—the total knowledge base can be considered to contain over 200 rules. The team, practicing the "art of structured design" and having learned from the much publicized mistakes of several forerunner expert systems (such as DEC's XCON), organized the rules by state of residence or jurisdiction. This method provides for easy maintenance. In the case of DEC's XCON, a system which assists in the configuration of DEC's one-of-a-kind computers, the knowledge base was composed of more than 10,000 rules. Rules were entered into the system in no particular order, making it a nightmare when a rule needed to be modified or erased. The new and enhanced version of XCON now contains a structured base—but DEC paid dearly to have it enhanced. Fortunately for Citibank, the design team combined its conventional data-processing experience, which is characterized by a love for the organized, with the new black art of expert system design to create a structured knowledge base.

DOLS can be considered a two-tier system. On the front lines is the user interface, or *Chinese menu,* permitting users to modify the tax parameters in the knowledge base. Bringing up the rear is the *overnight processor.* Issuing hundreds of thousands of checks is by no means a real-time application. In the dead of night the conventional component of DOLS performs mundane processing routines. On ready standby is the DOLS expert system, carefully embedded into the system architecture, eager to make decisions about withholding amounts for these complex check disbursements. Pension data is stored on a standard IBM VSAM file. One of Knowledgetool's strengths is the ability to integrate easily into the standard IBM VM or MVS batch or on-line environment. Interfaces exist for the IMS/VS, DB2, and SQL/DS databases as well as "hooks" for the PL/I, Cobol, Fortran, Pascal, and Assembler languages. This permits Knowledgetool to integrate fluidly with any existing application through one of the interfaces or hooks, as was the case with Citibank. In effect, the expert system acts similarly to any other called application, the only difference being in the sophistication of the processing.

Right on target, Citibank unveiled the most sophisticated pension processor on the Street. And the only one to use an expert system at its center.

Chase Lincoln's Financial Planner

People have always depended upon banks for advice. With the addition of new regulations and new products it's no longer as simple to give this advice.

Nowhere do they feel the pinch more keenly than in the United Kingdom. With the formation of the European market, complexity has reached a crescendo. According to Mike Pickup, a manager with the London-based company of Sema Group Business Strategy Advisors, this has forced UK firms to jump both feet first into the pool of expert systems for financial planning.

Although there is a large profession of independent financial advisers, bankers have long since realized the necessity of providing this service. Not only has financial planning been done since the days of yore, when Grandma Annie Oakley requested her bank manager to plan her investments for her, but it has the potential of becoming a profitable business line as more and more people become more and more confused about their financial options.

Joining the traditional financial planning system to an expert system opens new vistas. Obviously, it permits people with a more limited skill set to utilize the functionality of the system. This would open up the floodgates to provide financial planning services at a local branch level. Come in off the street to make a quick deposit and get a quick financial plan. And it is definitely a money-maker. Pickup's research has shown that people would gladly fork over from $50 to $200 to be able to walk out with a comprehensive financial plan.

And what a greater boon to the bank's information banks than to have all that financial data on its customers on its computers. This data could most certainly be used to market other banking products, providing the banks with a most valuable competitive weapon.

One bank that has taken this advice to heart is Chase Lincoln Bank, located in Rochester, New York. Its Chase Personal Financial Planning System is so innovative that it actually won an award from the American Association for Artificial Intelligence. Now, that's quite a feather in Chase Lincoln's cap.

With the help of Arthur D. Little consulting experts, the Chase Lincoln team worked for 5 long years to develop a system that takes the tedium out of working with 30,000 pieces of financial data. Geared to customers earning from $25,000 to $125,000 a year, this expert system handles more than 60 different investment options. The net result of the system is the publication of a 75- to 150-page laser-printed plan, replete with graphics, tailored specifically to the user. These statistics are mind-boggling when one puts the figure at about $10,000 for the cost of a very complicated financial plan that would consider many of these 30,000 variables.

Now with the use of this expert planner, Chase Lincoln's financial planning department is no longer losing money but making money.

References

1. C. Clark and J. H. Wolfarth, "A New Era in Bank Data Processing: Managers Look to DP for Strategic Capabilities," *Bank Administration,* January 1989, pp. 22–28.
2. From Gerald F. Lieberman, a professional teacher of humor who has coached the likes of Jackie Gleason.
3. V. Srinivasan and Y. H. Kim, "Designing Expert Financial Systems: A Case Study of Corporate Credit Management," *Financial Management,* Autumn 1988, pp. 32–43.

12

The Partnering Principle

There is no truer statement about system developers than that they are proud of their technological prowess. But sometimes this pride is carried out to a nonproductive end. There are literally hundreds of thousands of companies out there. What are the odds that at least some of the systems being built for Company A have already been built by Company B? And are being sold or shared by Company C?

Although IT professionals are the first to rush out to buy the latest techno-gizmo, they'd be aghast at the thought of going to another company to buy software for a particular business purpose. They'd be even more shocked if you suggested that they share computer resources with another company. The "not invented here" syndrome is all too prevalent the attitude of system developers who take great pride in their ability to develop systems. There are few pats on the back for these folks if the organization buys or shares a system.

In today's recessionary economy, the multiplicity of redundant and noncompeting projects funded by individual firms constitutes great waste, and ultimately siphons scarce resources from the projects that are crucial to the firm's economic well-being. Motivational issues aside, the sharing of information and/or information systems is one of the great productivity boosters of all time.

Partnering Lessons from Japan

It comes as no surprise that the Japanese are well positioned to act as competitors, if not market leaders, in many of the industries that Americans traditionally dominated. Since World War II, the Japanese have become extremely aggressive businesspeople. Although well-known dominators of the automobile market and the camera market, they are also moving aggressively into other spheres of American influence. A case in point is the global financial industry.

Measured by market valuation, the five largest companies in the world are Japanese, with four of the five being Japanese banks. The largest of these banks is Dai-Ichi. Comparatively, New York's Citibank ranks tenth after Dai-Ichi. In 1987, the Tokyo Stock Exchange became larger than the New York Stock Exchange. Around the same time period, Japan's share of the total value of major world stock markets increased from 17 percent to approximately 47 percent while the U.S. share decreased from 55 percent to below 30 percent.[1]

If there is one dominant factor in the background of all financial markets, domestic and otherwise, it is the use of information technology. Although financial institutions employ less than 5 percent of the U.S. work force, they account for approximately 35 percent of IT purchases.

Large IT expenditures cannot guarantee market dominance. And the threat to the American marketplace is very real, especially among those willing to give up some independence and move in the direction of resource sharing.

The Japanese are very aware of the large capital expenditures that the U.S. firms are making in information technology in financial services. And there is no doubt that they are positioning themselves to catch up, and then overtake, their U.S. counterparts. They just might succeed, since characteristically they employ a collaborative approach to the development of systems.

Good examples of this collaboration are easy to find. The four major Japanese securities firms have standardized their home-computing software on the Nintendo Family Computer. Additionally, they have standardized protocols, architectures, and commands. The collaboration occurred at the same time that American banks moved out of the home-banking market and companies began outsourcing strategic information systems to cut costs.

The Japanese have steadily increased their market share in the world financial markets. We can deduce that at least part of this success can be attributed to their collaborative mindset. Simply, the Japanese work together wherever they are not competitive. Perhaps, individually they lose some identity in the process, but in the long run all participating firms benefit in lower costs and greater efficiencies.

A Collaborative Approach to Technology

In the United States, this collaborative approach is beginning to catch on. Termed *partnering,* it is the process of working with external firms with the goal of sharing technological resources to reduce expenses.

Some innovators have been riding this trend for years. Take the major news bureaus. During the 1964 elections, many news bureaus (ABC, NBC, CBS, United Press, Associated Press) found that the statistics collected when covering elections were disturbingly dissimilar. This had the effect of confusing readers. For example, if one source said that candidate X was leading by 60 percent, another source said that candidate X was leading by 90 percent. These fiercely independent news bureaus decided that greater accuracy and economies of scale were worth more than independence. This decision begat the New York City-based News Election Service—a 20-year-old information technology services partnership.

Partnering comes in two varieties: competitor and client. Competitor resource sharing is a new phenomenon in the United States. Although antitrust legislation precludes U.S. firms from working in the exact same manner as the Japanese in the creation of heavily funded consortiums to develop new technologies, U.S. firms are beginning to see the wisdom of shared expenses in those areas where shared resources are possible. Information technology is most certainly one resource that is easily shared.

Client resource sharing is less a phenomenon than a logical outgrowth of the relationship a company has with its customers. The most common example of this is placing computer terminals on-site at the client so that the client may access, and even update, data.

When Partnering Means Survival

The computer industry is perhaps the newest of American industries to get into partnering. Just a dream a mere two and a half decades ago, the computer industry shot up out of nowhere into stratospheric profitability. But as the industry matured, and the economy soured, computer hardware and software manufacturers and vendors suddenly found themselves fighting for survival.

It's little wonder that Charles R. Wolf, a computer industry analyst at First Boston, called the IBM–Apple partnership the deal of the decade. He has forecast that this alliance will change the landscape of the industry. Given that IBM and Apple have been often bitter rivals since the inception of the personal computer in the early 1980s, Wolf's assessment of the situation is accurate.

The question is why. Although Apple is a prestigious and profitable computer company, the reasoning behind its agreement to this alliance is less profound than IBM's. Apple was the upstart computer company. As legend has it, the idea for a generic personal computer started in a garage in the minds of two school dropouts. Although quite popular for home and school use and in the arts industry, the Apple line of computers has never really caught on wholesale in the bread-and-butter business sector.

The big surprise is IBM. Its agreement to this alliance demonstrates the flexibility a firm must have if it is to survive in trying economic times.

Actually, IBM's alliance with Apple comes as no surprise to many who have been watching Big Blue. Over the last few years IBM has entered into several joint agreements with other companies. Additionally, its stance over the past few years, at least on the software side of the house, has been to develop a concept and then wait as its business partners developed the actual software that would deploy that concept. This is exemplified in its CASE strategy. IBM may push CASE, but its business partners, a diverse array of firms, have actually written this software. The Apple–IBM alliance is quite different. Apple is not, and never has been, a business partner. In fact, Apple has often been a bitter rival.

The reason behind this marriage of convenience is twofold. First, the industry has become so complex, so widely flung, and so diverse that no company can go it alone in developing technology and winning customers. Second, the computer industry once had only one standard—IBM's. But with the growing number of entries into the field, the number of standards has proliferated. This has occurred on both the hardware and the software side.

An example of fragmentation

Perhaps one of the better demonstrative examples of this industry fragmentation is in the CASE market. Since the idea of CASE was conceived, dozens of vendors have flooded the marketplace. Each of these vendors brought with them its own CASE tool. Customers who bought these disparate CASE tools are just finding out that many of them simply do not speak the same language.

Sometimes connecting one CASE tool to another is a lot like connecting that 3¼-inch pipe into the 3-inch hole. According to Howard Rubin, president of Howard Rubin Associates in Pound Ridge, New York, a lot of energy being wasted right now in constructing systems involves worrying about the binding process versus worrying about the individual components. The binding should be less of a headache, and we should be focusing on building the right components to assemble.

But in order for this vision of full-scale tool integration to take flight, one all-consuming issue must be resolved. This is the issue of standards. If plumbers hadn't developed, and adhered to, a set of standards, building a house today would be even more of a nightmare than it already is.

Building the technology for today's IT shop is very much like installing the plumbing for a new house. Mixed vendors and services. Given the increasing predilection toward becoming mixed-vendor shops, IT groups are very interested in heterogeneous solutions. Therefore, we must look at the set of services that has to be pervasive across all kinds of operating systems and different types of hardware in order to be really useful. This heterogeneity requires strict standards.

The real problem is not a lack of standards. The problem is too many standards leading to mass confusion and fragmentation of the marketplace. How confused *is* the marketplace? The world is dividing up into two camps. There's IBM and what is referred to as open systems. Hewlett-Packard, Unisys, Digital Equipment Corp. (DEC), Siemens, and Bull are all in open systems, along with some of the CASE vendors.

The migration of vendors into either one of these two camps is evidenced by the current consolidation of the CASE industry. Although there are plenty of market niches where a good CASE vendor can take root, the problem is one of distribution and perhaps user confidence. As more and more users are moving into the CASE marketplace, they are searching for some level of standardization. And they are looking to the bigger vendors for support, training, and stability. Because of this, some of the smaller players with good technology are finding themselves being shut out of the market. In order to survive, vendors must take the consolidation route by forming strategic alliances with other vendors or even merging with other vendors, as in the Index–Sage merger into the company known as Intersolv.

Losing control of the market

The alliance between Apple and IBM is clear proof of the fact that IBM has lost control over the very market that it helped create. IBM has become, in effect, just one more cog in the wheel competing with hundreds of lower-priced but equally capable machines. Even IBM's own machine has little that is IBM in it. An IBM PC's chips are Intel's, and its operating system is Microsoft—and much of the profits go to these two firms.

Therefore, many see the alliance between IBM and Apple as a merger specifically with the purpose of jointly gaining control over the dual issues of diversity of design and standards and proliferation of the marketplace.

Apple and IBM's letter of intent called for the formation of a new, independently managed company, whose goal is to create an advanced operating system. This new operating system will be used in both new and existing Apple and IBM computers and will be marketed to other companies. In the choice of an operating system as the prime vehicle for this alliance can be seen the underlying reason for the partnership. In a word, Microsoft.

It will come as no surprise to readers of the business pages that the relationship between Microsoft, the maker of the most popular operating system for the PC, and IBM has gone astray. What may be surprising is the level of acrimony between the two giants. It is perhaps in the deteriorating relationship between IBM and Microsoft that can be found the real reason for the IBM and Apple partnership.

Microsoft was the first business partner that IBM squired in the PC world. At the time, Microsoft was a young startup, so the partnership agreement between the two was nowhere near as significant as this most latest partnership between IBM and Apple. IBM was just entering the PC market and needed an operating system for that PC. Microsoft was the chosen partner. It appeared to be a relationship made in heaven and, in fact, did prove beneficial to both for quite a number of years. What IBM didn't count on was Microsoft's aggressive entry into more segments of the software market and its growing market share. Today, Microsoft is one of the most profitable, and dominant, computer companies of all time.

As Microsoft grew, it also grew more independent. The war with IBM over its newest operating system was the blow that broke the partnership apart, pushing IBM into the comforting arms of another. IBM's newest machines run under OS/2. IBM's relationship with Microsoft called for Microsoft to develop a newer and more robust version of OS/2. But Microsoft had a different agenda. Instead of OS/2, Microsoft spent its resources on developing newer versions of its original operating system, DOS, and something called Windows.

Windows is a software program that mimics the look and feel of the popular Apple computer operating system. But Windows placed this functionality on an IBM PC. Since Windows runs under DOS, Microsoft had no desire to move ahead with the IBM OS/2 agreement. Instead, Microsoft aggressively pushed Windows. Given the popularity of Windows, this was a good strategic business decision for Microsoft. But it did have the side effect of stirring great controversy in the industry and destroying the long-term relationship with IBM.

When IBM finally realized that Microsoft would never fulfill its agreement to develop the OS/2 operating system for the IBM PC, it began to understand that its one-time business ally had turned aggressive rival.

In situations such as these, a competitor is often pressured to choose what is perceived as the lesser of two evils. IBM must have surely been in a quandary. One the one hand, Microsoft had most surely severed its relationship with IBM by its actions. On the other hand, IBM viewed Apple as a prime competitor. But in considering its options, IBM must have realized that its only chance for survival in the personal computer wars would be to develop a partnership with its once most fearsome competitor—Apple.

The alliance is actually more extensive than the development of an Apple-based operating system for both the Apple and IBM platforms. The companies are developing products to make it easier for Apple Macintoshes to communicate and share information with IBM machines that are now widely used by corporations. The two companies will also develop a version of IBMs UNIX operating system (a high-end operating system that runs on advanced workstations) which will run programs written for the Macintosh. Apple will begin using an IBM microprocessor in future versions of the Macintosh. Finally, the two companies will develop common approaches to displaying images on displays and reproducing sounds.

The benefits that Apple derives from this partnership are perhaps even greater than those that IBM will enjoy. Once viewed as a loner, Apple will now take its place among the prime contenders in the IBM PC arena. It will be able to sell more computers to large corporations, which up to now have shied away from the Apple configuration and standardized on the IBM PC. Since the alliance will provide the ability to easily merge Apple computers into an all-IBM environment, the floodgates should open for Apple sales.

The IBM–Apple alliance is not the newest in the computer industry. Digital Equipment, Compaq, and Microsoft also have an arrangement. What is significant in the Apple–IBM partnership, though, is that two of the biggest names in the computer industry, and the two that were originally the most competitive, have joined forces in order to survive.

The computer industry leads the way in strategic partnering

Three months of 1991 provide an excellent overview of how partnering is changing the shape of the computer industry. It is presented here in calendar format:

April 9, 1991	Compaq, along with 20 other companies, launches the Advanced Computing Environment Consortium to establish a new standard to compete with Sun, Hewlett-Packard, and IBM.
April 12, 1991	The Federal Trade Commission widens its investigation into Microsoft for possible antitrust.
May 1, 1991	CompuCom purchases Computer Factory (both companies are retail computer stores).

May 6, 1991	NCR agrees to be purchased by AT&T.
June 4, 1991	JWP buys Businessland (both are computer retail chains).
June 13, 1991	Tandy, reversing its stance on independence, agrees to carry products from Apple, Compaq, and IBM in its stores.
June 18, 1991	Wang forges an agreement with IBM to resell IBM products.

And it continues—even into 1994. The computer industry shakeup is a portent of things to come in most American industries. Markets are so fragmented and competition is so aggressive that even the strongest of firms are increasingly finding that they cannot survive in isolation.

But partnering requires a great deal of effort from those firms that agree to join forces. The lines between these participating organizations tend to blur at contact. Being able to cope with the new rules of the game can make the difference between a successful partnership and one that ends in acrimony (i.e., IBM and Microsoft) and possible market repercussions.

Many in the computer industry, although lauding the IBM and Apple alliance, are taking a wait-and-see attitude. The question these critics raise is: "Can IBM and Apple put their differences aside and work together in unison to develop their line of products?" Only time will tell.

Crossing Wall Street As Partners

Running a back-office operation at a Wall Street brokerage firm costs an average of $300 million a year. By partnering and jointly operating the same operation, brokerage houses have the potential to save $50 million a year.

For many Wall Street brokerage firms, other benefits far outstrip this cash savings. By partnering their back-office operations, they should be able to create economies of scale, reduce head count, and even double the volume of trades.

These economies have spurred several nascent cooperative efforts—such as a plan for the building of a disaster recovery site with space for up to 1000 traders, a joint venture of several firms that wish to share their analytics libraries, and an initiative involving a shared electronic data interchange network.

In the bull market of the 1980s, securities firms built large data centers and hired large operations staffs. As new products were invented, more staff and more capacity were added. The rationale behind these excesses was that the introduction of the new product would more than pay for the additional overhead. Of course, that all changed with the stock market crash of 1987. Today, there are fewer new products and fewer opportunities to recoup the heavy investment costs of computers and people.

Securities firms simply built back offices for a business cycle that no longer exists. And with the need to pare down these cost burdens, securities firms have increasingly looked to sharing, or partnering, of their operations.

Unfortunately, the road to partnering is not smoothly paved. Perhaps the most exciting news of 1990 was the potential agreement between Prudential Securities and Shearson Lehman Brothers to merge their back-office computer operations to cut costs. Shearson had built a state-of-the-art data center which opened in 1986. In operation right before the crash, the Shearson data center had more than enough capacity to process Shearson and Prudential trade data easily. But merger talks broke down early in 1991 when American Express spun off the Shearson back office into a new company called Securities Information Group (SIG). This new involvement of American Express as a third party made the Prudential deal just too complex.

The competitive issue

What killed the deal was the competition bogey, an issue that the Japanese seem to have resolved. Some critics have said that partnering between competitors will never work in the securities industry. They ask: "What happens when both firms need to process something at the same time and there is computer capacity for only one of them?" These critics also question the confidentiality of data in a shared environment.

Perhaps the answer for these critics is the partnering method chosen by Kidder Peabody and First Boston. Kidder shares First Boston's data center but uses its own operations staff, as does First Boston. Still, even with the success of the Kidder–First Boston model, it is hard to persuade companies that are fierce competitors to cooperate. And even though this concept has been discussed on Wall Street for the last few years, little tangible results have occurred.

But unless some action is taken in this direction, the securities firms will remain at peak capacity. If the trading volume does not improve, too many firms will continue to compete for too few customers. And the firms, having to carry the burden of the fixed costs of their computer systems, will surely seek solace in price adjustments leading to lower margins for everybody.

Philadelphia National Bank's ATM Advantage

While the securities firms are just beginning to test the waters of partnering, a particular segment of the banking industry has already proved that the sharing of resources fosters economies of scale, reduces costs, and prevents erosion of market share.

The automated teller machine (ATM) is as ubiquitous nowadays as the corner candy store. Many consumers, in fact, base their banking decisions on which bank has more, or more conveniently available, "cash machines."

There is some debate, however, over just how easy or hard it is to gain competitive advantage through the use of ATMs. The issue is rooted in the many faces of the technology. Citibank in New York exemplifies the type of banking institution which offer ATMs on a *proprietary network*. Citibank's cash machines can be used only by Citibank customers. The question is: Did Citibank reap significant strategic advantage because of its proprietary network? Or did it realize a strategic advantage because it happened to be first among competitors to offer this service? The flip side of the ATM coin is the *shared network*, which is what this section is largely about.

A question often raised about shared technology is: Does it offer any strategic advantage at all? Wouldn't a proprietary network, like Citibank's, offer better positioning? These questions raise a complex issue which cannot be answered simply.

Certainly, at the outset Citibank received a competitive advantage by deploying its proprietary network in advance of competitors. But as those competitors caught up, an interesting phenomenon occurred. Consumers stopped thinking of ATMs as unique and started to think of them as a commodity. To use another example, the telephone itself has been a commodity for quite a while. There is little distinction, at this point, between phones from the AT&T phone store and those from AT&T's rivals. Still, AT&T must offer telephones for sale if it is to be competitive. The logic is similar with the market's newest commodity—the ATM. Truth of the ATM-as-commodity theory is further proved by Citibank's 1991 announcement that it will become a limited member of a competitor's shared ATM network. Obviously, Citibank felt that providing its customers with an extensive network far outweighed whatever advantages once were to be gained by supplying a proprietary network.

Shared networks offer significant advantages over proprietary networks. Eric K. Clemons,[2] a professor at the University of Pennsylvania's Wharton School, has nicely summarized this reasoning. A paraphrase follows:

- Necessities must be offered.

- Where competitive advantage is unlikely, these necessities should be provided at the lowest possible cost consistent with desired service levels.

- Shared development and cooperative operations often produce significant reduction in development costs, and often provide the least expensive means of achieving a desired level of geographic coverage.

Today, the benefits of sharing now exceed the benefits of remaining proprietary. But is there a strategic, economic, or other advantage to being the owner of a shared ATM service?

The uniqueness of MAC

The money access center (MAC) is a shared ATM network provided by the Philadelphia National Bank. MAC is the only single-owner shared system among the largest ATM networks. Other shared networks, like Yankee in Boston and NYCE in New York, have a shared ownership structure.

When MAC was launched in the 1970s, Philadelphia National Bank was a big player in commercial and wholesale banking, but its presence in retail was not significant. In 1977 a marketing research study performed by the bank revealed two major complaints among banking customers: long teller lines and short banking hours. At the same time, Philadelphia's Girard Bank had just launched George, a proprietary ATM network. Philadelphia National Bank recognized in George a possible reason for erosion of the bank's market share. As a result of this market study and George, Philadelphia National Bank decided to launch MAC.

MAC's requirements would be stringent. There would have to be enough ATMs in place to be relevant and justify aggressive marketing. The system would also have to have real-time access to account balances so that member banks would want to issue cards. Because of these factors, a proprietary network was unacceptable. In choosing a shared network, Philadelphia knew that a consortium of banks sharing costs and resources would not be feasible, since any bank having the resources was currently considering a proprietary network of its own. Thus the concept of marketing services to other banks was born. In 1979 the MAC network went live with 13 banks, all generically displaying identical advertising signs and receiving identical service.

Philadelphia National Bank (PNB), in providing the MAC service, is singularly responsible for all facets of the network and the software running on the network. These include the overall network strategy, program design and implementation, network maintenance, product development, marketing, and advertising. Banks that are members of MAC are charged no fees for these services—a definite advantage for these same banks. Funds for running MAC are derived from the normal transaction processing charge from PNB.

MAC provides several levels of services to member banks. For smaller banks, with teller machines but no network and supporting software, a turnkey operation is provided. Here, MAC provides a complete range of services, including start-of-day account balances, validation of cardholder, authorization of service, and record of accounting deposits made and withdrawals completed. Banks with the appropriate hardware and software are given what is known as *intercept service.*

MAC imposes two kinds of fees on banks sharing the network. All transactions that use the MAC switch incur a switch fee. The switch is typically invoked in those transactions that require interbank accounting—for example, a customer of a different bank withdrawing cash from an ATM located at a PNB bank. Switch fees increase as volume increases. In addition, MAC charges an interchange fee on all other transactions. These are transfer payments which MAC collects from the bank that issued the card used in the transaction. MAC then pays the bank that owns the card used.

From a competitive point of view, few bankers feel that a bank gains market share by joining a shared ATM network. In MAC's case, early joiners of the network adopted a defensive posture in meeting the threat posed by Girard Bank's George. In this posture, these banks were willing to place ATM service in the hands of a competitor. In later networks, such as New York's NYCE, member banks all use it on an intercept basis.

Even in the MAC network, more and more banks are moving in the more secured position of intercept processing. This is seen as a way to limit exit barriers to leaving the network if MAC becomes exploitive. At this point, these intercept processors can create their own alternative shared network in the manner of NYCE.

MAC's stance is now of acquisition. By acquiring competing networks, MAC has become one of the larger of the ATM networks in the United States. As the ATM networks consolidate and the industry restructures, MAC is in a comfortable position.

According to Clemons of the Wharton School, past a certain point both the economies of scale and decreasing network costs diminish, making the concept of a single local network or a single national interconnection network infeasible. Even though ATMs are now seen as a full commodity service—that is, there is no competitive advantage to having them but there is competitive disadvantage to not having them—PNB enjoys what is known as *first mover advantage.*

For those firms that enter a market first and strongly, considerable advantage occurs. Firms entering the marketplace at a later time need an aggressive plan and sufficient resources to compete. Although PNB appears to have covered costs, and is making a modest profit, MAC is not seen as a highlight to its bottom line. It is in an intangible area where PNB has benefited the most. PNB has embellished its reputation as a banker's bank among competitors at the same time as it has strengthened its reputation among customers.

Negotiating the Sharing of Information

Information partnerships between corporations may be the next wave of the future, running the gamut from links between suppliers and customers to joint ventures between companies in the same industry to collaborate on R&D or marketing (like the Apple–IBM venture).

In all these partnerships, the common entity will be a *shared information resource.* Sharing of information will require exacting managerial efforts as widely dispersed companies, out of necessity, must provide a commonality of data definitions, relationships, and even search patterns. Even into the 1990s companies are having difficulty in creating an *internal information resource,* common to all divisions within a single company. Thus attempting to develop an intercompany information resource will be even more difficult.

Flexibility, cooperation, and computer power seem to be the key words of a workable, and mutually profitable, partnership—as exemplified by Corning. Corning's approach to strategic alliances is one of adapting to great change. This ability to accommodate is, perhaps, the deciding factor between success and failure. A partnership is only as successful as the partners' abilities to make it work. And to make it work, each partner may have to change more than just the way business is performed. The partners may have to change corporate culture as well.

Corning is no stranger to this phenomenon, since it has a large number of strategic alliances and joint ventures. For an information services department bearing the brunt of development for the new relationship, it means having to accommodate clients that are external to the company. For Corning's information services department this has meant determining costs, negotiating rates, and sending out bills. These are activities that Corning's internal information services group never had to do before.

The way Corning's information services group works with partners is directly related to the nature of the partnership and the needs of the various participants. In one notable instance, 50 percent of a Corning division was divested into a joint-venture company. The new company's information services group had to be apportioned from the central group. In addition, the new joint venture decided to purchase some services from the central group as well requiring the central group to begin monitoring the new company's usage in order to calculate billables.

Much like Corning, other developers of intercompany information resources will have to overcome multiple political problems, priority problems, and jargon problems. Developing a negotiating game plan can be of invaluable assistance. Let's look at how to avoid the pitfalls and achieve successful cooperation.

Standardize the terms that all companies use

Greenwood Mills, located in Greenwood, South Carolina, found that standardization of jargon was a necessity if it was to successfully implement a system which linked the textile company to its customers and suppliers. Greenwood was used to keeping track of material using standard sizes such as 36 or 48 inches. In reality, those measurements represented the minimum size on the bolt. In essence, a 36-inch bolt of material might very well be 37 inches wide. This was a big issue to Greenwood's customers, since many of them were using sophisticated numerical control equipment that could pick up on this difference, requiring them to remeasure the fabric.

Greenwood also discovered a jargon problem in the naming of colors. Greenwood designated names for shades, while its customers used a value that described the amount of variance from a standard color.

Choose a board of directors

In joint-venture partnerships all partners are created equal. This, of course, is just theory. In practice, it is possible that the information services group will find itself beholden to several masters. Since the partnership is being formed around a joint goal, an insistence on a many-master approach to the information services group will most surely result in lowering efficiencies. Information services must serve one master only. In joint partnerships this can be accomplished through election of a board of directors whose function is to oversee the information services efforts.

The board of directors should have equal representation from all partners. Its function is to determine both the short- and long-term plans of the information services group. This includes the determination of priorities of all development projects as well as the resolution of any political confrontations.

When a firm that has formed an alliance with one or more companies also permits those companies to utilize a proprietary information system, it is reasonable to expect requests for modifications to that system. All too often, in these situations, those external companies are handed a phone number of the technician in charge of that system. The technician is then confronted with having to fit these requests into an already filled agenda. On many occasions these requests for change are not desirable to the owner company. A better control of the situation is desired.

In these cases, a user liaison should be appointed to run interference between these external companies and the owner company. This liaison will be responsible for taking requests for change and then working with the user team as well as the information services group to determine if the change is desirable, and when and if it can be accommodated.

Determine the boundaries of exchange

Data links between two companies can be *unidirectional* or *bidirectional*. A supplier posting new product information may require only a one-way link. Some partnering agreements require a two-way link. For example, not only does McKesson Drug transmit information to its pharmacy clients, but the pharmacies are able to transmit order information back up the link as well.

Eliminate redundancies

In a joint venture separate firms, each having its own information services department, join forces for a common goal. In cases such as these, each firm may desire to retain its own independent information services group.

Efficiencies are lowered when a processing function is performed more than once. In addition, redundant data often becomes inconsistent. For example, each of three allied firms uploads market data to its respective marketing research department for analysis. Each market research department has its own computer system. It is possible that three different results will be obtained because of the differences in data processing. Additionally, the longer the raw data sits in diverse databases, the stronger the chance that the data will be altered and, thus, differ from data in its sister databases.

It is recommended that all data be processed in one location to negate these potentialities. This calls for the creation of a joint processing center servicing the legitimate needs of the partnership. If this is not possible, or desirable, then one location should be chosen as master with the ability to update. The remaining locations should have the ability to download in a read-only mode to prevent the data from becoming redundant and corrupted. To ensure that data analysis is performed singularly, software should be located on a network for shared use or the same analytical programs should be made mandatory.

Allow for varying levels of sophistication

In information systems serving multiple partners, it should be remembered that each partner will exhibit its own level of sophistication, and have its own set of requirements.

In building its system, McKesson Drug had to deal with the fact that its pharmacy customers lacked the degree of sophistication of its own internal staff. In providing hand-held terminals as well as scannable inventory labels, McKesson recognized, and provided for, its own level of sophistication.

Many firms develop a joint system with multiple interfaces: one for the least sophisticated user, one for the average user, and one for an extremely knowledgeable, or power, user.

Be ready to compromise

In a single-user system, the user can tailor the system for a specific purpose. This is usually not possible in jointly held systems. Although many of the problems of partnership systems can be resolved through the appointment of a board of directors, companies involved in process should be on the ready to compromise some of their specific requirements.

A Checklist for Exploiting Partnering

1. List the possible reasons your company might form a partnership. For example:

   - Counter threat from a competitor
   - Achieve greater efficiencies
   - Provide services to customers, creating dependence

2. How would information technology fit into the partnership? Would it service the partnership? Would it be the basis around which the partnership is formed?

3. Consider developing information systems from scratch for the partnership. Kluging existing systems to add new functionality may not start the venture off on the right foot. Developing from scratch enables the partners to tailor a joint system.

4. Research newer technologies when developing partnership systems. As long as the partnership is presented with the opportunity to develop from scratch, a serious effort should be made to incorporate state-of-the-art technologies when appropriate.

5. Consider spinning off an information services group to run independently of the partnership companies.

6. Consider unusual productivity boosters for the new partnership. Assuming that the partnership will create an independent entity, complete with its own information resources group, consider Eli

Berniker's proposal for superproductivity. Berniker, an associate professor of management at Pacific Lutheran University, proposes to divide the profits of the joint venture in four parts. The first part is given to the workers as a bonus; the second is split among the partners as addition to profits. The third part is used to fund the future productivity of the team—in particular, funding R&D and then implementation of new technology. Berniker recommends that the fourth part be used to improve the quality of life in the community.

References

1. Richard Van Slyke, "Rust on Wall Street," *Information Strategy: The Executive's Journal,* vol. 5, no. 10, Winter 1990.
2. Eric K. Clemons, "MAC—Philadelphia National Bank's Strategic Venture in Shared ATM Networks," *Journal of Management Information Systems,* vol. 7, no.1, Summer 1990.

13

Some Thoughts on
IT Productivity and Quality

Let's take a long, hard view on things—not just on measuring the productivity of the software engineering process, but on the concept of technology and productivity in general. What this chapter offers up are ruminations about obtaining quality from some of the best-known companies in the industry.

Whereas the pieceworker's productivity is easy to measure, the information worker's productivity is difficult to quantify. It is just as difficult to measure not only the quality of the software system being utilized, but also the effectiveness of the software developer.

Through the use of measurements, or *metrics* as they are commonly called, it is possible to understand and manage the software development process. Perhaps more important, it is possible to measure the impact of change when a shift in methodologies (such as CASE) or training procedures occurs.

The self-perception of software developer as artist has evolved to that of engineer. The term *software engineering* is indicative of this change in perception from art to science. Software "artists" insisted that measuring their work was as impossible as measuring the work of Rembrandt. But with the emphasis on engineering comes the viewpoint that the software development cycle is process-oriented. Therefore, a method of measuring is not only possible, but required.

Why Bother to Measure?

The idea of measuring productivity is relatively new. Jerrold M. Grochow, a vice president of American Management Systems, Inc. (AMS) of Arlington, Virginia, has queried over 2500 people at up to 500 organizations over the last 3 years. He found that few IT organizations are quantitatively measuring productivity or quality.

As an industry, we have a dismal performance in this area. There is no other industry that knows so little about itself in a quantitative way.

The organizations measuring, or just getting into measurement, are primarily doing it for the same reasons. Software is becoming more complex and user demands and expectations are increasing. The need to develop better software, faster, translates to a need to quantify the project's progress and the system's attributes.

A variety of productivity/quality metrics are available; choosing the most appropriate one can be as tricky as picking winning lottery numbers. (See Figure 13.1.)

Measuring does have its detractors. Many "artists" still refuse to be measured. Ironically, measuring often produces the unusual effect of increasing productivity in just the areas that are measured.

In most situations, the term *metric* is used in conjunction with the programming process only. But programming is the smallest part of

1) Lines of Code
2) Pages of documentation
3) Number and size of tests
4) Function count
5) Variable Count
6) Number of modules
7) Depth of nesting
8) Count of changes required
9) Count of discovered defects
10) Count of changed lines of code
11) Time to design, code, test
12) Defect discovery rate by phase of development
13) Cost to develop
14) Number of external interfaces
15) Number of tools used and why
16) Reusability percentage
17) Variance of schedule
18) Staff years experience with team
19) Staff years experience with language
20) Software years experience with software tools
21) MIPs per person
22) Support to development personnel ratio
23) Nonproject to project time ratio

Figure 13.1 Productivity/quality metrics.

the systems development life cycle. For an effective measurement program, each component of the cycle must include its own measures—or a measure must be used that encompasses the entire spectrum of development.

The software development process is one of the most complex processes a human can perform, according to T. Capers Jones, chairman of Software Productivity Research (SPR) in Burlington, Massachusetts. Software development includes numerous formidable tasks. Although variations abound in the number of executable steps in a life cycle, most IT organizations perform the same functionality.

Metrics must consider several esoteric items, such as user involvement, which is positively correlated with productivity increases. Human factors must also be taken into account, such as the square footage allocated per programmer. (Jones's research has shown that a full 78 square feet of floor space increases programmer productivity more than any CASE tool.) Design, programming, and quality factors must also be weighed.

Quality measurements are frequently overlooked in the race to implement on or before deadline. However, no matter what the time pressure, certain measures undertaken seriously can enhance the quality of output of any software investment.

Measurement of quality is often thought of as a manufacturing process. But this view is changing, and the hardware manufacturers are leading the way. Geoffrey Roach, a marketing executive in the Marlboro, Massachusetts, office of Digital Equipment Corporation (DEC), described the automated methodology used to run the 22,000 quality checks on the VAX Cobol compiler.

With 22,000 tests, it is impossible to test the compiler thoroughly, so DEC wrote VaxScan, which looks at many micro-oriented measures such as rate of change and how much the program was tested. It also measures the introduction of new errors, plus performs many other tests.

Roach tells the story of Deming, who fought unsuccessfully for quality measurements within the automobile industry. Deming took his message to the Japanese, who listened. The rest is history. Deming's message is being taken seriously by the likes of Roach and others on the hardware side. That message is slowly getting through to mainstream corporate data centers.

The Original Metric

Those who measure most often use a simple *source lines of code* (SLOC) metric. With this metric, however, there is room for variation. In *Software Engineering Metrics and Models,* S. D. Conte and his associates proposed this definition of SLOC:

A line of code is any line of program text that is not a comment or blank line, regardless of the number of statements or fragments of statements on that line. This specifically includes all lines containing program headers, declarations and executable and nonexecutable statements.[1]

The SLOC metric is often further redefined into distinguishing the number of *noncomment* source lines of code (NCSLOC) from the lines of code containing *comment* statements (CSLOC).

Along with SLOC measurements, the weekly time sheet provides other gross statistics often used for productivity measurement. The total number of labor-hours expended, divided by the total number of NCSLOC, provides an overall statistic that can be used to compare productivity from project to project.

One problem with the SLOC measurement is that it does not take into account the complexity of the code being developed or maintained. Lines of code and labor-months hide some very important things. For example, the SLOC measurement for a name and address file update program might be 600 lines of code per day. SLOC not only fails to account for complexity; it also fails to account for the compactness of the language with respect to the application. One can, for example, in 20 lines of Lisp, encode the same list-processing problem that might take 50 lines of C.

To further this last point, the output for software that tracks satellites might be in the range of 40 to 50 lines of code per day. To look at this output on a purely gross statistical level, one would conclude that the name and address project was more productive and efficient than the satellite project. This conclusion would be wrong.

So starting from this base, two researchers at the Massachusetts Institute of Technology's Center for Information Systems Research examined the complexity issue. Chris F. Kemerer and Geoffrey K. Gill studied the software development projects undertaken by an aerospace defense contracting firm from 1984 to 1989.[2]

The Kemerer and Gill team began its research by reviewing the original measure for complexity as developed by Thomas McCabe, now president of McCabe & Associates, a consulting group in Columbia, Maryland. McCabe proposed that a valid measurement of complexity would be the number of possible paths in a software module.[3] In 1978, W. J. Hansen interpreted McCabe's mathematical formula into four simple rules that would produce a numerical measure of complexity (i.e., the higher the number, the more complex):[4]

- Add 1 for every IF, CASE, or other alternate execution construct.

- Add 1 for every iterative DO, DOWHILE, or other repetitive construct.

- Add 2 less than the number of logical alternatives in a CASE.

- Add 1 for each AND or OR in an IF statement.

The results of the Kemerer and Gill study showed that increased software complexity leads to reduced productivity. They recommend the use of more experienced staff and a reduction of the complexity of the individual software module. To reduce complexity, they suggest the establishment of a complexity measure that could be in use as the code is written, and adherence to this preset standard.

The goal of these studies is to transfer the generally accepted processes of measurement from the manufacturing arena to the software arena. The problem with the software industry is that developers think everything they're doing is new.

Peeling Back Layers of Quality Equation

In the short term, companies in search of a silver bullet to the software development quality and productivity quandary will find themselves firing blanks. One of the big problems in this country is that we tend to look for one silver-bullet solution to the productivity problem. Simply throwing technology or methodology at the problem is not enough. IT departments must also use peopleware solutions. (See Figure 13.2.)

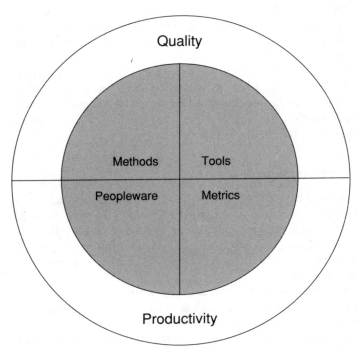

Figure 13.2 Layers to productivity/quality. (*Sourse: Techinsider*)

For example, one way to improve development is to hire better developers. This solution is the closest thing to a silver bullet.

Rather than spend lots of money trying to bring in a new methodology, why not just bring in better people? Since we know that there is a 25-to-1 differential between the best and the worst people, and a 4-to-1 differential between the best and the worst teams, maybe the best way to improve productivity and quality is just to improve your hiring practices.

A good peopleware improvement to productivity is to help managers improve their skills, as well as to foster a teamwork approach among developers. Peopleware solutions boost productivity and quality more than any tools or techniques.

The companies that will win the competitive battles of the 1990s are those that will leverage their technology investments to create new possibilities. To make a productive contribution, IT needs good management, good technical staff (including good estimators and testers), good measurements, good tools, and a good methodology.

And there is definitely a relationship between methodology and measurement. Until you master a methodology and have time to implement that methodology in a complete product, you can't measure it. It takes a good 3 or 4 months to get a mastery of the methodology; then it takes a good 6 months to implement it in an entire project life cycle. So you're a year down the road before you can find out if the methodology even worked. Only then can you begin measuring what differences you can get out of it.

Vaughan Merlyn, partner at Ernst & Young's Center for Information Technology and Strategy in Boston, is reported to have said, "The important part is learning to understand method." What he meant is that once an organization has established a methodology as a way of doing things, the CASE tool is disposable.

Quality in an Era of Paradigm Shifts

Who among us doesn't remember the soulful tale of Alice? In her journey through Wonderland she comes upon the Queen of Hearts, who, at one point in the fantasy, makes sport of the game of chess with live chess pieces, including our very own Alice. The Queen makes Alice run so fast, but Alice finds that she is merely running in place—running so very fast just to catch up.

This story is a good analogy to describe where the information technology industry is vis-à-vis productivity and quality. In essence, our productivity is masked by system complexity and continually rising demand for new systems, so like Alice, it seems like we're merely running in place.

Has productivity and quality risen? Or, like Alice, are more and more firms merely running in place—too tired from continual day-to-day operational battles or too shell-shocked from retrenching to support the new paradigms of client/server architectures and object orientation to pay heed to what is now being referred to as total quality management (TQM)?

Although there's certainly a lot of noise about quality programs, it's a little hard to tell at this time how many of these programs are actually bearing fruit. In fact, quality improvements may have less to do with putting certain methodologies in place than with modifying human behaviors.

This phenomenon is known as the Hawthorne effect. In the 1920s, social scientists studying the productivity of workers at a Western Electric plant in Hawthorne, Illinois, discovered that when they turned up the lighting, productivity went up. They also found that when they turned down the lighting, productivity went up again. These social scientists concluded that when the Hawthorne workers realized that people were paying attention to them, they started to do better work.

TQM Meets the Black Hole

Even though the jury is still out on the effects of TQM on the process of information technology, there's no doubt that the industry itself is extremely interested in its potential. Less than 5 percent of IT organizations are doing this sort of thing. Even though TQM is strongly rooted in many industries as a whole, IT tends to be a black hole.

You start off the TQM process by understanding a single principle— that change is painful and lengthy. In fact, to effectuate any kind of change you need something like a 10-year plan. But 10 years is a long time and management's patience is short. So how can you motivate change over that time period?

The secret is to make management extremely dissatisfied with the status quo. And to do that you need to look at the cost of the status quo. One way of accomplishing this is to examine the cost of poor quality. By answering questions such as "What are we spending on detecting defects?" and "What are we spending on repairing defects?" the IT organization can begin to accumulate the statistics it needs to make the push for change. The data needn't be hard to track—in most cases it's already available through project management systems that track walkthroughs, reviews, defect rates, and the like. Merlyn calculates that 40 to 50 percent of the IT budget is spent on fixing defects stemming from poor quality. With statistics like this, it should be rather easy to motivate massive change.

New Tools for More Complex Development

The 1990s is most certainly the decade of fear in our industry. At the same time that quality has become a "hot ticket," so too has a cadre of new developmental and implementation paradigms dramatically shifted IT's perception of itself. When we moved away from the glass house (i.e., the mainframe) we upped the complexity of software management. Most organizations have not upped management practices to manage that. What I'm alluding to here is the developmental shift that must take place when the move is made from mainframe-based applications to the world of client/server. The issue is really how to manage distribution. When you go into a distributed system it is very important to have planned the data in different places: How will it be used? Is it in the right place for efficiency?

Since efficiency and productivity are ever present in the minds of today's IT managers, we might question whether or not the migration to today's more complicated technologies has served to increase productivity—or decrease it. New tools have been introduced that are more complex, but demand for systems has gone up so greatly that it gives the appearance that our productivity has gone down. In essence, our productivity is masked by complexity and demand for new systems. The key is the development environment. This is where CASE research is coming to fruition. Let CASE environments do a lot of the complex background work for the users.

The effect of the extra layer of complexity added by the new developmental techniques of GUI, client/server, and the like, must be mitigated by newer and more robust forms of CASE.

Measurement in the Brave New World

But moving into these new paradigms of development presents the IT organization with a quandary. What type of metrics should be utilized that will effectively measure development in this brave new world? Is the old standard, lines of code, dead? Has the new kid on the block, function points, lost its utility?

The measurement field hasn't been changing very much at all to incorporate new technologies like GUI and client/server. Although function points are the measure of the moment, many agree that function points do have their limitations in dealing with today's more GUI-oriented systems. Function points were created with a transaction notion of input and output. What do you do with the notion of color and motion? This is not reflected in the internal measure.

Today's systems very much stress the envelope of measurement. There were really no good solid standards of measurement even for traditional environments looking back to the world of the 1970s, and people are now trying to build on those very same things to deal with GUIs and object-oriented systems. There's a risk that a lot of technical size measures might start to fall apart. Recognizing the inadequacies of current measurement practices when used on today's more complex systems, Howard Rubin, of Howard Rubin Associates in Pound Ridge, New York, has developed what he terms a "consumer reports scorecard structure." Rubin's scorecard includes 13 categories of measures which can be further refined down to 156-business oriented measures. This scorecard, or EKG, approach is so palatable to some developers that recently a very large northeastern bank managed a merger with another large bank using this approach.

Rubin is the first to admit that not all metrics are appropriate to all methodologies. As far as function points are concerned, he finds that people are trying to stretch function points to work with the object-oriented world. He doesn't believe that they're stretchable. We might as well use something new. We can't always use the past for the future.

Research is under way at MIT to do just that—find something new. Forever the researcher, Dr. Chris Kemerer authored a paper entitled "Towards a Metrics Suite for Object-Oriented Design."[5] This paper, co-authored with Shyam Chidamber, also of the Sloan School, asserts Kemerer's position as perhaps the first person to talk about measurement for object-oriented systems. Since most client/server systems of the future and all GUI systems are object-based, the IT world is beginning to take notice of just this type of research.

Kemerer's paper proposes a series of six metrics that serve to measure the depth and breath of object-oriented design. While he is currently collecting statistics to verify his proposal, his list of six is worthwhile mentioning even without validation. Figure 13.3 summarizes Kemerer's contribution. By perusing this figure it is easy to pinpoint how Kemerer's metrics differ from conventional measurements. Object-oriented metrics are specifically oriented to object-oriented methodologies which are quite different from conventional methodologies. The notion is to try to go after those things that are different about the object-oriented approach. The one that is the easiest to explain to most people is the notion of inheritance. Kemerer's metric is to measure depth of inheritance. In this way we can determine to what degree people are using inheritance. The goal here is to address the optimal mix between complexity and usability.

What Kemerer is referring to is actually the optimal use of the depth of inheritance. When a programmer uses no inheritance, then he is not taking advantage of reusability and therefore negates productivity gains of the object-oriented technique. When the programmer "goes really deep" then, according to Kemerer, this may also be bad, since it

Metric 1:   WMC—Weighted Methods Per Class. Relates to the definition of complexity of an object. The number of methods and the complexity of methods involved is an indicator of how much time and effort is required to develop and maintain the object.

Metric 2:   DIT—Depth of Inheritance Tree. DIT is a measure of how many ancestor classes can potentially affect a class. It is useful to have a measure of how deep a particular class is in the hierarchy so that the class can be designed with reuse of inherited methods.

Metric 3:   NOC—Number of Children. NOC is a measure of how many sub-classes are going to inherit the methods of a parent class. NOC gives an idea of the potential influence a class has on the design. If a class has a large number of children, it may require more testing of the methods in that class.

Metric 4:   CBO—Coupling between Objects. This is a count of the number of non-inheritance related couples with other classes. Excessive coupling between objects outside of the inheritance hierarchy is detrimental to modular design and prevents reuse. This measure is useful to determine how complex the testing of various parts of the design are likely to be.

Metric 5:   RFC—Response for a Class. The response set is a set of methods available to the object. Since it specifically includes methods called from outside the object, it is also a measure of communication between objects. If a large number of methods can be invoked, the testing and debugging of the object becomes more complicated.

Metric 6:   LCOM—Lack of Cohesion in Methods. LCOM uses the notion of degree of similarity of methods. Fewer disjoint sets implies greater similarity of methods. Cohesiveness of methods within a class is desirable, since it promotes encapsulation of objects.

Figure 13.3   Metrics for object-oriented design. (*Source: Chidamber and Kemerer, MIT.*)

will be hard to test it—indeed it may get to be too much for one person to keep in mind.

Even though Kemerer is well on his way to inventing the latest state of the art in the form of measurement he, as is Rubin, is still keen on function points. Measurements could coexist. Measurements might address two parts of the same problem, One is size; the other is design complexity.

Given the trend toward complexity in software, coupled with a desire for increased quality, is there any wonder that IT managers all across the country are having a difficult time adjusting to the new status quo and are actively seeking out role models? In looking for role models to interview for this chapter, the author decided to look straight to hardware/software vendors. After all, they are developers too. And developers of software that is highly complex and has pushed into the new frontiers of client/server and GUI development. What better than to find out from the heads of development, then, just how they cut the mustard.

A View from the Top

In ensuring that quality reigns supreme Unisys uses the SEI matrix to self-access their readiness for quality. A number of years ago Unisys concluded that it didn't have a sufficient emphasis on software engineering quality issues.

As a result, Unisys implemented a TQM program in which quality and productivity is "everybody's job." Their first step was to train everyone, including programmers, in the basics of modern quality thinking. This course was not specifically geared to software engineering but rather emphasized the Deming approach to quality. The Unisys quality course includes everything from statistical process control to why quality is everyone's job and why quality leads to productivity.

What this translates to is some general TQM thinking where different software engineering organizations get to apply that thinking to their own development life cycles. Where this approach has really paid off is in the lowering of the Unisys defect rate. Using an in-house automated system named PRIMUS, Unisys staff, and customers, can track defects both before and after release enabling Unisys to improve tests to make sure that we don't let software out that has bugs in it.

This emphasis on improved quality of their software product has broadened into more sophisticated issues that relate to completeness and marketability of their products. Unisys's quality goals force them to concentrate on three key areas: defect rates, predictability of software performance and product completeness.

This is demonstrated by Unisys's commitment to bring to the table products that can be used both internally and externally for automatic testing and in funding extensive R&D in the area of measurement.

In the first instance, Unisys markets the highly regarded LINC Interpretive test Environment, which is CASE software that eliminates the need to regenerate systems during the test stage of application creation. Unisys LINC developers can change code and immediately verify proper operation to implement changes faster. This interpretive test environment comes complete with an on-line debugger for locating, analyzing, testing and correcting logic errors as well as a statistics gathering feature to ensure code efficiency.

At the other end of the spectrum, Unisys has played a pivotal role in the funding of function point measurement research by the esteemed

Dr. Eberhard Rudolph, Professor of Information Systems at the Hochschule Bremerhaven in Germany. He is a well-known authority on productivity in application software development and in particular on Fourth Generation Languages, CASE tools and the function point technique. His most recent study, released in November 1991, surveyed the effectiveness of the Unisys LINC software development environment. According to the study:

> The results indicate that LINC users can develop larger application systems than installations using conventional Cobol environments. Productivity gains of 5:1 to 10:1 were observed for application systems exceeding 2000 function points. Applications over 5000 function points can have gains of 20:1 and more.

Though the Rudolph study measured solely the Unisys LINC environment one can extrapolate that the newer software methods can play a large role in fostering productivity.

Digital Equipment Corporation knows this lesson only too well. DEC is another hardware/software vendor with a need for consistent quality and enhanced productivity across hardware platforms and software types.

Over the years DEC has refined some techniques that can be successfully used to develop quality software. The most important of these techniques is a clear definition, at the outset of the project, of its usability goals. If you are developing a spreadsheet how will you know that someone can use it effectively, what other products will this be positioned against, what are some sample tasks and is the rate at which you do these tasks important?

In essence, DEC arrives at these goals by working with his customers. As it turns out this is really a study in human factors. And in performing this human factors study DEC has developed a number of techniques that run the gamut from knowledge acquisition to development of quantifiable measurement parameters some of which are shown in the form of questions to be asked in Figure 13.4. One of these

---

1. How stable are the project's requirements?
2. Are you aware and up to speed on your competitor's products?
3. What are you doing to build a better project?
4. What do you need to do, or need to have, to improve quality?
5. At this stage of the project, what process are you using to help you understand where you are in quality?
6. What test coverage is planned?

Figure 13.4 DEC quality review questions. (*Source: Tom Harris, Digital Equipment Corp.*)

is "contextual inquiry" In the context of someone doing their job, rather than put that person in a lab and watch—why don't you work with the person in the context of his job by running a small video camera off to the side. The DEC approach to fostering quality can be summed up with a couple of phrases: a consistent process, good change control, and good testing tools.

Oracle Corporation, maker of the Oracle relational database software, echoes DEC in its insistence on fostering quality. Oracle's development strategy is very specific. First Oracle decides on what the users want to do, what is actually intended, what are its major features. Then Oracle does a full analysis of how that product should be developed. This analysis is based on discussions with both users and technologists. Not only does Oracle consider internal users but they have a wide base of cooperative business partners with whom they spend a lot of time. These are the Boeings and the Shells with whom Oracle spends much time in identifying what they require and how it should work.

Before Oracle is ready to delve into development on any one particular product they match the project to a set of guidelines, or rules of thumb which includes:

"No product will come out before it's ready."

"How many different development streams can we manage at one time?"

"How much development can we actually afford?"

"What is the list of features and functions that we must support?"

This list serves to streamline the long list of possible projects that is presented to Oracle at any given time. At some point Oracle says "we can do this much and not more". When that point has been reached, Oracle prioritizes the projects that do remain.

Oracle is so intent on quality that they are gung-ho on ISO 9000 certification. From Oracle's perspective, quality goes hand in hand with development. So alongside every development plan Oracle has a quality plan. And for each plan they have a list of deliverables or what they call acceptables.

Oracle's many development teams use the concept of acceptables to "prove" that they are delivering usable and quality oriented software. Oracle's quality plan is something that each of the development managers has to produce to demonstrate that product quality is acceptable. It details how they are going to assure that what they deliver is adequate. Oracle has also implemented a formal process that Oracle developers undergo in this vein. They utilize something they call a formal structured hand-over. These sessions, which take about half a day, are attended by four people—one for each stage of development. This includes the supplier—whoever it was that thought of the previous stage, the author—the coder of the current stage, the designer and the receiver who is the person that is supposed to do something with the product. There is also a moderator. The idea behind the formal structured hand-over is that if you put the person who wrote the specification, the designer and the programmer together and they go through the design document in detail with the user a higher end-quality will result.

Perhaps the name that looms largest on the horizon in terms of heavy-duty software development is Computer Associates. Makers of a wide variety of software products which are available on an even wider array of hardware platforms, CA offers the reader an excellent role model.

CA considers that developing a process is bigger than just a coding job. It's something that ties in the appropriateness of the product, performance, the way it integrates into the environment as well as just looking at a particular design for implementing a particular feature.

The centerpiece of the CA development strategy is their CA90 architecture. When developing new code one of the things that they look for is how the new release is going to implement the CA90 architecture. CA90 has a lot of business focus to it. It also has a lot of technical focus. It makes heavy use of common components and tools in creating software. This, almost by itself, contributes to a higher level of quality because CA makes very heavy use of common components and tools in creating their software.

Although the CA90 architecture was conceived at least ten years ago to deal with developing software that needed to integrate easily into the ever-changing IBM operating environment, the architecture provides CA real benefits in today's rapidly changing environment where multi-platform, GUI oriented software is the norm. By insisting that all CA software adhere to a common set of rules all defined neatly within an architecture, CA assures itself that reusable and quality code are the yardstick by which it measures itself.

And in an era of rapidly changing technologies it is perhaps this yardstick that will matter the most.

References

1. S. D. Conte, H. E. Dunsmore, and V. Y. Shen, *Software Engineering Metrics and Models,* Benjamin/Cummings Publishing, Reading, Mass., 1986.
2. Chris F. Kemerer and Geoffrey K. Gill, unpublished study.
3. Thomas McCabe, "A Complexity Measure," *IEEE Transactions on Software Engineering,* SE-2(4):308–320, 1976.
4. W. J. Hansen, "Measurement of Program Complexity by the Pair (Cyclomatic Number, Operator Count)," ACM SIGPLAN Notices, March 1978.
5. Chris Kemerer and Shyam Chidamber, "Towards a Metrics Suite for Object-Oriented Design," October 1991. Presented at ACM Object-Oriented Programming, Systems, Languages, and Applications Conference.

14

A Quick Guide
to Total Quality

In Tracy Kidder's book *Soul of a New Machine,* he details the riveting story of a project conducted at breakneck speed, and under incredible pressure. Driven by pure adrenaline, the team members soon became obsessed with trying to achieve the impossible. For more than a year, they gave up their nights and weekends—in the end logging nearly 100 hours a week each! Somewhere buried in the midst of Kidder's prose we find that at the end of this project the entire staff quit. Not just one or two of them, but every single one!

The information technology field is rife with stories such as this one. Software development projects are usually complex and often mission-critical. As a result the pressure on staff to produce is great. And sometimes, as in the Kidder example, even with success comes failure.

Successful software development projects (i.e., get the product done on time—and *not* lose staff members) have something in common. Each of these projects, in some way, shape, or form, followed one or more principles of quality and productivity. Some of these principles are clearly intuitive. But most are learned or culled from vast experience over a number of years and projects.

In today's competitive environment, information technology is a major partner with the business units. And because of this the push is on for enhanced software productivity and quality. Intuition just won't cut the mustard any longer. Nor can an organization wait until software developers learn their quality lessons over so many projects in as many years.

This final chapter presents a departure from the tone, but not the substance, of the rest of this book. I've stated from the very outset, that IT is besieged. But it's more than just bad press and bad consultants;

it's also being besieged by an overwhelming amount of advice. While much of it is good, much of it is impractical.

Let me explain what I mean. I've been a system developer for what feels like a million years. I have constant deadlines and constant migraines. I really don't have the luxury of stopping work to figure out how to apply some esoteric new way of doing things. Take function points, for example. It's a wonderful metric. But the manual on how to implement it is long and hard to understand. As a result, function points simply have not achieved a level of success commensurate with its benefits.

If you think about it, in spite of everything we've been talking about, in spite of everything you've been reading in the papers, and in spite of everything the industry soothsayers tell us to do, as a whole IT is pretty much where it was 10 years ago. That's because our "experts" have failed to understand one thing. Any technique deployed to IT must ultimately be practical. Not academic or esoteric but practical.

Now if I'm too busy working on tangible projects for my firm and the company I work for spends its money only on bottom-line projects, then how can I improve both productivity and quality?

This is a tough question.

I'd like to say that we should force our managements to understand the importance of IT productivity and quality. Many do. But more ignore it and instead concentrate on the company's profit centers. Perhaps IT should become a profit center then.

Alas, this book can't solve this age-old dilemma. What I *can do* is to provide some real, workable ways to start you on the road to productivity and quality. Toward that end, this final chapter provides a series of checklists. No funny words here. No little anecdotes. Just tried and true policies, procedures, and advice that works.

Each checklist is an abstract from a larger work (footnotes direct you to the source on applicable checklists). Each of these checklists was chosen because I felt that, given your busy work schedules, it was something you could both absorb and try out in short order.

Yes, there are many, many other paths to quality and productivity. But these checklists provide a practical, workable way to get you, at least, out the front door.

Who knows, with a little success, maybe your management will see the light and invest in IT. One can only hope.

The Meaning of Quality

Although quality and productivity are foremost on the minds of management, few truly understand how to correlate the tenets of quality to the process of information technology.

Total quality management, or TQM as it has come to be known, was actually born as a result of a loss of competitive edge to countries such as Japan. In fact, the father of TQM, W. E. Deming, finding no forum for his radical new ideas on quality in the United States, found eager listeners in Japan. Today, Deming's 14 points on quality, listed in the next section, are considered the basis for all work on quality in this country as well as Japan.

But Deming's studies were only the start of a flood of research in the field. For example, Y. K. Shetty, a professor of management at Utah State University's College of Business and the coeditor of *The Quest for Competitiveness* (Quorum Books, 1991), suggests that even though most corporate executives believe that quality and productivity are the most critical issues facing American business, many do not know how to achieve it. Shetty lists 16 organizations that have vigorously attacked this challenge: Caterpillar, Dana Corp., Delta, Dow Chemical, General Electric, Hewlett-Packard, IBM, Intel, Johnson & Johnson, Marriott, Maytag, McDonald's, Procter and Gamble, Texas Instruments, 3M, and Xerox.

What Shetty found was that these organizations shared some characteristics in common. He refers to these as the Seven Principles of Quality.[1]

Principle 1:   Quality improvement requires the firm commitment of top management. All top management, including the CEO, must be personally committed to quality. The keyword here is *personally*. Many CEOs pay only lip service to this particular edict. Therefore, top management must be consistent and reflect its commitment through the company's philosophy, goals, policies, priorities and executive behavior. Steps management can take to accomplish this end include: establish and communicate a clear vision of corporate philosophy, principles, and objectives relevant to product and service quality; channel resources toward these objectives and define roles and responsibilities in this endeavor; invest time to learn about quality issues and monitor the progress of any initiatives; encourage communication between management and employees, among departments, and among various units of the firm and customers; and be a good role model in communication and action.

Principle 2:   Quality is a strategic issue. It must be a part of a company's goals and strategies and be consistent with and reinforce a company's other strategic objectives. It must also be integrated into budgets and plans and be a corporate mission with planned goals and strategies. Finally, quality should be at the heart of every action.

Principle 3:   Employees are the key to consistent quality. The organization must have a people-oriented philosophy. Poorly managed people convey their disdain for quality and service when they work. It is important to pay special attention to employee recruitment, selection, and socialization and to reinforce the socialization and quality process with continuous training and education. It is also a good idea to incorporate quality into performance appraisal and reward systems and to encourage employee participation and involvement. Effective communication throughout the department, between departments, and throughout the organization is required to reinforce the deep commitment of management and creates an awareness and understanding of the role of quality and customer service.

Principle 4: Quality standards and measurements must be customer-driven. It can be measured by:

- Formal customer surveys
- Focus groups
- Customer complaints
- Quality audits
- Testing panels
- Statistical quality controls
- Interaction with customers

Principle 5: Many programs and techniques can be used to improve quality such as:

- Statistical quality control
- Quality circles
- Suggestion systems
- Quality-of-work-life projects
- Competitive benchmarking

Principle 6: All company activities have potential for improving product quality; therefore teamwork is vital. Quality improvement requires close cooperation between managers and employees and among departments. Total quality management involves preventing errors at the point where work is performed and ultimately every employee and department is responsible for quality.

Principle 7: Quality is a never-ending process.

- Quality must be planned.
- Quality must be organized.
- Quality must be monitored.
- Quality must be continuously revitalized.

TQM Methodologies

Since early TQM programs were largely manufacturing-oriented, Information technology (IT) researchers, academicians, and consulting firms were required to interpret and extrapolate TQM tenets and create quality paradigms that could be used to significant advantage. As a result, there is no single TQM methodology in use today that has garnered wholesale industry acceptance. All of these methodologies, however, are based on TQM tenets and all, if used properly, will provide organizations with a clear path toward better quality in their systems.

Be warned, though. One size does not fit all. In a joint report by Ernst & Young and the New York City think-tank, American Quality Foundation, the notion was challenged that quality programs were universally beneficial for all organizations. Based on a study of 584 firms in North America, Japan, and Germany, the report noted that total quality management practices are not generic. What works for some organizations may well turn out to be detrimental to the performance of others.

The problem with quality

Information technologists have long realized that there was something askew. Deadlines were often stretched, more and more money was being poured into never-ending development projects, and an ever-larger percentage of the budget was being allocated to maintenance to fix problems that should never have occurred in the first place.

According to Tom DeMarco, in 1984 15 percent of all software projects with more than 100,000 lines of code failed to deliver value. And in 1989, according to Capers Jones, of all software projects with over 64,000 lines of code, 25 percent failed to deliver anything; 60 percent were significantly over budget and behind schedule; and only 1 percent finished on time, on budget, and met user requirements. In the fall of 1993, I surveyed over 500 managers in charge of large, complex systems. Only 2 percent of those surveyed indicated that they had delivered their project on time, within budget, and with less than a 5 percent error rate.

The Systems Engineering Institute (SEI) at Carnegie-Mellon has developed a five-level framework—shown in the next section—that can be used to assess the quality of the software development process in an organization. It is disheartening to note that SEI has determined that over 86 percent of companies assessed fall in Stage 1, while only 1 percent of firms achieve Stage 5.

It comes as no surprise, therefore, that the majority of software development projects are late, over budget, and out of specification. Project managers point to a number of technical problems, most of which are related to technical tasks specific to software development.

Understanding the symptoms of the quality problem is the first step in recovery. The most common reasons given by project managers for failure to meet budget, time scale, and specification are these:

- Incomplete and ambiguous requirements
- Incomplete and imprecise specifications
- Difficulties in modeling systems
- Uncertainties in cost and resource estimation
- General lack of visibility
- Difficulties with progress monitoring
- Complicated error and change control
- Lack of agreed metrics
- Difficulties in controlling maintenance
- Lack of common terminology
- Uncertainties in software/hardware apportionment
- Rapid changes in technology
- Determining suitability of languages
- Measuring and predicting reliability
- Problems with interfacing
- Problems with integration

Organizations auditing their systems development departments as a result of these problems find several shortcomings in how their projects are structured and managed:

- Lack of standards
- Failure to comply with existing standards
- Nonadherence to model in use
- No sign-off at end of states
- Lack of project plans
- No project control statistics recorded or stored
- No quality assurance (QA) procedures
- No change control procedures
- No configuration control procedures
- Records of test data and results not kept

Software quality management in today's environment

While total quality management and software quality management (TQM/SQM) are laudable goals, most organizations realize that these are truly long-term goals. What processes, then, can be instituted on a short-term basis to provide the organization with a shortcut to quality improvement? F.J. Redmill[2] offers us a series of quickhit tactics:

1. *Training.*   Project manager and team must be trained in TQM concepts and facilities.

2. *Management commitment.*   Must always be seen to be 100%.

3. *Standards.*   A comprehensive set of standards for all aspects of work should be instituted and used. The project life cycle must be covered as well as other pertinent issues.

4. *Guidelines, procedures, and checklists.*   Assist both workers to meet the standards and QA agents to check the products.

5. *Quality assurance.*   Should be carried out at all stages of the life cycle and for all end-products:

   - QA team should be independent of the development team.

   - Audits should be carried out during the project to ensure that management and QA procedures are being adhered to. The project manager should always initiate a review of the auditors' recommendations and of all resulting corrective actions.

6. *Planning.*   The project manager should be fastidious in drawing up plans and ensuring their use for control. Plans should include the project plan; stage plans; and a quality plan, which details the quality requirements of the project.

7. *Reporting.*   A reporting system, to ensure that problems are quickly escalated to the management level appropriate to the action needed, and should be instituted.

8. *Feedback.*   Statistics that assist in project control and the improvement of quality should be collected, analyzed and used.

9. *Continuous / review.*   The whole quality system (components, mode of operation and quality of results) should be reviewed and improved continuously.

10. *Project manager.*   Must not be too technically involved. Technical duties should be delegated to a development team manager who reports to project manager.

11. *Nontechnical support team.*   Should be appointed to assist in nondevelopmental matters, including coordination and interpretation of resource and time statistics, recording all expenditures and tracking against the budget (tracking milestone). This team should report to the project manager.

SEI's Software Process Maturity Framework

The Software Engineering Institute at Carnegie Mellon is the bulwark of engineering productivity research. In their studies of thousands of firms they've discovered some common characteristics that can be used to pinpoint how progressive a firm is in terms of its maturity in the quest for productivity and quality.

The five levels of process maturity are outlined below:

Stage 1:   Initial

- Ad hoc
- Little formalization
- Tools informally applied to the process

Key actions to get to next step:

- Initiate rigorous project management, management review, and quality assurance.

Stage 2:   Repeatable

- Achieved a stable process with a repeatable level of statistical control

Key actions to get to next step:

- Establish a process group.
- Establish a software development process architecture.
- Introduce software engineering methods and technologies.

Stage 3:   Defined

- Achieved foundation for major and continuing progress

Key actions to get to next step:

- Establish a basic set of process managements to identify quality and cost parameters.
- Establish a process database.
- Gather and maintain process data.
- Assess relative quality of each product and inform management.

Stage 4:   Managed

- Substantial quality improvements
- Comprehensive process measurement

Key actions to get to next step:

- Support automatic gathering of process data.
- Use data to analyze and modify the process.

Stage 5:   Optimized

- Major quality and quantity improvements

Key actions to get to next step:

- Continue improvement and optimization of the process.

Productivity/Quality Metrics Checklist

There are as many metric systems as there are firms using them. I've compiled a list of the most frequently and easily implemented.

1. Lines of code
2. Pages of documentation
3. Number and size of tests that you perform on the code
4. Function count
5. Variable count
6. Number of modules
7. Depth of nesting
8. Count of changes required
9. Count of discovered defects
10. Count of changed lines of code
11. Time to design, code, test
12. Defect discovery rate by phase of development
13. Cost to develop
14. Number of external interfaces
15. Number of tools used and why
16. Reusability percentage
17. Variance of schedule
18. Staff years experience with team
19. Staff years experience with language
20. Software years experience with software tools
21. MIPs per person
22. Support to development personnel ratio
23. Nonproject to project time ratio

Quality Factors Checklist

Quality is eminently quantifiable. In this section I provide a checklist that can be used to assess the perceived quality of any delivered system. Rate the items 1 to 5.

1. How easy is it to use?   1 2 3 4 5
2. How secure is it?   1 2 3 4 5
3. Level of confidence in it?   1 2 3 4 5
4. How well does it conform to requirements?   1 2 3 4 5
5. How easy is it to upgrade?   1 2 3 4 5
6. How easy is it to change?   1 2 3 4 5
7. How portable is it?   1 2 3 4 5
8. How easy is it to locate a problem and fix it?   1 2 3 4 5
9. Is the response time fast enough?   1 2 3 4 5
10. How easy is it to train staff?   1 2 3 4 5
11. Ease of testing?   1 2 3 4 5
12. Is the software efficient in terms of computing resources?   1 2 3 4 5
13. Ease of coupling this system to another?   1 2 3 4 5
14. Does the system utilize the minimum storage possible?   1 2 3 4 5
15. Is the system self-descriptive?   1 2 3 4 5
16. Does the system exhibit modularity?   1 2 3 4 5
17. Is there a program for on-going quality awareness for all employees?   1 2 3 4 5
18. Do you check supplier quality?   1 2 3 4 5
19. Is there a quality department?   1 2 3 4 5
20. Is this the "right" system to be developed?   1 2 3 4 5

Rubin Measurement Assessment Questions[3]

Howard Rubin, a professor of Computer Science at Hunter College and a principal of Rubin Associates of Pound Ridge, New York, uses the following questionnaire to assess an organization's ability to manifest change.

1. How intense is the organization's desire to improve its performance?
   (0) No desire   (5) Intense
2. How much is the organization willing to invest to improve its performance?   (0) $0   (5) Up to $100,000 per professional
3. What is the current level of the systems skills inventory in regard to software engineering?   (0) Abstractions and models not used at all (5) Formalization and models used by all

4. To what extent are basic software engineering concepts known and understood by the systems staff? (0) No staff have been exposed (5) 100% trained

5. Is the systems culture adverse to using new tools, techniques, or innovations (0) 100% against (5) Anxious to implement

6. To what extent is a support structure in place to foster measurement software engineering technology transfer? (0) None (5) In place team of critical mass exists

7. What is the current software engineering platform? (0) dumb terminals (5) client-server workstations

Rubin's Questions About Management Practices[3]

Rubin takes a long, hard look at the organization's infrastructure in terms of management practices.

1. How are planning and prioritizing done?
2. How does the organization translate requests into systems?
3. How defined is the systems development life cycle?
4. What is in the organization's tool inventory and what is actually used? (tool penetration)
5. What is organization's current software process maturity level? (Perform a formal or informal SEI assessment)

Malcolm Baldrige Quality Award Ratings

The Malcolm Baldrige quality award looks at quality from a total firm perspective—IT makes up only one component. However, since IT is but a microcosm of the whole organization the Baldrige criteria are equally applicable to IT as to the whole organization.

Since these criteria do change, the reader is advised to obtain the most current copy.

Rate your organization in the space provided.

1.0 Leadership
    1.1 Senior Executive Leadership
    1.2 Quality Values
    1.3 Management for Quality
    1.4 Public Responsibility

2.0 Information and Analysis
    2.1 Scope and Management of Quality Data and Information
    2.2 Competitive Comparisons and Benchmarks
    2.3 Analysis of Quality Data and Information

3.0 Strategic Quality Planning
    3.1 Strategic Quality Planning Process

Quick Hit Productivity Ratios

Productivity is never easy to measure. Use the following three business-oriented metrics to give you an overall feeling for productivity in your organization.

$$\text{Raw productivity} = \frac{\text{system size}}{\text{work hours}}$$

$$\text{Delivery rate} = \frac{\text{system size}}{\text{elapsed weeks}}$$

$$\text{Defect density} = \frac{\text{number of defects}}{\text{system size}}$$

Deloitte & Touche Misuses of Methodology

It probably comes as no surprise but you can misuse as well as use any technology. The following list reflects the collected wisdom of one of the largest consulting firms.

1. *Religious fanaticism.*   This is the situation where an organization holds to the theory that there can be nothing else but the methodology. A "methodology-centric" view of the world if you'll permit the use. Such rigidity is seldom useful or productive. It may also be a symptom of other poor management practices.

2. *Bureaucracy.*   Here the methodology gets wrapped up in a less than effective organization which adds yet another layer of protection and excuse as to why no products are produced. Using a methodology in an organization which may already have top down communications problems and seven or more management layers between the programmers and the management will not help. It will just cause people to push more paper.

3. *The end in itself.*   Very similar to step 2 is the failure resulting from the total focus on the process of developing systems and not on the end results. Personnel are indoctrinated into the process and become wedded to the idea that step "16" must come after "15" and before "17," and that every last step must be completed and documented, even when it is obvious that performing the activities in a step will add no value to the result or that what they are doing has no real business benefit.

4. *Using the wrong one.*   This is rare but is sometimes seen. The few cases I have seen personally seem to arise because a methodology in place has failed to keep up with the times. For example, having no methods that focus on joint application development (JAD) (i.e., where development staff work closely with the end users to develop systems in a RAD-like environment) or on structured testing or, trivially, a customer's methodology which still requires the use of a paper screen layout form when screen painters and prototyping provide far faster and more effective user interaction. A methodology incorporating no guidance in data modeling would be of little help in implementing a system using a modern relational database system.

5. *Lack of organizational penetration.*   The most common problem is still lack of consistent use, starting with lack of commitment by management. Project leaders who get trained and start off by trying to conform will tend to fall by the wayside if not encouraged and coached to do better. In *Strategies for Software Engineering,*

Martyn Ould identified "fourteen dilemmas of software engineering" that he concluded impeded the introduction of new techniques into organizations. Among the more notable examples of these "catch 22's" are:

- We can't use a new method on a project until we have seen it work on other projects.
- We could justify the use of a new method if we could quantify the costs of using it. But we use traditional methods even though we are unable to quantify the costs of using them, resulting in a continuation of the status quo and generally unreliable estimates
- Tools that are generally applicable are generally weak. Strong tools are very specific and therefore generally inapplicable.
- An important feature of new methods is that they tend to be powerful in particular areas. This makes them generally inapplicable. The traditional methods are weak in all areas. This makes them generally inapplicable as well.

Pressman's Common Management Questions[4]

Roger Pressman is one of the luminaries in the field of IT. Here Roger poses some pertinent questions about the relationship between change and management.

We are very set in our ways, is change really possible? The modus operandi of every software development organization appears to be cast in concrete. The fact is that organizations change regularly: new tools, new people, new policies new products and applications, and even new organizational structures are commonplace in the software development community. Even if your organization is "set in its ways," a move toward a software engineering culture (and the changes it portends) is often essential for the continued production of high quality systems. Change is certainly possible, but only if both managers and technical staff take a systematic approach to it.

We're going a million miles an hour, how can we make the time? This question is often asked by managers of young, high technology companies that are growing at a precipitous rate, or in large, well-established companies that are experiencing a significant growth in software demand. It is true that rapid growth stretches resources to their limit. But it is also true that rapid growth exacerbates any underlying software development problems that do exist. The need for change becomes more important.

OK, we have to change, what do we do first? If this question is asked, the first thing has already been done—the speaker has recognized that change is required. Once the decision to change has been made, many managers and most technical people feel that immediate action is necessary. Although a "bias for action" is commendable, the road to a new software engineering culture must be viewed as a journey with many steps. Before beginning the journey, you must understand where you are now. Understanding your current "location" is the first thing that you should do.

We've worked hard to develop internal standards and procedures, isn't that enough?   Although standards and procedures can help to guide technological change, they are not enough. Many software development organizations have fallen into an "S & P trap." That is, they have expended time and resources developing voluminous standards and procedures documents that few staff members understand or use. just because an approach to software development has been codified, does not guarantee that it will be followed.

Should technological change be driven from the top down or from the bottom up?   When successful technological change occurs, it usually occurs in a way that might best be called a "sandwich." Senior management establishes goals and provides resources, driving the process from the top down. At the same time, technical staff obtain education and apply methods and tools driving the process from the bottom up. Both meet in the middle.

Software engineering requires a new approach and a substantial learning curve, won't this cause upheaval?   It is true that cultural change can cause upheaval if it is not managed properly. Therefore, our primary goal in implementing change is to do it in a manner that does not negatively impact the progress of on-going projects. In a later section we discuss a strategy for implementing change that will minimize upheaval while at the same time having a reasonable likelihood of success.

What about project managers, won't they resist?   If software engineering is viewed as a destabilizing influence, project managers will resist it. To gain the support of project managers, we must look at software engineering from their point of view and ask the question: "What's in it for me?" The answer is simple—control. Software engineering procedures, methods, and tools will improve the manager's ability to control a project, something that every manager desires. Once the project manager recognizes this benefit, resistance will disappear.

Money is always tight, how do I get resource commitment from management?   Too many requests for resources (to be allocated to software engineering transition) continue to use the "trust me" school of justification. That is, a request for resources attempts to sell middle and senior management on the overall qualitative benefits of new software engineering technology, without translating these benefits to the bottom line. Although this approach sometimes works, it is being viewed with increasing skepticism by many senior managers. For this reason, it is necessary to develop concrete measures of the software development process and establish a historical baseline that will enable quantitative justification to be made.

Why can't we just buy some good CASE (computer-aided software engineering) tools and leave the rest alone?   Any power tool can be a wonderful thing. Whether you are cutting wood, washing dishes or building computer software, a power tool can improve the quality of your work and the productivity with which you do it. But this is true only if you understand the methods and procedures that must be applied to properly use the tool. If a power tool is used without an understanding of underlying procedures and methods, it can be both unproductive and even dangerous. Most of us wouldn't use a large chain-saw without first understanding the procedures and methods that guide its use. Few people would attempt to wash socks in a dishwasher. Yet, many software developers attempt to use sophisticated CASE tools with little more than a passing understanding of software engineering methods and procedures. Then, they wonder why "these tools don't work for us."

Bouldin's Questions to Ascertain Readiness for Technological Change[5]

In *Agents of Change,* Barbara Bouldin lists the following criteria as benchmarks for readiness for technological change.

1. Is your organization newly formed?
2. Are the functions your organization performs new to your organization?
3. Is your organization growing at a reasonably rapid rate?
4. Is your organization responsible for the development of new systems?
5. Is there a general attitude of optimism, and is morale high?
6. Are your [technical] staff utilizing tools or methods that improve productivity?
7. Does your management support the concept of productivity in any way?
8. Is staff experiencing motivation problems?
9. Is your staff responsible for mature systems that are primarily in the maintenance mode?

10. Does your organization have a backlog of user [or customer] requests...?

Coopers & Lybrand Quantitative Measurement System

Coopers & Lybrand uses the following measurement system to gauge the predictability, business impact, appropriateness, reliability, and adaptability of any system.

Issue: Predictability

    Attribute: Schedule

        Metric: Deviation from estimated number of elapsed weeks

    Attribute: Effort

        Metric: Deviation from estimated number of hours per phase

        Metric: Deviation from estimated number of rework hours per phase

    Attribute: Cost

        Metric: Deviation from estimated number of hours × cost per phase

        Metric: Deviation from estimated number of rework hours × cost per phase

Issue: Business Impact

    Attribute: Time to market

        Metric: Number of elapsed weeks

        Metric: Deviation from schedule

    Attribute: Cost savings

        Metric: Personnel cost savings

        Metric: Hardware, software, and facility cost savings

        Metric: Cost of quality savings

        Metric: Turnaround time

    Attribute: Customer satisfaction

        Metric: Turnaround time

        Metric: Number of support hours

        Metric: Number of problem reports

        Metric: User satisfaction rating

Issue: Appropriateness

    Attribute: Satisfaction of system requirements

        Metric: User satisfaction rating

        Metric: Percent of requirements that can be traced to code

        Metric: Number of design changes

        Metric: Number of perceived goals met

Metric: Number of hours spent in requirements collection

Attribute: Fitness for use
Metric: Number of prototype iterations

Attribute: Conformance to business objectives
Metric: Percent of business objectives that can be traced to requirements
Metric: Number of design changes

Issue: Reliability

Attribute: Correctness
Metric: Number of defects
Metric: Number of rework hours times cost
Metric: Number of rework hours per process product

Attribute: Availability
Metric: Percent of time system is up

Issue: Adaptability

Attribute: Responsiveness to changes
Metric: Number of rework hours
Metric: Problem request completion date

Attribute: User support
Metric: Number of problem reports
Metric: Percent of problem reports completed

W. E. Deming's 14 Quality Points

W. E. Deming is considered the expert who got away. Ignored in the United States, he took his ideas and headed for Japan where he was responsible for their meteoric rise in productivity, quality, and competitiveness. Although there are software interpretations of Deming's ideals, my tendency toward a business-perspective much prefers Deming's original words.

1. Create constancy of purpose toward improvement of product and service, with the aim to become competitive, to stay in business and to provide jobs.
2. Adopt a new philosophy. We are in a new economic age. Western management must awaken to the challenge, must learn its responsibilities and take on leadership for change.
3. Cease dependence on inspection to achieve quality. Eliminate the need for inspection on a mass basis by building quality into the product in the first place.
4. End the practice of awarding business on the basis of price tag. Instead, minimize total cost. Move toward a single supplier for any one item, on a long-term relationship of loyalty and trust.

5. Improve constantly and forever the system of production and service, to improve quality and productivity, and thus constantly decrease costs.
6. Institute training on the job.
7. Institute leadership (see point 12). The aim of leadership should be to help people and machines and gadgets do a better job. Leadership of management is in need of overhaul, as well as leadership of production workers.
8. Drive out fear, so that everyone may work effectively for the company.
9. Break down barriers between departments. People in research, design, sales and production must work as a team, to foresee problems of production and use that may be encountered with the product or service.
10. Eliminate slogans, exhortations and targets for the work force asking for zero defects and new levels of productivity.
11. *a.* Eliminate work standard (quotas) on the factory floor. Substitute leadership.
    b. Eliminate management by objective. Eliminate management by numbers, numerical goals. Substitute leadership.
12. *a.* Remove barriers that rob the hourly worker of his or her right to pride of workmanship. The responsibility of supervisors must be changed from sheer numbers to quality.
    b. Remove barriers that rob people in management and in engineering of their right to pride of workmanship.
13. Institute a vigorous program of education and self-improvement.
14. Put everyone in the company to work to accomplish the transformation. The transformation is everybody's job.

W. S. Humphrey's Principles of Software Process Management[6]

Watts Humphrey is the father of the concept of the "software factory." Here he elucidates on the major principles of the management of the software process.

People Management
1. The professionals are the key to the programming process, and they must be intimately involved in its development and improvement.
2. Management must focus on programming defects not as personal issues but as opportunities for process improvement.

Process Support
1. Special process groups need to be established.
2. Necessary management and professional education is provided.
3. The best tools and methods are obtained and used.

Process Methodology
1. The process is formally defined.
2. Goals and measurements are established.
3. Statistical data are analyzed to identify problems and determine causes.

Process Control
1. Management practices are established to control change.
2. Periodic process assessments are conducted to monitor effectiveness and identify necessary improvements.
3. Procedures are established to certify process quality and implement corrective actions.

Motorola's Six Sigma Defect Reduction Effort[7]

In 1987 Motorola set in motion a 5-year quality improvement program. The term *Six Sigma* is one used by statisticians and engineers to describe a state of zero defects. The result of this program has produced productivity gains of 40 percent as well as winning the Malcolm Baldrige National Quality award in 1988. Benefits include:

- Increased productivity by 40 percent
- Reduced backlog from years to months
- Increased customer service levels
- Shifted IS time from correcting mistakes to value-added work
- More motivated staff
- Saved $1.5 billion in reduced cost

Here is how it's done:

1. *Identify your product.*   Determine what is the service or product you are producing. IS must align what they do with what the customers want.
2. *Identify customer requirements.*   IS must determine what the customer perceives as a defect-free product or service. The unit of work that the user is dealing with must be considered. For example, in a general ledger system in which the user worries about defects per journal voucher and not defects per thousand lines of code.
3. *Diagnose the frequency and source of errors.*   Four categories of metrics were established to target defect reduction:
   - New software development

- Service delivery
- Cycle time
- Customer satisfaction, which is composed of a detailed service with the intent of validating the first three metrics

4. *Define a process for doing the task.*   Motorola refers to this process as mapping but closely aligned to the re-engineering process. The process involves using personal computer-based tools to determine flow-through of processes and answering the following questions:
   - Which processes can be eliminated?
   - Which processes can be simplified?

5. *Mistake-proof the process.*   By streamlining a process and eliminating any unnecessary steps, it is possible to make the process mistake proof. By using metrics a process control mechanism is put into place so that problems can be addressed before it affects output.

6. *Put permanent control measures in place.* Once Six Sigma is reached, this level must be maintained. At this step, the Six Sigma metrics are set up to be used to continuously monitor the process:
   - Monthly quality review meetings are held where each person gets up and discusses their metric, its trend, diagnosis of source cause of errors, action plan to correct

Ernst & Young Center for Information Technology and Strategy TQM Solution

The basic tenet behind Ernst & Young's TQM consultancy is to get organizations to understand a single principle—that change is painful and lengthy. In order to effectuate any kind of change, you need a ten-year plan and management's patience is short. So, how do you motivate change over that time period?

The secret is to make management extremely dissatisfied with the status quo. And to do that you need to look at the cost of the status quo. One way of accomplishing this is to examine the cost of poor quality.

By answering questions such as, "What are we spending on detecting defects?" the IT organization can begin to accumulate the statistics it needs to make the push for change. The data need not be hard to track; in most cases, it is already available through project management systems that track walkthroughs, reviews, defect rates, etc.

The following nine steps constitute Ernst & Young's quick-hit approach to tackling TQM in IT departments:

1. Create a massive discomfort with the status quo. This can be accomplished in any one of a number of ways, including using numerical data or using a customer survey.

2. Use what was found in step 1 to get management sponsorship. Use what was found in step 1 to get management sponsorship of the TQM process.

3. Develop a commitment to quality. Top management needs to make a visible and personal commitment to any quality program.

4. Involve others. Customers/suppliers must be involved in the TQM process.

5. Define what the processes are.

6. Determine value measurements. Have customers of the processes outputs determine what value measurements are.

7. Form teams. Form process (quality) improvement teams that use these measures

8. Innovate/improve the process. Come up with ways to innovate or improve the process.

9. Continue to improve. Create an environment where the processes continually improve

Coopers & Lybrand TQM Methodology[8]

Coopers & Lybrand have taken appropriate elements of TQM and successfully applied them to software delivery organizations. It has developed a specific four-phase methodology, dubbed *software quality management* (SQM), which provides a framework for managing continuous improvement for software delivery.

Assessment

The purpose of the *assessment* phase is to evaluate the organization's current environment and determine how well the organization meets or is likely to meet its customers' software quality requirements. In any assessment phase, a measurement system must first be designed as a tool and to establish a quality baseline. The Goal/Question/Metric approach described below can be used to produce this measurement system.

During assessment, it is important to understand the activities involved in the software development process as well as the organizational roles and responsibilities. The measurements currently being used by the organization must also be identified and assessed. Whenever possible, existing measures should be used as part of the quality assessment to promote familiarity and acceptance.

Nevertheless, the overall approach is to develop questions and metrics that have the greatest importance to the organization. This is achieved by focusing on the three dimensions of the goals of the assessment: the phase under scrutiny, the relevant quality issue and the role from which the phase and quality issue are viewed.

When conducting an assessment, it may also be necessary to hold briefing sessions with respondents to clarify the meaning of some of the metrics. Moreover, respondents who feel that they are being imposed upon or are fearful of the measurement effort are likely to provide questionable data. It is especially important to make clear that the metrics are not being used as a mechanism for punitive actions. Since many sensitive and perhaps embarrassing issues may arise during the assessment, it is often easier for an outside third party to manage the process and gather data.

It is also desirable to collect the data during a fixed period of time with a specific deadline. During the assessment period, the collection team should be available to answer questions and clarify procedures. After the data is collected, it is compiled, analyzed, and translated into graphic depiction's of the major findings. The key outcome of the assessment is the identification of opportunities for improvement by studying the consolidated findings. This resulting list of opportunities is essential for the planning and implementation of pilot improvement projects.

Getting consensus from management as to the validity of the analysis and the opportunities for improvement is also essential. Specifically, the assessment team must be sensitive to the possible misinterpretation of the findings and conclusions which may result in blame laying. Prior to moving on to planning, the management sponsor must help the team identify potential trouble spots and devise methods for defusing them.

Planning

The analysis of the data collected during the assessment provides the foundation for the quality improvement plan. The assessment defines the organization's quality profile and identifies opportunities for improvement. The objectives of the *planning* phase are to establish strategic and tactical direction, as well as consensus and commitment for improvement is identified in the assessment. A *process improvement plan* is the final outcome of this strategic planning effort.

Typically, two different types of problems surface as a result of the assessment: ones with relatively simple, quick solutions and ones more deeply rooted in organizational practices, requiring a longer period to solve. To address the first type of problem, the organization must devise short-term, measurable projects with a consistent sequence encompassing the Plan/Do/Check/Act process. The second type of problem requires an effort aimed at longer-term organizational and behavioral changes. The focus of the planning effort will be on these long-term projects.

Nevertheless, a critical success factor for any SQM project is the perception that quality improvement is attainable. The quality improvement team's ability to achieve successes on the short-term projects will help to pave the way for the entire process. Furthermore, quick management decisions on short-term projects will show development staff that their improvement ideas have been taken seriously and that management is willing to take actions based on staff input.

Because participation and consensus of management is essential to the planning effort, there is always considerable risk of delay. The planning team must, therefore, conduct an intensive quality planning session with managers early in the process. Ideally, all of the planning work could be accomplished at such a session. At a minimum, the result of the meeting will be to define the "quality vision" and to establish the roles and responsibilities of the groups to be charged with the organization's quality program.

The organization's vision of what quality software means and where it expects to be must be agreed upon early in the planning effort. Most organizations find that there are several areas where improvement efforts can be focused; however, trying to do too much at once is not a good idea. Priorities should be assigned to targets based on the following criteria:

- Criticality
- Cost
- Resources
- Timing
- Risks
- Opportunity for near-term success

The projects that are selected as top priorities will require further discussion and decisions regarding the manner in which the improvements are to be implemented. The result will be a prioritized statement of quality objectives, the process improvements to be achieved and the measurements that will demonstrate success. In addition, each quality improvement project should have:

- A mission statement that includes improvement goals
- Schedules and resource and cost estimates for each project
- An organization structure responsible for quality management
- Measurement procedures to validate the meeting of goals

In addition to establishing procedures, it is essential that top management realize the implications of committing to SQM. It must be understood that SQM is not a pilot program but an ongoing process to enhance the way the software organization conducts business. SQM requires changing procedures, cooperating with other departments, emphasizing the process and changing management philosophies that are ineffective yet pervasive. If senior management is not willing to commit themselves, their organization and their people to the process, an SQM program is probably not worth starting.

Planning for software quality improvement requires more than just top management commitment and sponsorship. It also calls for attention to cultural and behavioral issues. For example, the initial reaction of staff to a measurement program may be apprehension, fear and resistance. It must be shown that the program and data collected will be used for improvement purposes and not punishment. One or more short-term successes will demonstrate the real value of the measurement system. Also, a measurement system should indicate process and product strengths that need encouragement as well as weaknesses that need improvement.

The primary goals of the planning phase of SQM are to define quality objectives and strategies for instituting improvement solutions. It is also important for the plan to establish the roles and responsibilities for the individuals and teams whose mission is to promote and oversee continuous quality improvements. The final product is a plan that prioritizes the quality objectives, details the means for achieving improvements in the short term, identifies and analyzes quality-related risks, and creates an agreed upon framework to achieve long-term quality improvement objectives.

Implementation

Introducing measurement systems and the concept of continuous improvement will require far reaching changes to an organization. During the *implementation* phase, these changes begin to occur. Implementing the quality improvement plan means incorporating the measurement and improvement efforts into the organizational culture and discovering which behavioral changes need to occur. This effort, therefore, requires a corresponding change in the reward structure. A reward system should motivate the staff to change development procedures in a way that is consistent with the goals of the improvements efforts.

Once a new reward system is in place, implementation should turn to those short-term projects that were identified in the planning phase. These may include:

- Project tracking techniques and tools

- Formalizing reviews and walkthroughs
- Implementing *joint application design* (JAD) sessions
- Applying new approaches to testing

Most of the efforts at improvement will require training of staff and project management in the relevant techniques and tools. These training efforts must be undertaken with the same commitment and level of support given to the entire SQM effort. If staff is not supported in its effort to change, all of the assessments and strategic planning sessions in the world will not effect change. For an SQM program to be successful, staff and management must be encouraged to experiment, take risks, and take charge of improving the process.

Once the framework of rewards, training, and empowerment is established, the long-term process improvements can be attempted. These may include:

- Implementing risk management techniques
- Introducing a structured development methodology
- Instituting Rapid Prototyping techniques
- Evaluating and implementing new CASE tools

Institutionalization

Institutionalization requires that the lessons learned during implementation be captured and transformed into organizational assets to form the basis of a continuous improvement culture. As a first step, the experiences gained in near-term improvement projects should be analyzed, packaged, and communicated to everyone in the organization. Successes must be validated and publicized. The experience is packaged into self-contained units including approach, results, techniques, tools, manuals, and training, to transform the knowledge gained into the organization's culture.

The basic techniques for institutionalizing continuous quality improvement include:

- Analyzing the results of short-term projects and comparing the results with the targets defined in planning
- Synthesizing the experience into lessons learned, domain expertise, rules, and models
- Packaging the experience as products that can be delivered to the organization

Institutionalizing SQM requires comprehensive reuse of the experience from several projects or several phases of a project. Much of the work done at this stage of the program involves educating the individuals who develop and maintain software. This education involves not only formalized training on specific process improvements, but also formal and informal quality awareness education via the promotion of quality improvement successes.

Corbin's Methodology for Establishing a Software Development Environment[9]

The *software development environment* (SDE) is actually the integration of a number of processes, tools, standards, methodologies, and related elements whose purpose is to provide a framework for building quality software. This section discusses the elements of SDE and shows how to develop one.

1. The elements of SDE are
   - Project management
   - Business plan
   - Architecture
   - Methodologies
   - Techniques
   - Tools
   - Metrics
   - Policies and procedures
   - Technology platform
   - Support
   - Standards
   - Education and training

2. The benefits of SDE are
   - Improved problem definition
   - Selection of the "right" problem according to the customer
   - Joint customer/IS responsibility and accountability
   - Acknowledgment of customer ownership of system
   - Reduced costs of systems development and maintenance
   - Reusability of software, models, and data definitions
   - Acceptance of the disciplined approach to software engineering using a consistent methodology
   - Productivity improvements through team efforts and tools such as CASE

3. Sample goals of SDE are

   - Reduce systems development costs
   - Reduce maintenance costs
   - Reduce MIS turnover rate

These goals should be quantifiable wherever possible. For example, the first goal could be stated as "reduce systems development costs by 50% over the next five years."

4. Architecture.   Many organizations do not have a formal, documented architecture. There are three types:

   - *Business architecture* is a model of the business and identifies such things as processes and entities in the form of models.
   - *Computing architecture,* at a minimum, identifies hardware, software, and data communications. This breaks out into components such as operating systems, data resource management, network protocols, user interface
   - *Enterprise architecture* is a combination of the Business and Computing Architectures

5. Business plan

   - Create a steering committee that provides direction to the MIS function
   - Translate the organization's business plan into an actionable MIS plan that supports the business's goals and objectives
   - The steering committee should be responsible for funding projects, setting priorities, resolving business issues, and reviewing MIS policies and procedures

6. *Education and training*   Make sure that analysts, programmers, and users are all trained and ready to start the development project. Training might include the following:

   - Software engineering concepts
   - Prototyping
   - System development life cycle
   - Joint application development
   - Software quality assurance and testing
   - Project management
   - Data and process modeling
   - CASE

7. *Methodologies*   Whether the methodology chosen by the MIS department is a standard one, from a vendor or developed inter-

nally, the MIS group must follow one to ensure consistency from project to project. This will enable staff to be able to move from project to project without retraining while, at the same time, ensuring consistent deliverables. Questions to ask when selecting a methodology are

- Does your methodology support the entire systems development life cycle?
- Does it include maintenance?
- Is it clearly documented?
- Does it focus on deliverables instead of activities?
- Is it CASE tool independent?
- Can you use your metrics and techniques with it?

8. *Project management*   Questions to ask include

- Do you have a formal project management discipline in place?
- Do you have a training program to support this?
- Is a software tool used?
- Do you have program planning and control to help manage the project?
- Do you get routine reports showing the project work breakdown structure, status reports, resource loading, and cost projections?
- Is there a formal reporting mechanism done on a timely basis to resolve problems?

9. *Standards*   Some of the areas in which standards are required are

- Systems analysis and design
- Data administration
- Database administration
- Systems testing
- Prototyping
- Documentation
- Data entry
- Systems production
- Change/configuration management

Questions to ask:

- Have you identified all of the standards that are required to support your SDE?
- Do you have someone responsible for developing and maintaining standards?

10. Support options
    - External consulting
    - A sharing arrangement where you can provide services in exchange for those needed
    - User groups
    - Special interest groups

11. Automated tool questions
    - Have you identified the tools you need in the SDE?
    - Have they been approved, acquired, and installed?
    - Do they support the methodologies?
    - Do they support the technology platform?
    - Do they support the standards?
    - Is technical support available to support the tools?
    - Do you have templates for use in systems development?
    - Do you have a data dictionary, or repository for your data?
    - Do you have tools to support each phase of the life cycle?

Simmons Statistics Concerning the Effect That Communications Has on Group Productivity[10]

This section details the many factors that dominate software group productivity. Simmons defines dominator as a single factor that causes productivity to decline ten-fold. The two dominators that are discussed are communications and design partition.

What follows is a set of rules and statistics that the reader can use as a comparison in his or her own efforts to increase productivity.

1. Factors that developers must cope with in developing large systems:
    - Personnel turnover
    - Hardware/software turnover
    - Major ideas incorporate late
    - Latent bugs

2. A Delphi survey performed by Scott and Simmons to uncover factors that affect productivity found that the main factors are
    - External documentation
    - Programming language
    - Programming tools
    - Programmer experience

- Communications
- Independent modules for task assignment (design partition)
- Well-defined programming practices

3. Improvement statistics:

   - Any step towards the use of structured techniques, interactive development, inspections, etc., can improve productivity by up to 25 percent.
   - Use of these techniques in combination could yield improvements of between 25 and 50 percent.
   - Change in programming language can, by itself, yield a productivity improvement of more than 50 percent.
   - Gains of between 50 and 75 percent can be achieved by single high achievers or teams of high achievers.
   - Gains of 100 percent can be achieved by database user languages, application generators, and software reuse.

4. *Dominators* are factors that can suppress the effects of other factors and can reduce software group productivity by an order of magnitude.

5. Poor design partition can dominate group productivity. To obtain high productivity in the development of large software systems, the designer must break down the system in chunks that can be developed in parallel. The difference between great and average designers is an order of magnitude.

6. Communications can dominate productivity. Most project problems arise as the result of poor communications between workers. If there are n workers on the team, then there are $n(n - 1)/2$ interfaces across which there may be communications problems.

7. Productivity of individual programmers varies as much as 26 to 1.

8. An individual working alone has no interruptions from fellow group members and, therefore, the productivity can be quite high for a motivated individual. It is estimated that one programmer working 60 hours a week can complete a project in the same calendar time as two others working normal hours, but at three-quarters the cost.

9. Small groups of experienced and productive software developers can create large systems. An example is given of a company, Pyburn Systems. They scour the country for the best analytical thinkers. Its senior programmers typically earn $125,000 a year and can be paid bonuses of two to three times that amount. They work in small teams, never more than five, to produce large, com-

plex systems. In comparison, most MIS departments produce large systems using normal development teams with developers of average ability.

10. In general, the difference between the cost to produce an individual program to be run by the program author and the cost to produce a programming system product developed by software group is at least nine times more expensive.

11. There is a point where coordination overheads outweighing any benefits that can be obtained by the addition of further staff. Statistics that support this were pioneered during the nineteenth century in work on military organization. It was noted that as the number of workers who had to communicate increased arithmetically, from 2 to 3 to 4 to 5..., the number of communication channels among them increased geometrically, from 1 to 3 to 6 to 10...From this study, it was concluded that the upper limit of effective staff size for cooperative projects is about 8.

12. In studies, it has been shown that when the number of staff increased to 12 or more, the efficiency of the group decreased to less than 30 percent.

13. The productive time of a typical software developer during a working day can vary from 51 to 79 percent. It was found that the average duration of work interruption was 5 minutes for a typical programmer. The average time to regain a train of thought after an interruption was 2 minutes. Thus, the average total time spent on an interruption was 7 minutes. It we assume five productive hours each day, then each interruption takes 2.33 percent of the working day, ten interruptions would take up 23 percent of the day, and 20 interruptions would take approximately 50 percent.

14. The optimum group size for software development team is between five to eight members. The overall design should be partitioned into successively smaller chunks, until the development group has a chunk of software to develop that minimizes intragroup and intergroup communications.

Burns's Framework for Building Dependable Systems[11]

The role and importance of nonfunctional requirements in the development of complex critical applications have, up until now, been inadequately appreciated. It has been shown, through experience, that this approach fails to produce dependable systems.

Nonfunctional requirements include dependability (e.g., reliability, availability, safety, and security), timeliness (e.g., responsiveness, orderliness, freshness, temporal predictability, and temporal controllability), and dynamic change management (i.e., incorporating evolutionary changes into a nonstop system).

The purpose of the framework described in this section is to:

- Impose a design discipline that ensures that appropriate abstractions are used at each level of the design

- Allow assertions to be developed that the nonfunctional requirements can be met by the design if implemented in a particular environment.

- Allow interactions between these nonfunctional requirements to be analyzed so that dependencies can be identified

- Allow the nonfunctional and functional requirements to be traded off against each other

Burns's framework consists of the following steps and procedures:

1. A constructive way of describing the process of system design is a progression of increasingly specific commitments which define properties of the system design which designers operating at a more detailed level are not at liberty to change. For example, early in the design there may already be commitments to the structure of a system, in terms of module definitions and relationships.

2. Those aspects of a design to which no commitment is made at some particular level in the design hierarchy are the subject of obligations that lower levels of design must address. For example, the behavior of the defined committed to modules is the subject of obligations which must be met during further design and implementation.

3. The process of refining a design—transforming obligations into commitments—is often subject to constraints which are imposed primarily by the execution environment.

4. The execution environment is the set of hardware and software components on top of which a system is built. It may impose both resource constraints (e.g., processor speed) and constraints of mechanism (e.g., data locking).

5. The framework controls the introduction of necessary implementation details into the design process by distinguishing two phases in the construction of an architectural design of any application:

- *Logical architecture.* Embodies commitments which can be made independently of the constraints imposed by the execution environment and is aimed at satisfying the functional requirements
- *Physical architecture.* Takes constraints into account and embraces the nonfunctional requirements.

6. The nonfunctional requirements of an application can be considered as projections onto the physical architecture. Distinct projects apply to timeliness, safety, and so on. The physical architecture makes it explicit where projections interact and enables criteria to be developed that cater to these interactions.

7. The framework is grounded in the object-oriented approach to system design. The object-oriented approach is widely regarded as offering a conceptual framework for mastering the complexities of the design process:

   - Objects are an adequate modeling tool for the functional requirements of the system.
   - They can be used to provide traceability through all stages of the design process.
   - They are an adequate basis for expressing nonfunctional requirements.
   - They provide an appropriate granularity for replication, checkpointing, dynamic change management, configuration, and dynamic reconfiguration.
   - They assist error containment through encapsulation.
   - They can support dynamic security by accessing right mechanisms on operations.
   - They can represent schedulable entities.
   - Commonly encountered standard architectures can be implemented by means of redefined classes and methods.

8. The logical architecture is concerned with defining a set of object classes, their interfaces, and relationships which together meet all the functional requirements. In the logical architecture, communication between the classes is represented by invocation of methods.

9. The physical architecture is concerned with objects, that is, instances of the classes defined in the logical architecture. It refines the logical architecture in two ways:

   - It instantiates objects from the classes defined in the logical architecture and maps them onto the target execution environment.
   - It annotates the objects and their methods with attributes (such as deadlines) derived from the nonfunctional requirements.

Farbey's Considerations on Software Quality Metrics During the Requirements Phase[12]

In this section Farbey expands on the general view of quality as the difference between what is expected and what is experienced, namely,

$$Quality = expectations - experience$$

Four questions are addressed:

- *Effectiveness.* Does the specification, considered as a solution, solve the right problem?
- *Serviceability.* Does the specification, considered as a starting point, provide a firm basis on which to proceed?
- *Prediction.* Does the requirement specification (together with the system test specification) provide useful measures for predicting the final quality outcome?
- *Process.* Does the process by which the specification is produced encourage effectiveness, serviceability, and quality prediction?

1. *Effectiveness*   The first question concerns the quality of the specification as a solution—how well does the specification capture the problem? The ultimate effectiveness of a system depends not on the quality of software or specification, but on the degree to which the problem is correctly perceived. Focus on the specification as a product by asking these questions like the ones that follow:

   - Is the process by which it has been produced conducive to bringing out and clarifying objectives?
   - Is it complete in that it exhausts the objectives and needs that are known?
   - Is the specification maintainable?
   - Is it readable?

Quality attributes covered in this question include:

- *Functionality.* Does the specification capture all of the required functions?
- *Performance.* Does the specification meet the users' demands?
- *Usability.* Does the specification promote ease of use, learning, and relearning?

2. *Serviceability*   The second question concerns the quality of its content and implications for later system development. The following is a list of questions of efficiency, in this context meaning "doing things right":

- Are the requirements consistent?
- Are the requirements unambiguous?
- Are the requirements compatible with the methods of later development stages?
- Are the requirements readable?
- Are the requirements modifiable?
- Are the requirements traceable?
- Are the requirements usable after implementation?
- Are the requirements maintainable?
- Are the requirements in compliance with documentation standards?

3. *Prediction* The third question concerns the value of measures of quality that will act as predictor measurements for the eventual quality of the finished software. A predictor metric is used to predict the value of a property of a system that will only become directly observable during a later stage of system development

4. *Process* Three processes of development are worth considering:
   - Life-cycle process such as SSADM (Structured Systems Analysis and Design), which is based on a waterfall model. In this model requirements specification occurs at an early stage and is then fixed as would any associated metrics.
   - Prototyping approach offers an early normalization but also offers a more flexible model of system development that recognizes the problem of changing requirements.
   - Approaches that recognize specifically the social setting in which requirements specifications takes place. Control of quality during any process will probably be one of instituting checklists together with a program for completing them and acting on the results.

   Questions to ask at this point include:

- Is the system easy to learn?
- Is the system easy to relearn?
- Is there stability and maturity in the system?

Hewlett-Packard's TQC (Total Quality Control) Guidelines for Software Engineering Productivity[13]

Engineering productivity is extremely important to HP because they rely on new product development to maintain their competitive strength. HP introduces an average of one new product every business day. Seventy percent of HP's engineers are involved in software development. Half of all R&D projects are exclusively devoted to software development.

It was this significant investment in software development that prompted HP's president to issue a challenge to achieve a ten-fold improvement in software quality within 5 years. He also asked that new product development time be reduced by 50 percent.

This section points out the techniques HP utilized to meet this vast quality and productivity challenge.

1. HP's productivity equation:

$$\text{Productivity} = \underset{\text{the right things}}{\text{function of doing}} \times \underset{\text{things right}}{\text{function of doing}}$$

2. Cultural and organizational issues addressed to be able to motivate and support positive changes:
   a. Productivity managers are used in each division to
      (1) Understand productivity and quality issues
      (2) Evaluate, select, and install CASE tools
      (3) Communicate best software engineering practices
      (4) Train personnel
      (5) Establish productivity and quality metrics
   b. A group productivity council is created to share the best R&D practices across divisions, such as
      (1) Metrics definition
      (2) Metrics tracking
      (3) Productivity councils
      (4) Software quality and productivity assessment
      (5) Communication of best practices
3. A software metrics council is created, composed of both R&D and QA managers and engineers, whose objective is to identify key software metrics and promote their use.
4. Project/product quality metrics are as follows:
   a. Breakeven time measures return on investment. It is defined as time until development costs are offset by profits. The three numbers plotted are: (1) R&D investment in dollars, (2) operating profit in dollars and time, and (3) sales revenue in dollars and time.
   b. Time-to-market measures responsiveness and competitiveness. It is defined as time from project go-ahead until release to market.
   c. A Kiviat diagram measures variables that affect software quality and productivity. It is a bulls-eye chart which graphs results of quality and productivity assessment.
5. Process quality metrics:
   a. Progress rate measures accuracy of schedule. It is defined as the ratio of planned to actual development time.

    b. Open critical and serious KPRs measure effectiveness of support processes. It is defined as the number of service requests classified as known problems (of severity level critical or serious) that are not signed off.

    c. Postrelease defect density measures effectiveness of design and test processes. It is defined as the total number of defects reported during the first 12 months after product shipment.

6. People quality metrics:
       a. Turnover rate measures morale. It measures that percent of engineers leaving the company.
       b. Training measures investment in career development. It is defined as the number of hours per engineer per year.

7. Basic software quality metrics:
       a. Code size (KNCSS, which is thousands of lines of noncomment source statements)
       b. Number of prerelease defects requiring fix
       c. Prerelease defect density (defects/KNCSS)
       d. Calendar months for prerelease QA
       e. Total prerelease QA test hours
       f. Number of postrelease defects reported after 1 year
       g. Postrelease defect density (defects/KNCSS)
       h. Calendar months from investigation checkpoint to release

8. Strategy for code reuse:
       a. Share code (use exactly as is) whenever possible
       b. If sharing is not possible, try to leverage (minimal modifications)
       c. If neither sharing nor leveraging is possible, look for similar algorithms (design reuse)
       d. As a last resort, invent something new

9. The Systems Software Certifications program established to ensure measurable, consistent, high-quality software. The four metrics chosen were
       a. *Breadth.* Measures the testing coverage of user-accessible and internal functionality of the product
       b. *Depth.* Measures the proportion of instructions or blocks of instructions executed during the testing process
       c. *Reliability.* Measures the stability and robustness of a product and its ability to recover gracefully from error conditions
       d. *Defect density.* Measures the quantity and severity of reported defects found and a product's readiness for use

Specification Thoroughness Survey

Circle the appropriate number for each item below as it applies to your current project. The desired result from this test is a preponderance of marks in the 1 or 2 categories.

	Often				Seldom
1. Program specifications contain (hidden) errors and omissions.	1	2	3	4	5
2. Design decisions are made on personal preferences.	1	2	3	4	5
3. Program design process is informal.	1	2	3	4	5
4. Programmers begin to code before design is complete.	1	2	3	4	5
5. Software objectives are inadequately defined.	1	2	3	4	5
6. Programmers spend too much time correcting errors that are the result of poor specifications.	1	2	3	4	5
7. Poor and inadequately enforced standards contribute to poor quality programs.	1	2	3	4	5
8. Far too many omissions and errors are discovered after implementation.	1	2	3	4	5
9. Inadequate commitment to quality software by management.	1	2	3	4	5
10. Inadequate commitment to quality software by end users.	1	2	3	4	5

Criteria Definitions for Software Quality

Traceability Those attributes of the software that provide a thread from the requirements to the implementation with respect to the specific and operational environment.

Completeness Those attributes that provide full implementation of the functions required.

Consistency Those attributes that provide uniform design and implementation techniques and notation.

Accuracy Those attributes that provide the required precision in calculation and notation.

Error tolerance Those attributes that provide continuity of operation under nonnominal conditions.

Simplicity Those attributes that provide implementation of functions in the most understandable manner (usually avoidance of practices which increase complexity).

Modularity Those attributes that provide a structure of highly independent modules.

Generality   Those attributes that provide breadth to the functions performed.

Expandability   Those attributes that provide for expansion of data storage requirements or computational functions.

Instrumentation   Those attributes that provide for the measurement of usage or identification of errors.

Self-descriptiveness   Those attributes that provide explanation of a function.

Execution efficiency   Those attributes that provide for minimum processing time.

Storage efficiency   Those attributes that provide for minimum storage requirements.

Access control   Those attributes that provide for control of the access of software and data.

Access audit   Those attributes that provide for and audit the access of software and data.

Operability   Those attributes that determine operation and procedures concerned with the operation of software.

Training   Those attributes that provide a transition from current operation to initial familiarization.

Communicativeness   Those attributes that provide useful inputs and outputs that can be assimilated.

Software system independence   Those attributes that determine the software's dependency on the software environment (operating systems, utilities, input/output routines, etc.).

Machine independence   Those attributes that determine the software's dependency on the hardware system.

Communications commonality   Those attributes that provide the use of standard protocols and interface routines.

Data Commonality   Those attributes that provide the use of standard data representations.

Conciseness   Those attributes that provide for implementation of a function with a minimum amount of code.

Steps to Refocusing IT Activity

The process of squeezing extra resources from systems can be broken down into three steps, each with several components.

Step 1:   Streamline the current systems environment

Objectives: 15 to 20 percent of real cost reduction with payback in 6 to 12 months.

Activities:

1. Choose relevant organization units for analysis.
2. Allocate costs to end products.
3. Generate ideas for streamlining costs.
4. Plan implementation.

Step 2: Focus on high-value priorities.

Objectives: 30 to 40 percent reduction in current development projects, with resources reallocated to highest impact investments.

Activities:

1. Identify cost drivers and leverage points.
2. Group planned projects around leverage points.
3. Identify new opportunities and possible cutbacks.
4. Restate priorities.

Step 3: Build ongoing organizational capabilities.

Objectives: (1) Consolidation of gains on ongoing basis and (2) maintenance of major improvements in organizational effectiveness.

Activities:

1. Evaluate planning and decision-making procedures.
2. Interview users and participants regarding the effectiveness of those procedures.
3. Identify weaknesses and opportunities for improvement.
4. Design procedural changes.

End Note

In the end, IT will be plagued with problems of productivity and quality for many years to come. There will always be "experts" who use your watch to tell you the time, writers who "confuse" their advice to you, and managers who are long on dictatorial style but short on real skills. All this subtly contributing to the decrease in productivity.

But we will also be blessed with many opportunities. New methodologies to spur you to the greatest ever heights of reliability, new software tools to make it easier for you, and new measurement systems to prove to your management what you knew all along.

The question is: Are you ready to take advantage of what's being offered you?

References

1. Y. K. Shetty, "A point of view: Seven principles of quality leaders," *National Productivity Review* (Winter 1991–1992) pp. 3–7.

2. F. J. Redmill, "Considering Quality in the Management of Software-Based Development Projects," *Information and Software Technology,* vol. 32, no. 1. January/February 1990, pp. 18–33.
3. Howard Rubin, Rubin Associates, Pound Ridge, New York.
4. Roger Pressman, *A Manager's Guide to Software Engineering,* McGraw-Hill, 1993.
5. Barbara Bouldin, *Agents of Change,* Yourdon Press, 1989.
6. Watts Humphrey, "Software and the Factory Paradigm," *The Software Engineering Journal,* IEEE Publishing, Stevenage, Herts, England.
7. G. Rifkin, "No more defects," *Computerworld,* July 15, 1991, pp. 59–62.
8. W. Smillie, "Improving the Quality of Software Development," in *The Software Engineering Productivity Handbook,* J. Keyes (ed.), McGraw-Hill, 1993.
9. D. S. Corbin, "Establishing the Software Development Environment," *Journal of Systems Management,* September 1991, pp. 28–31.
10. D. B. Simmons, "Communications: a software group productivity dominator," *Software Engineering Journal,* November 1991, pp. 454–462.
11. A. Burns and A. M. Lister, "A framework for building dependable systems," *The Computer Journal,* vol. 34, no. 2, April 1991, pp. 173–181.
12. B. Farbey, "Software quality metrics: considerations about requirements and requirement specifications," *Information and Software Technology,* vol. 32, no. 1, January–February 1990, pp. 60–64.
13. Hewlett-Packard, *Software Engineering Productivity,* 1989.

Bibliography

Ansoff, H. I. *Corporate Strategy,* McGraw-Hill, New York, 1965.

Andrews, K. R. *The Concept of Corporate Strategy,* Irwin, Homewood, Ill., 1971.

Applegate, L., J. Cash, and D. Mills. "Information Technology and Tomorrow's Manager," *Harvard Business Review,* November–December 1988.

Barr, A., E. A. Feigenbaum, and Paul Cohen. *The Handbook of Artificial Intelligence,* vols. I, II, and III, William Kaufmann, Los Altos, Calif., 1981.

Brown, F. *The Mythical Man-Month,* Addison-Wesley, Reading, Mass., 1975.

Bullen, C., and J. Bennett. "Groupware in Practice: An Interpretation of Work Experiences," MIT Center for Information Systems Research, 1990.

Conference Board, New York. *Information Technology: Initiatives for Today-Decisions That Cannot Wait,* Report 577, 50 pages, 1972.

Conference Board, New York. *Information Management: The New Strategic Weapon,* Report 220, 22 pages, conference presentations, 1988.

Conference Board, New York. *Information: The Great Equalizer,* ATB, July–August 1986, pp. 5–6.

Conference Board, New York. *Taming The Information Monster,* ATB, November 1986, pp. 33–38.

De Marco, T. *Software Systems Development,* Yourdon Press, New York, 1982.

Deming, W. E. *Out of the Crisis,* MIT Press, 1986.

Drucker, P. "The Coming of the New Organization," *Harvard Business Review,* January–February 1988.

Drucker, P. *Management: Tasks, Responsibilities, Practices,* Harper & Row, New York, 1974.

D'Souza, Dinesh. *Illiberal Education,* Vintage Books, New York, 1992.

Feigenbaum, E. A., and P. McCorduck. *The Fifth Generation,* Signet, New York, 1984.

Finkelstein, C. B. *An Introduction to Information Engineering,* Addison-Wesley, Reading, Mass., 1989.

Finkelstein, C. B. *Information Engineering: Strategic Systems Development,* Addison-Wesley, Reading, Mass., 1992.

Frenzel, L. E. *Understanding Expert Systems,* Howard W. Sams, Indianapolis, 1987.

Gane, C., and T. Sarson. *Structured Systems Analysis,* Prentice-Hall, Englewood Cliffs, N.J., 1979.

Gray, D. H., "Uses and Misuses of Strategic Planning," *Harvard Business Review,* January–February 1986.

Hamilton, M. "Zero-defect software: the elusive goal," *IEEE Spectrum,* 23(3):48–53, 1986.

Hanks, K. *Motivating People,* Crisp Publications, 1991.

Harmon, P., and D. King. *Expert Systems,* Wiley, New York, 1984.

Hayes-Roth, F., D. A. Waterman, and D. B. Lenat. *Building Expert Systems,* Addison-Wesley, Reading, Mass., 1983.

Huff, A. S., and R. K. Reger. "A Review of Strategic Process Research," *Journal of Management,* vol. 13, no. 2, 1987.

Jones, C. *A Short History of Function Points and Feature Points,* Software Productivity Research, Burlington, Mass.

Keyes, J. *Infotrends,* McGraw-Hill, New York, 1992.

Keyes, J. *The New Intelligence,* HarperBusiness, New York, 1990.

Keyes, J. *The Software Engineering Handbook,* McGraw-Hill, New York, 1993.

Marca, D. "Coordinators: Guidelines for Groupware Developers," *Proceedings of the 5th International Workshop on Software Specification and Design,* May 1989.

Martin, J., and C. B. Finkelstein, *Information Engineering,* Savant Institute, Carnforth, Lancashire, U.K., 1981.

Maus, R., and J. Keyes. *The Handbook of Expert Systems in Manufacturing,* McGraw-Hill, New York, 1991.

Mishkoff, H. C. *Understanding Artificial Intelligence,* Texas Instruments, Dallas, Texas, 1985.

Morton, M. S. Scott. *The Corporation of the 1990s: Information Technology and Organizational Transformation,* Oxford University Press, New York, 1991.

Musa, J., A. Iannino, and K. Okumoto. *Software Reliability: Measurement, Prediction, Application,* McGraw-Hill, New York, 1987.

Nagy, T., D. Gault, and M. Nagy. *Building Your First Expert System,* Halstead Press, New York, 1983.

Nolan, R. L. "What Transformation Is," in *Stage by Stage,* R. L. Nolan (ed.), Norton & Co., Boston, 1987.

Orr, K. *Structured Systems Development,* Yourdon Press, New York, 1977.

Peat, F. D. *Artificial Intelligence: How Machines Think,* Bean Publishing, New York, 1988.

Porter, M. E. "How Information Technology Gives You Competitive Advantage," *Harvard Business Review,* July–August 1985, p. 149.

Porter, M. E. *Competitive Strategy,* Free Press/Macmillan, New York, 1980.

Pressman, R. *Making Software Engineering Happen,* Prentice-Hall, Englewood Cliffs, N.J., 1988.

Rich, Elaine, *Artificial Intelligence,* McGraw-Hill, New York, 1983.

Schoen, S., and W. Schoen. *Putting Artificial Intelligence To Work,* Wiley, New York, 1987.

Tanimoto, S. L. *The Elements of Artificial Intelligence,* Computer Science Press, Rockville, Md., 1987.

Waterman, D. A. *A Guide To Expert Systems,* Addison-Wesley, Reading, Mass., 1985.

Yourdon, E., and L. Constantine. *Structured Design: Fundamentals of a Discipline of Computer Program Systems Design,* Prentice-Hall, Englewood Cliffs, N.J., 1978.

Index

ABOUT THE AUTHOR

Jessica Keyes is president of Techinsider/New Art Inc., a
technology consultancy/research firm specializing in produc-
tivity and high-technology applications. She is publisher of
Techinsider Reports as well as the *Computer Market Letter*.
Organizer and leader of Techinsider seminars, Keyes has
given seminars for such prestigious universities as Carnegie
Mellon, Boston University, University of Illinois, James
Madison University, and San Francisco State University.
Prior to founding Techinsider, Keyes was Managing
Director of Technology for the New York Stock Exchange
and has been an officer with Swiss Bank Co. and Banker's
Trust, both in New York City. She has over 15 years of tech-
nical experience in such diverse areas as artificial intelli-
gence, multimedia, CASE, and re-engineering. She holds a
M.B.A. from New York University.

A noted columnist and correspondent with over 150 arti-
cles published in such journals as *Software Magazine,
Computerworld, AI Expert*, and *Datamation*. Keyes is also
the author of six books, including *The Software Engineering
Productivity Handbook* (McGraw-Hill) and *Infotrends: The
Competitive Use of Information* (McGraw-Hill), which was
chosen as one of the best business books of 1992 by the
Library Journal.